The JOY of Cataloging:

Essays, Letters, Reviews,
and Other Explosions

The JOY
of Cataloging:
Essays, Letters, Reviews,
and Other Explosions

by Sanford Berman

ORYX PRESS
1981

The rare Arabian Oryx, a desert antelope dating from Biblical times, is believed to be the prototype of the mythical unicorn. The World Wildlife Fund found three of the animals in 1962 and, aware that they were nearing extinction, sent them to the Phoenix Zoo as the nucleus of a breeding herd in captivity. Today the Oryx population is nearing 200 and herds have been returned to breeding grounds in Israel and Jordan.

Library of Congress Cataloging in Publication Data

Berman, Sanford, 1933–
   The joy of cataloging.

   Bibliography: p.
   Includes index.
   1. Cataloging—Addresses, essays, lectures.
2. Subject cataloging—Addresses, essays, lectures.
I. Title.
Z693.B47   025.3   80-20525
ISBN 0-912700-51-3

Contents

Abbreviations and Acronyms

AACR	*Anglo-American Cataloging Rules*
ACP	Annotated Card Program (Library of Congress)
AJL	Association of Jewish Libraries
ALA	American Library Association
BL	British Library
CCRC	Catalog Code Revision Committee (American Library Association)
CCS	Cataloging and Classification Section (ALA Resources and Technical Services Division)
CIBC	Council on Interracial Books for Children
CIP	Cataloging-in-Publication
COSMEP	Committee of Small Magazine Editors and Publishers
CSD	Children's Services Division (American Library Association)
CSLA	Church and Synagogue Library Association
DC&	*Dewey Decimal Classification Additions, Notes, and Decisions*
DCD	Decimal Classification Division (Library of Congress)
DDC	*Dewey Decimal Classification*
HCL	Hennepin County Library
ISBD	*International Standard Bibliographic Description*
ISBN	International Standard Book Number
LA	Library Association (Great Britain)
LC	Library of Congress
LCSH	*Library of Congress Subject Headings*
LIV	*Legislative Indexing Vocabulary*
LRTS	*Library Resources & Technical Services*
MARC	Machine-Readable Cataloging
MISR	Makerere Institute of Social Research
MULS	*Minnesota Union List of Serials*
NST	*New Serial Titles*
NUC	*National Union Catalog*
PAIGC	African Independence Party of Guine and the Cape Verdes
PER	Unclassified Periodical (Hennepin County Library)
PLA	Public Library Association
RCIA	Retail Clerks International Association, AFL-CIO
RSA	Republic of South Africa

RTSD	Resources and Technical Services Division (American Library Association)
SAC	Subject Analysis Committee (ALA Resources and Technical Services Division)
SCD	Subject Cataloging Division (Library of Congress)
SDIS	Southdale Information Services (Hennepin County Library)
SRRT	Social Responsibilities Round Table (American Library Association)
SWAPO	Southwest African People's Organisation
TSD	Technical Services Division (Hennepin County Library)
ULS	*Union List of Serials*
URM	Unclassified Reference Material (Hennepin County Library)
WASP	White Anglo-Saxon Protestant
YASD	Young Adult Services Division (American Library Association)
X-REF	Cross-Reference

Introduction

Cataloging should be fun. And challenging. And useful. But too often it's none of those things. Too often it's regarded not as an art nor craft, but merely as a process, a procedure, something clerical, mechanical. It's widely assumed either that our governing codes and schemes are so irredeemably bad and foolish, and so permanent, that it's just not worth trying to do anything about them—or, conversely, that our illustrious code- and scheme-makers, including the Library of Congress, the principal source of cataloging copy for most libraries, are so completely sensible and trustworthy that they merit deep, unending gratitude rather than constant criticism and complaint.

Such attitudes and assumptions, coupled with a growing, almost religious faith in automation—a belief that the machine, the computer, will itself bring Bibliographic Salvation—have already produced fewer, and generally less creative and autonomous, catalogers; demonstrably poorer catalog access to library resources; greater mystification; more frustration for both library patrons and staff; and an alarming passivity, even nihilism, among catalogers and reference librarians alike.

The writings that follow variously document the *un*reliability of standard "authorities" and centrally generated cataloging products; demonstrate that codes, schemes, and practices *can* be reformed and made more functional, both at local and higher levels; emphasize the inescapable responsibility of *each* library to establish and maintain a catalog that works for *its* users; and illustrate the potential value, excitement, and—yes—joy of cataloging. Also, these papers, letters, and reviews exemplify and elaborate the three principles or objectives that should underlie and animate all cataloging:

- Intelligibility. Bibliographic data—the substance and format of catalog entries—should be helpful to catalog users. And should make sense.

- Findability. Access should be quick and liberal. (This involves the use of contemporary, familiar language; entering works under the author's title-page name; and assigning enough added entries for titles, subtitles, collaborators, and subjects to make the material findable where people are likely to look for it.)

- <u>Fairness</u>. That is, fairness to the material being cataloged and, with particular respect to subject cataloging, to the topics themselves. (For instance, it's *not* fair to the whole category of materials called *audiovisual* or *nonprint* to either not catalog them at all or to treat them in a second-class way by comparison to books. And, as another example, it's not fair to employ rubrics for age, sex, or ethnic groups that are not their own, preferred names.)

The JOY of Cataloging:
Essays, Letters, Reviews, and Other Explosions

MANIFESTOS

These two selections, both dating from 1977, capsulize and exemplify what John Berry dubbed the "Cataloging Revolution." They criticize inherited orthodoxy and propound new visions, new modes. Everything that follows elaborates and refines the themes and issues raised here.

The Cataloging Shtik

Friends, we've been conned into believing

- That making materials quickly and painlessly accessible through the catalog is much *less* important than picking, buying, stamping, labeling, pocketing, and preserving those same materials.
- That our illustrious "experts," "leaders," and "authorities" (mostly from academia and the research conglomerate) really know better than we do what's good for public, school, and college libraries.
- That universal "standards" like *ISBD* are sacred and inevitable, to be implemented everywhere regardless of whether they make any sense or contribute to better service.
- That PLA, RTSD, CSD, YASD, etc. can be trusted to behave like consumer advocates (rather than stockholders or sweethearts) with respect to LC, Baker & Taylor, Josten's, Brodart, and other cataloging products.

What we *don't* need

- Abbreviations; e.g., not the original "illus." nor lately reduced "ill." (Users and staff alike are already bombarded—in fact, overloaded—with acronyms, symbols, and contractions.)
- Secret punctuation—like slashes, dashes, and equal signs—that only the "elect" can comprehend.
- Mandatory author statements following titles when the name is identical to the main entry and thus redundant; e.g.,

> Herndon, Brodie.
> Time clocks; by Brodie Herndon.

- Brackets (understood—if at all—exclusively by library types and utterly insignificant to everyone else).
- Pointless, space-wasting "1st ed." statements.
- Mysterious Latin ciphers—e.g., [s.l.], [s.n.]—that could well make the uninducted feel like stupid jerks.

Reprinted from *Library Journal* (June 1, 1977): 1251–3. Published by R.R. Bowker Co. (a Xerox company). Copyright © 1977 by Xerox Corporation.

- Roman pagination (seldom extensive nor of any tangible value).
- Centimer spine sizes. (Call numbers for tall works ordinarily indicate the odd size by means of something like a "folio" prefix, anyway, so who needs "34 cm."?)
- ISBN numbers and prices, the former because no one (outside of acquisitions) gives a damn, the latter because the figure's likely to be much higher even *before* the card gets filed.
- Bibliography and index notes, so common that they've become meaningless.
- Archaic, foolish, clumsy, inauthentic, and biased subject terms that hamper searching, damage the library's credibility, and peddle misinformation. (Examples: MAMMIES; ILLEGITIMACY; MOTOR-TRUCKS; RIME; GIPSIES; CRUELTY TO CHILDREN; WATER-CLOSETS; EUROPEAN WAR, 1914–1918; YELLOW PERIL; AGED; DEGLUTITION DISORDERS; MOVING-PICTURES; DWELLINGS; FORE*MEN*; STATES*MEN*; REFUSE COLLECTION VEHICLES.)
- The concealment of material on current and often vital topics by subject-cataloging it under remote or improbable rubrics. (Examples: "Reggae music" under JAZZ ENSEMBLES; "Cohabitation" under SEX AND LAW or COLLEGE STUDENTS—SEXUAL BEHAVIOR; "Food co-ops" under COOPERATIVE SOCIETIES or FOOD INDUSTRY AND TRADE; "Sexism in education" under SEX DIFFERENCES IN EDUCATION; "Political repression in America" under COMMUNISM—UNITED STATES—1917- ; "Homesteading" under AGRICULTURE—HANDBOOKS, MANUALS, ETC.; "Job hunting" under APPLICATIONS FOR POSITIONS; "Third World literature" under LITERATURE, MODERN—20TH CENTURY; "Smoking and health" under TOBACCO—PHYSIOLOGICAL EFFECT; "Laetrile" under CANCER—PERSONAL NARRATIVES.)
- DDC Phoenixes—completely "remodeled" schedules "prepared with little or no reference to earlier editions"—that wreck call-number integrity and frustrate browsing at all but the few libraries that can afford to reclassify their existing stock.
- CIP entries frequently so incomplete and based on such scanty data that they're virtually unusable.
- Hierarchical filing that wrongly assumes users know (or can guess) what mischievous librarians have decided to file first, last, and in the middle.

What we *do* need

- Determination of authors' names from the title page or container, recognizing that some authors write or compose under various names, all of them being equally "legitimate." (As a practical result, mysteries by Gordon Ashe, Michael Halliday, Kyle Hunt, J.J. Marric, Anthony Morton, and Jeremy York would have been entered—and shelved—under "Ashe," "Halliday," "Hunt," "Marric," "Morton," and "York" instead of being totally lumped together under the late author's semi-sanctified *real name*, John Creasey. "Creasey" and the six pseudonyms, of course, could be easily connected by notes; e.g., "For works written by this author under other names, see: . . .")

- Shortened imprint statements; e.g.,

Da Capo Press, 1973.	*instead of*	Amsterdam, Theatrum Orbis Terrarum; New York, Da Capo Press, 1973.
Doubleday, 1974.	*instead of*	Garden City, N.Y., Doubleday, 1974.
MIT Press, 1973.	*instead of*	Cambridge, Mass., MIT Press [1973]
Springer-Verlag, 1973-	*instead of*	Berlin, New York, Springer-Verlag, 1973-

- Appropriate notes to highlight special features; e.g., the manifold, government-ordered deletions in Marks and Marchetti's *CIA and the Cult of Intelligence.*
- Code-breaking cross-references; e.g.,

Amin Dada, Idi, 1925-

x   Dada, Idi Amin, 1925-
    General Amin, 1925-
    President Amin, 1925-

Cocaine

x   "Blow" (Drug)
    "C-dust" (Drug)
    "Coke" (Drug)
    "Flake" (Drug)
    "Snow" (Drug)
    "Stardust" (Drug)

Rodgers, Mary

x   Rogers, Mary

United Automobile, Aerospace
  and Agricultural Implement
  Workers of America

x   Auto Workers Union
    Automobile Workers Union
    U.A.W.
    United Automobile Workers of
    America

United States.
  Occupational Safety
  and Health Administration

x   O.S.H.A.
    OSHA
    Occupational Health and
    Safety Administration

Urban Coalition of Minneapolis

x   Minneapolis Urban Coalition

- Development of a contemporary, relevant, and accurate subject thesaurus, replete with generous cross-references and including entries for key fictional characters (e.g., Christopher Robin, Sam Spade, Harry Paget Flashman, Inspector Maigret, Perry Mason).

- The regular assignment of enough specific subject tracings to fairly and adequately reflect a work's content, irrespective of whether the material is juvenile or adult, print or A/V, fiction or nonfiction.
- Added entries for all significant, likely-to-be-remembered, or quasi-topical subtitles and catch-titles; e.g.,

CIA and the cult of intelligence.
    Added entry: The cult of intelligence.

The rise and fall of the city of Mahagonny.
    Added entry: Mahagonny.

The persecution and assassination of Marat as performed by the inmates of the Asylum of Charenton under the direction of the Marquis de Sade.
    Added entry: Marat/Sade.

The Anarchist collectives; workers' self-management in the Spanish Revolution, 1936-1939.
    Added entries: Workers' self-management in the Spanish Revolution, 1936-1939. The Spanish Revolution, 1936-1939.

Black anti-Semitism and Jewish racism.
    Added entry: Jewish racism.

Man's most dangerous myth: the fallacy of race.
    Added entry: The fallacy of race.

The case of the fabulous fake.
    Added entry: The fabulous fake case.

- Age- and media-integrated catalogs that freely intermix children's and adult materials, as well as print and A/V items, favoring no one genre nor medium over another. (Among other things, this means no "special" subheads for—JUVENILE LITERATURE,—PHONODISCS,—VIDEO CASSETTES,—KITS, etc.)
- The timely creation of new DDC numbers to handle contemporary subjects like "Alternative energy sources," "Feminism," and "Workers' control."
- A comprehensive index to the *Dewey Decimal Classification* that swiftly and directly links topics and numbers. (Try finding "Prison reform," "Wife beating," "Intellectual freedom," or "Vasectomy" in the 18th edition index.)
- A national cataloging center for nonresearch libraries *if* LC and the major vendors refuse to shape up.

Catalogue of Horrors

Critics of standard, LC-type cataloging charge that it too often frustrates the catalog user and actually "buries" or "hides" much of the library's wares. Among the most common accusations are: Unintelligible punctuation and abbreviations; irrelevant data; insufficient access points (e.g., for subjects, subtitles, and catchwords); author forms that hardly (if at all) relate to title-page names; and variously biased, archaic, and imprecise subject terminology. Is there any substance to that indictment? Well, decide for yourself. Below, on the left, appear bona fide Library of Congress entries. On the right are alternatives, indicating how the same works *might* have been handled.

Standard

Robinson, David Ernest, 1945–
    The complete homesteading book; proven methods for self-sufficient living/David E. Robinson; illustrated by Paula Savastano; diagrs. by Douglas Merrilees. Charlotte, Vt.: Garden Way Pub., [1974]
    249 p., [8] leaves of plates: ill.; 24 cm.
    Includes bibliographies and index.
    1. Agriculture—Handbooks, manuals, etc. 2. Agriculture—United States. I. Title.

    630   74-75462

Alternative

Robinson, David E., 1945–
    The complete homesteading book; proven methods for self-sufficient living. Illustrated by Paula Savastano. Diagrams by Douglas Merrilees. Garden Way, 1974.
    249 pages.
    Includes unpaged photos.
    1. Homesteading. I. Garden Way Publishing Company II. Title. III. Title: Self-sufficient living.

    630.43

Reprinted with permission from *Emergency Librarian*, v. 4, no. 4 (March/April 1977):6–10, now published by Dyad Services, P.O. Box 4696, Station D, London, Ontario, Canada N5W 5L7.

Standard

Giant talk; an anthology of Third World writings/ compiled and edited by Quincy Troupe and Rainer Schulte. 1st ed. New York: Random House. [1975] xliv, 546 p.; 24 cm.
Bibliography: P. [523] 528.
1. Literature, Modern—20th century. I. Troupe. Quincy. II. Schulte, Rainer, 1937–
808.88   75-11549

Schickele, Peter
The definitive biography of P.D.Q. Bach, 1807–1742?/Professor Peter Schickele. 1st ed. New York: Random House, c1976
xxi, 238 p.; ill.; 22 cm.
Includes index.
1. Music—Anecodotes, facetiae, satire, etc. 2. Biography—Anecdotes, facetiae, satire, etc. I. Title.
813.54   75-31682

Wortis, Joseph, 1906–
Tricky Dick and his pals: comical stories, all in the manner of Dr. Heinrich Hoffman's Der Struwwelpeter/by Joseph Wortis; and funny pictures by David Arkin. New York: Quadrangle/New York Times Book Co., [1975] c1974.
[28] p.: col. ill.; 25 cm
SUMMARY: Chronicles the adventures of a naughty boy and his pals.
1. [Stories in rhyme.] 2. [Conduct of life—Fiction.] I. Arkin, David, III. II. Title.
[Fic] 73-92230

Patri, Giacomo, 1898–
White collar: a novel in linocuts/Giacomo Patri. Millbrae, Calif.: Celestial Arts, 1975.
127 p.: chiefly ill.; 22 cm
1. Patri, Giacomo, 1898– 2. United States—History— 1933–1945—Pictorial works. 3. United States in art. I. Title.
769.924   75-9440

Alternative

Troupe, Quincy, 1943– editor.
Giant Talk; an anthology of Third World writings. Compiled and edited by Quincy Troupe and Rainer Schulte. Random House, 1975.
546 pages.
"Achebe/Asturias/Baldwin/Baraka/ Brooks/Cesaire/Cruz/Ellison/Marquez/Neruda/ Paz/Reed/Senghor/Wong and others."
1. Third World literature. I. Schulte, Rainer, editor. II. Title. III. Title: Third World writings.
808.89917

Schickele, Peter, 1935–
The definitive biography of P.D.Q. Bach, 1807–1742? Random House, copyright 1976.
238 pages.
Includes photos, drawings, musical notations, bibliography, and discography.
1. Music— Anecdotes, facetiae, satire, etc. 2. Bach, P.D.Q., 1807–1742?—Fiction. 3. Bach Family—Cartoons, satire, etc. 4. Composers, German—Anecdotes, facetiae, satire, etc. I. Title.
780.207 or 817.54

Wortis, Joseph, 1906–
Tricky Dick and his pals; comical stories, all in the manner of Dr. Heinrich Hoffman's Der Struwwelpeter. Funny pictures by David Arkin. Quadrangle/New York Times Book Company, copyright 1974.
28 pages.
1. Nixon, Richard Milhous, 1913– —Cartoons, satire, etc. 2. Watergate Scandal—Anecdotes, facetiae, satire, etc. 3. Cautionary tales and verse. 4. Wickedness—Poetry. 5. Bullies and bullying— Poetry. 6. Hoffman, Heinrich, 1809–1894. Der Struwwelpeter— Adaptations. I. Arkin, David, illustrator. II. Title.
973.924 or 817. 54

Patri, Giacomo, 1898–
White collar; a novel in linocuts. Introduction by Rockwell Kent; afterword by John L. Lewis. New edition. Celestial Arts, 1975.
127 pages.
"A classic from the Great Depression."
1. Stories without words. 2. Capitalism—United States—Fiction. 3. Depressions— 1929—United States—Fiction. 4. Labor solidarity—Fiction. 5. "White collar" workers—Fiction. 6. The Thirties— Fiction. I. Celestial Arts. II. Lewis, John L., 1880–1969. III. Kent, Rockwell, 1882– IV. Title.

Standard

Alternative

Sommer, Robert
 Street art/Robert Sommer. New York: Links. [1975]
x, 66 p., [42] leaves of plates: ill. (some col.); 21
cm.
 Bibliography: P. 65–66.
 1. Art and society—United States. 2. Art.
Amateur—United States. 3. Street decoration—
United States. I. Title.
 709.73   74-78867

Sommer, Robert
 Street art. Links, 1975.
 66 pages.
 Includes 84 unpaged plates, some in color
 1. Mural painting and decoration, American. 2.
Graffiti—United States. 3. Ethnic art—United States.
4. Radical art—United States. 5. Art and society—
United States. I. Title.
 751.73

Marchetti, Victor.
 The CIA and the cult of intelligence [by] Victor
Marchetti and John D. Marks. Introd. by Melvin L.
Wulf. [1st ed.] New York, Knopf, 1974.
 xxvi, 398, xxi p. 22 cm. $8.95
 1. United States. Central Intelligence Agency. I.
Marks, John D., joint author. II. Title.
 327.12'06173   74-4995

Marchetti, Victor.
 The CIA and the cult of intelligence; by Victor
Marchetti and John D. Marks. Introduction by Melvin
L. Wulf. Knopf, 1974.
 398 pages.
 "The first book the U.S. Government ever went to
court to censor before publication . . . In this edition,
passages the CIA originally ordered excised—and
then reluctantly permitted to be reinstated—are
printed in bold face type. Firm deletions, including
the 140-plus passages cleared but still tied up in
litigation, are indicated by blank spaces preceded
and followed by parentheses: (DELETED). The
spaces correspond to the actual length of the cuts."

 "Appendix: The Bissell philosophy; minutes of the
1968 'Bissell Meeting' at the Council of Foreign Relations as reprinted by the Africa Research Group."
 1. CIA. 2. Censorship—United States—Case
studies. 3. Security classification (Government
documents)—Case studies. 4. Espionage,
American. I. Marks, John D., joint author. II. Title. III.
Title: The cult of intelligence. IV. Title: The Bissell
philosophy.
 327.12

Young, Ian.
 The male homosexual in literature: a bibliography/
by Ian Young; with essays by Ian Young, Graham
Jackson, and Rictor Norton. Metuchen, N.J.: Scarecrow Press, 1975.
 ix, 242 p.; 22 cm.
 Includes index.
 1. English literature—Bibliography. 2. Homosexuality—Bibliography. I. Title.
 016.82'08'0353 75-25611

Young, Ian.
 The male homosexual in literature; a bibliography.
With essays by Ian Young, Graham Jackson, and
Rictor Norton. Scarecrow press, 1975.
 242 pages.
 PARTIAL CONTENTS: The bibliography.—The
flower beneath the foot: a short history of the gay
novel, by I. Young.—The theatre of implication:
homosexuality in drama, by G. Jackson.—The
poetry of male love, by I. Young.—Ganymede
raped: gay literature—the critic as censor, by R.
Norton.
 1. Gay men in literature. 2. Gay men in literature—
Bibliography. 3. Homophobia in literary criticism. I.
Title.
 016.80989'2'81'6
or
809.892'81'6

Standard

Richler, Mordecai, 1931–
   Jacob Two-Two meets the Hooded Fang/
Mordecai Richler; illustrated by Fritz Wegner.
Toronto: McClelland and Stewart, c1975.
   83 p.: ill.: 24 cm.

   I. Title

      75-333180

McDermott, Beverly Brodsky.
   Sedna: an Eskimo myth/adapted and illustrated
by Beverly Brodsky. 1st ed. New York: Viking Press.
1975.
   [30] p.: col. ill.; 22 x 26 cm.
   Bibliography: P. [2]
   SUMMARY: Sedna, mother of all sea animals, tells
the story of her life and helps the starving Inuit.
   1. Eskimos—Legends. 2. Indians of North
America—Legends. 3. [Eskimos—Legends.] I. Title
      398.2'454   75-4979

Alternative

Richler, Mordecai, 1931–
   Jacob Two-Two meets the Hooded Fang. Illustrated by Fritz Wegner. McClelland and Stewart,
copyright 1975.
   83 pages
   1. Child prisoners—Fiction. 2. Children—Rights—
Fiction. 3. Children's liberation—Fiction. 4.
Ageism—Fiction. 5. English Medal Award books. I.
Wegner, Fritz, illustrator. II. Title. III. Title: Two-Two
meets the Hooded Fang. IV. Title: The Hooded Fang.
[Fic]

Brodsky, Beverly
   Sedna, an Eskimo myth. Viking, 1975.
   30 pages.
   1. Mythology, Inuit. 2. Mother-goddesses, Inuit. I.
Title.
      299.7

Yes, the LC examples were deliberately chosen for their very
"badness." But they're also very *real*. And they genuinely—even if a
bit dramatically—illustrate what's wrong with so much standard
cataloging, which libraries increasingly accept (as CIP, ready-made
cards, or MARC tapes) with little or no critical revision. The net
results are further erosion of the catalog's usefulness; wasted pur-
chase and processing money when materials are underexploited
because of poor access; and a worsened image of the library itself
as dowdy, antique, and unresponsive.

What to do about it? If the kind of cataloging represented by the
alternatives seems significantly better than the standard variety,
there are two ways to "make it happen," both complementary: (1)
Insist that your own library undertake as much "critical revision" as it
can afford, and (2) lobby the primary sources of "outside copy" to
overhaul their approach.

The catalog *should* be effective, modern, easy-to-use tool, not a
thing of dread, confusion, embarrassment, or horror.

AACR

The long-gestating second edition of the *Anglo-American Cataloguing Rules (AACR2)* finally appeared in late 1978. The new Rules 22.2C ("Pseudonyms") and 22.3A ("Fullness") substantially embody the suggestions made in the 1975 "Brief." In addition, the editors thoroughly reformed the prior edition's rampantly sexist prose and male-oriented examples, systematically employing the equally readable "non-sexist terminology" mentioned in the "Brief" and providing a "more equitable distribution among male and female entries." Joan Marshall, HCL's head cataloger, and ALA's Social Responsibilities Round Table had lobbied for just such reforms as early as Fall 1974 (for documentation, see "Midwinter Mish-mash," *SRRT Newsletter,* no. 34 [March 1975]: 4, and *"AACR:* Overhauling a Pompous, Macho Code," *HCL Cataloging Bulletin*, nos. 11–13 [March 15, 1975]: 9–12).

The proposed *AACR2* "options and addenda" attempt to render the code more appropriate for "non-archival" libraries, in particular eliminating much descriptive rubbish and elitist "honorifics," showing how to construct popular team names, and mandating more title added-entries, as well as greater small press access.

"Planning for *AACR2*" addresses the problem of what the new rules mean to individual libraries, reporting a strategy for code implementation and catalog management actually applied at one medium-sized public institution.

A Brief
for Title-Page Cataloging

On April 16, 1976, HCL's head cataloger sent the following letter to John D. Byrum, who chairs the ALA Catalog Code Revision Committee:

> The Winter 1975 *Catalogue & Index* (#39) reports on page four that the Library Association/British Library *AACR* Committee has proposed "adoption of the present alternative rule [42B] as the main rule," as well as recommending that "headings for personal names should take the form of the name most commonly used" (Rule 43).
> Alternative Rule 42B declares:

> > If the works of an author appear under several pseudonyms or under his real name and one or more pseudonyms, enter each work under the name he used for it. Make *see also* references to connect the names.

> > Dodgson, Charles Lutwidge
> >   *see also his pseudonym:* Carroll, Lewis.
> > Carroll, Lewis
> >   *see also his real name:* Dodgson, Charles Lutwidge.

Particularly because of the tremendous benefits to libraries with large and active fiction collections, I strongly urge CCRC to endorse the LA/BL position. Instituting the alternative rule will finally allow ordinary readers to find Jeremy York novels, for example, under Y (where they would naturally be expected) instead of C (for "Creasey," the multipseudonymed author's real name). Enclosed as possible prototypes are several examples—culled from recent *HCL Cataloging Bulletins*—of "linking" or "connecting" notes between various forms of an author's name.

Re "Fullness" (Rule 43): Again, the British proposal for "most commonly used"—rather than "fullest"—forms deserves CCRC support. This should result in faster and much less puzzling searches for library patrons and staff alike. Now, for instance, the popular comedian "Bill Cosby" is ludicrously (and frustratingly) entered under "Cosby, William H." (see 1974 *NUC*, v. 4, p. 426).

* * *

P.S. To conform, of course, with CCRC's commitment to nonsexist terminology, a recast Rule 42B should read something like:

> If an author's works appear under several pseudonyms, or under a real name and one or more pseudonyms, enter each work under the name actually used for it . . .

Reprinted from *HCL Cataloging Bulletin,* no. 22 (July 1, 1976): 6.

Proposed: *AACR2* Options and Addenda for School, Public, and Community College Libraries

Description

- Use no English nor Latin abbreviations unless they actually appear in the work being cataloged; e.g.,

The wolves of Willoughby Chase; illustrated by Pat Marriott.	*not*	The wolves of Willoughby Chase; ill. by Pat Marriott.
510 pages	*not*	510 p.
3 volumes	*not*	3v.

- Spell out "copyright"; e.g., Horizon Press, copyright 1978. *not* Horizon Press, c1978.
- Do not record "1st edition."
- Do not repeat an author's name following the title when that name, apart from dates, is identical to the main entry.
- When including an author statement following the title and no "by" appears in the work itself, preface the statement with "by" for clarity; e.g.,

> Marketing; by Theodore N. Beckman, William R. Davidson and W. Wayne Talarzyk. 9th edition.

- Omit roman-numeral paging and spine size from collations.

Reprinted from *HCL Cataloging Bulletin*, no. 38 (January/February 1979): 24–6.

- If a work contains significant graphic or other matter, indicate such features in a short, intelligible note; e.g.,

> Includes "225 plates in full color, reproducing more than 400 specially made photographs."
>
> Includes "over 175 photographs, drawings, and maps; lists of suggested readings; and a glossary of animals found in the paintings."
>
> Includes critical descriptions and ordering data for 300 films, slide sets, videotapes, and filmstrips, as well as a subject index, bibliography, and still illustrations.
>
> "Illustrated with 120 two- and three-color line drawings." Includes glossary, together with material on "congenital abnormalities," arteriosclerosis, strokes, aneurysms, hypertension, pacemakers, and "preventive maintenance."

- Use contents' notes or jacket quotes to reveal aspects of a work not obvious from the title alone and which perhaps merit subject or other analytics; e.g.,

Butler, Sandra, 1938-
  Conspiracy of silence: the trauma of incest.

  PARTIAL CONTENTS: The children.—The aggressors.—The mothers.—The family.—History of a survivor.

Adair, Casey.
  Word is out: stories of some of our lives.

  Includes "in-depth commentary on the making of the film," personal statements by each of the 6 filmmakers, biographical sketches of the 26 Gay interviewees, complete interview texts, an "extensive bibliography/reading list," and "more than 100 photographs."

Arlen, Michael J.
  The view from Highway 1: essays on television.

  PARTIAL CONTENTS: Media dramas of Norman Lear.—Kidvid.—White Man still speaks with forked tongue.—Three views of women.

Kutz, Meyer, 1939-
  Rockefeller power.

  Includes material on philanthropic projects, art collecting, politics, Rockefeller Center, Attica, and conservation.

- Do not display prices and ISBN numbers, nor use brackets, slashes, and equal signs.

Form of Entry

- Employ the title-page form of personal names, adding no more than dates, when known, and establishing links between pseudonyms; e.g.,

Highwater, Jamake.	*and*	Marks, J.
For works by this author written under another name, see: Marks, J.		For works by this author written under another name, see: Highwater, Jamake.
Lawrence, D.H., 1885-1930	*not*	Lawrence, D.H. (David Herbert), 1885-1930

- Do not include honorific titles like "Sir," "Lord," and "Lady" in personal name forms unless there is no other way to distinguish between two or more identically named persons; e.g.,

Chaplin, Charlie, 1889-1977	*not*	Chaplin, Sir Charlie, 1889-1977
	not	Chaplin, Charlie, Sir, 1889-1977

- Enter a sports team under its most familiar and popular name, making cross-references from variants; e.g.,

Minnesota Twins.	Minnesota Kicks.	Minnesota Vikings.
x Twins (Minnesota baseball club)	x Kicks (Minnesota soccer club)	x Vikes (Minnesota football club) Vikings (Minnesota football club)

Added Entries

- Trace all titles, without exception.
- Trace subtitles and portions of titles that are likely to be remembered and sought; e.g.,

Baraka, Imamu Amiri, 1934-
    Raise race rays raze.
    I. Title. II. Title: Race rays raze raise. III. Title: Rays race raze raise. IV. Title: Raze race rays raise.

Anker, Charlotte.
    Last night I saw Andromeda.
    I. Title. II. Title: I saw Andromeda last night. III. Title: Andromeda last night.

• Trace small, local, and alternative presses; e.g.,

> Ferretti, Fred.
> Afo-A-Kom: sacred art of
> Cameroon. Third Press, 1975.
> I. Third Press.

> Arguelles, Jose, 1939-
> The transformative vision.
> Shambhala, 1975.
> I. Shambhala Publications.

> LeSueur, Meridel, 1900-
> Rites of ancient ripening.
> Vanilla Press, 1975.
> I. Vanilla Press.

> The national prison directory:
> organizational profiles of
> prison reform groups in the
> United States. Urban Infor-
> mation Interpreters, 1972.
> I. Urban Information
> Interpreters.

Planning for *AACR2*:
The Hennepin Experience

I want to outline, chronologically, what we've already done at Hennepin County Library to plan for *AACR2*. My hope is that the process, if not also some of the specific issues and outcomes, can be adapted or transferred elsewhere.

As background:

- Hennepin produces an annual book catalog, updated by quarterly fiche supplements.
- In dictionary format, the HCL catalog fully integrates print and A/V, as well as adult and juvenile, entries.
- The bibliographic database—i.e., all the individual records for items in the collection—is *machine readable*, or automated.
- Authority control—i.e., control of name and subject forms to ensure consistency and avoid conflicts—is effected through the *Authority File* (on fiche) which both clerks and catalogers check.[1]
- New records for most print items are based either on MARC printouts or CIP data, as modified according to HCL cataloging policy.[2]
- New records are keyboarded—added to the database—in-house.
- HCL does *not* accept nor employ such ISBD elements as mandatory author statements, denotative punctuation (like slashes), Latin abbreviations, and ISBN numbers. Our reason is simply that they are either unneeded, unintelligible, or both.[3]
- Like many other public libraries, we don't indicate place of publication in imprints nor "1st edition," nor do we permit elaborate and frequently confusing collations. For instance, we don't show roman pagination and centimeter spine sizes, and we prefer short, fully comprehensible notes rather than orthodox hieroglyphics to reveal special features: photos, color plates, folded tables, bibliographies, glossaries, maps, etc. Also, we long ago

Remarks made on October 29, 1979, at an Institute in St. Paul jointly sponsored by the Minnesota Library Association, University of Minnesota Library School, and Minnesota Office of Public Libraries and Interlibrary Cooperation.

abandoned the mystifying "ca." in dates, routinely replacing it with a question mark (e.g., "Pann, Anton, 1797?–1854" instead of "Pann, Anton, ca. 1797–1854").

- In short, these decisions and practices—coupled with an audio-visual cataloging code developed and implemented in 1972—represented *our* response or posture toward Part I of *AACR2*, "Description," even before the final text had been published.[4] So about one-half of the new code, the initial 273 pages, didn't have to be seriously examined nor accommodated.

- Regarding Part II: Again, like many public libraries, we already performed "title-page cataloging." Therefore, we were substantially in accord—beforehand—with the new rules governing "Choices among different names" and "Pseudonyms" and "Fullness." Additionally, we had evolved a policy concerning added entries for persons, groups, and titles that not only harmonizes with *AACR2* stipulations, but often exceeds and extends them.[5]

On February 7, 1979, our technical services director circulated a memo to all HCL agencies, inviting staff volunteers—with no limitation placed on grade or place of work—to participate in two task forces: one to assess *DDC 19*'s probable impact on library users and operations and to make recommendations about what HCL should do about it; the other to do the same with respect to *AACR2*.

By March 1, several public service staffers had volunteered for the *AACR2* Task Force. The head cataloger was named the non-voting chair of that group, and three other people from the Technical Services Divison (TSD) agreed to serve as nonvoting consultants.

On March 1, the head cataloger sent to all task force members and consultants the new code itself, several background articles and reports (mainly extracted from the *HCL Cataloging Bulletin*, LC *Cataloging Service Bulletin* and *LC Information Bulletin*),[6] and a memo that sought to "isolate or pinpoint the principal issues—relating largely to the *form* of personal and corporate names—that the task force should address and resolve." These were the isolated issues:

When an *AACR2* personal name is either fuller or simpler than the form we're already using; e.g.,

HCL Now	AACR2
Lawrence, David Herbert, 1885–1930	Lawrence, D.H. (David Herbert), 1885–1930

A corollary question is whether we should express full names in parentheses when only initials appear in the actual name form or eliminate such redundant data from the displayed name, but perhaps store the information on our *Authority File* to resolve a future "conflict" (i.e., distinguish between two otherwise identical names).

When an *AACR2* corporate name, most notably for business firms and universities, differs drastically from the established HCL form; e.g.,

HCL Now	*AACR2*
Minnesota. University.	University of Minnesota
Bowker (R.R.) Company, New York	R.R. Bowker Company,

In general, the new rules favor "natural word order" rather than inversions; hence, "University of . . ." and "R.R. . . ." What needs primarily to be determined is whether to accept the natural-order pattern as basic HCL policy. In short, do we prefer "Minnesota. University." or "University of Minnesota," "R.R. Bowker" or "Bowker (R.R.) . . ."? If we endorse the *AACR2* approach, there will be *no* problem regarding natural-order name forms that arise here for the *first* time. That is, if we later this year receive material for which the main entry is "University of Newfoundland" and "Newfoundland. University." never before appeared in our catalog, there's no conflict. However, if we get more material that requires either a main or added entry for "University of Minnesota," *that* form *will* conflict with the already used "Minnesota. University." What we can then do, among other things, is to let the two conflicting forms coexist, perhaps linking them with notes; e.g.,

University of Minnesota.	Minnesota. University.
For material by or about this institution added to the collection before June 1979, see: Minnesota. University	For material by or about this institution added to the collection after June 1979, see: University of Minnesota.

If we do *not* approve *AACR2*'s natural forms, we can nonetheless introduce them as cross-references; e.g.,

Bowker (R.R.) Company, New York
  x R.R. Bowker Company, New York

When an *AACR2* geographic name is more fully qualified than an established HCL form or is qualified differently; e.g.,

HCL Now	*AACR2*
Paris	Paris (France)
Minneapolis	Minneapolis (Minn.)
Birmingham, England	Birmingham (West Midlands, England)

To be decided: whether to add a qualifier like "France" to "Paris" if there's otherwise no confusion nor conflict among "Paris" entries, to interpose the name of a county or region in British place-names (as in the

"Birmingham" example), and to employ parentheses or simply stick to commas; i.e.,

---

Hennepin County, Minnesota *instead of* Hennepin County (Minn.)

That March 1 memo also spotlighted an ancillary issue:

> Whether literary *anthologies* or *collections,* in particular, might not be better entered under the editor or compiler's name rather than following the current LC practice of "main entry under title" (see also *AACR2,* p. 286, rule 21.1C: "Enter a work under its title when . . . it is a collection or a work produced under editorial direction"). Some research on information-gathering behavior suggests that when a personal name is known to be associated with a given work, it's the name, not the title, that's sought.[7]
>
> As an example, should the main entry for *The American Rivals of Sherlock Holmes,* a collection edited by Hugh Greene, be under the title or the editor's name? A major consideration is that the choice of main entry, especially for fiction, will also dictate shelf location. In this Sherlockian example, the physical volume would be shelved either in the *A*'s or *G*'s, depending on main-entry choice. The possible virtue of editor/compiler-as-main entry is that all such collections put together by Greene would be collected or shelved in one place, intermixed with any works actually *authored* by the same person.

By April 27, the task force had formally submitted its recommendations to the TSD director, who circulated them on May 2 to the entire system for comment and suggestions. Deadline for reactions was May 15.

On May 25, following TSD analysis of the task force recommendations and subsequent systemwide responses, a final memo went to all agencies specifying just what the Library would do in each of those isolated areas; for instance, it declared that HCL:

> Will *not* follow *AACR2* re personal names that are either fuller or simpler than the forms already established at HCL, nor indicate full names in parentheses following initials. For example, the established HCL name,
>   Eliot, Thomas Stearns, 1888–1965
> will not be converted on either existing or future titles to the *AACR2* form,
>   Eliot, T.S. (Thomas Stearns), 1888–1965.
> And for new authors, full names will not be shown in parentheses following initials unless necessary to resolve conflicts; for instance, if the title page shows "E.H. Evans" as the author and this form is not identical to any other appearing in the HCL catalog, the name will be recorded as "Evans, E.H." instead of the *AACR2* form, "Evans, E.H. (Edward Howard)." When available, a person's birth and/or death dates will always be added to the name forms; e.g.,

---

Evans, E.H., 1937–

Will follow *AACR2* re corporate names not beginning with initials, abbreviations, and/or forenames; e.g.,

---

| University of California [*AACR2* form] | *not* | California. University. [present HCL form] |

Will *not* follow *AACR2* re corporate names beginning with one or more initials, abbreviations, or forenames followed by a surname; e.g.,

DuPont de Nemours (E.I.) and Company [present HCL form]	*not*	E.I. DuPont du Nemours and Company [*AACR2* form]
Bowker (R.R.) Company	*not*	R.R. Bowker Company
Coughlin (Michael E.), Publisher	*not*	Michael E. Coughlin, Publisher
Penney (J.C.) Company	*not*	J.C. Penney Company[8]

Will continue present HCL practice re geographic names, only adding qualifiers to resolve conflicts and employing a comma, rather than parentheses, to separate the basic place-name and qualifier;[9] e.g.,

Chicago	*not*	Chicago (Ill.)
Hennepin County, Minnesota	*not*	Hennepin County (Minn.)

Will *not* follow *AACR2* re "works produced under editorial direction" (Rule 21.1C, p. 286), but will follow *AACR1* (Rules 4.A and 5.A, pp. 17–9). Works such as collections and anthologies will be entered under editor or compiler rather than under title, e.g.,

Greene, Hugh, editor. The American rivals of Sherlock Holmes. [*AACR1* entry; shelved under G]	*not*	The American rivals of Sherlock Holmes; edited and introduced by Hugh Greene. [*AACR2* entry; shelved under A]
Cole, William, 1919– compiler Beastly boys and ghastly girls. [Shelved under C]	*not*	Beastly boys and ghastly girls; compiled by William Cole. [Shelved under B]

Interestingly, a number of staff members independently suggested two discrete name conversions, irrespective of what the old *or* new rules mandated:

Gaulle, Charles Andre Joseph Marie de	*to*	De Gaulle, Charles
	and	
Gogh, Vincent van	*to*	Van Gogh, Vincent.

Those two changes were immediately instituted, not only in the catalog, but also on cards and pockets bearing the old name forms as main entries, as well as on book spines, cards, and pockets when the call numbers required recuttering.

Since May 25, then, we have officially been using *AACR2,* as modified by earlier decisions and the task force results. And coincidentally, there have been two separate, but closely related, developments in our purely descriptive practice:

- In January 1979, as a direct consequence of staff and patron requests, we began spelling out nearly all A/V-connected abbreviations:

b&w	*became*	black and white
col.	*became*	color
diagr.	*became*	diagram
enl.	*became*	enlarged
fr.	*became*	frames
in.	*became*	inches
l.	*became*	leaves
min.	*became*	minutes
pt.	*became*	part
sd.	*became*	sound
si.	*became*	silent

- As it happens, this policy is also supported by the only relevant research I know of: Jane Schlueter's and Robert D. Little's survey of high school and college students which found that this sample group repeatedly failed to identify 15 of 18 standard abbreviations in A/V cataloging.[10]

In April and March, we conducted an inexpensive, but objective, survey of abbreviation recognition among 50 ordinary library users and 25 staff members. The surveyor, Larry Legus, concluded that "a substantial number of people do not understand many of the abbreviations used in the catalog.[11] "Co.," "Dept.," "p.," and "no." were relatively well recognized but not "c" (for "copyright"), "comp.," "b." ("born"), "d." ("died"), "tr.," "suppl.," "v.," "ed.," "Pub.," and "rev." So, believing it irresponsible to continue using abbreviations that many—or most—users just plain don't understand, we decided to spell out all the poorly recognized forms. And that experience inspired me to write this letter to the chair of ALA's Cataloging and Classification Section:

Enclosed is Larry Legus' March 22d report on the survey he lately conducted here. What he discovered regarding public and staff recognition and understanding of standard bibliographic abbreviations prompted the HCL policy changes specified in the attached April 4th memo. I'm forwarding these documents for consideration by the RTSD bodies responsible for *AACR* revision.

To my knowledge, there has so far been no serious, empirical study of how well ordinary catalog users, as well as library staff, actually understand basic bibliographic elements, despite frequent suggestions by critics that the intelligibility and utility of *AACR2* be researched before finalizing and implementing the code. The HCL survey, easily designed and conducted at minimum cost, not only disclosed that certain long-accepted cataloging conventions—like the abbreviations "v.," "c.," "d.," "comp.," "b.," and "ed."—are *not* comprehended by the average library patron and so prove inappropriate and dysfunctional, but powerfully suggests that if many *abbreviations* don't work for the public, perhaps the same obtains for other descriptive cataloging practices (e.g., Latinisms, slashes, colons, equal signs, ISBN numbers, spine measurements, and direct entry of corporate names—like E.I. DuPont de Nemours—under initials). At any rate, I firmly believe it's time to finally and objectively evaluate fundamental aspects of descriptive cataloging: Do they make sense to catalog users? Do they help or confuse? And if—as we found with abbreviations—the answers are that they *don't* make sense and *do* confuse, professional integrity dictates reform. There is simply no excuse for continuing practices that demonstrably damage rather than enhance catalog intelligibility and effectiveness. The Legus Study shows that such research can be quickly and inexpensively undertaken. It's now the responsibility of RTSD and our library schools to do the job.

That was sent on May 1, 1979. I'm still waiting for a reply. In fact, I'm still waiting for even an acknowledgement.

Notes

1. A cumulated, "export" edition of the *HCL Authority File*, on 42x microfiche, is available to subscribers at $30.00 per annum. Single cumulations—each including all currently employed name, subject, and series' forms, together with cataloger's notes, cross-references, and public notes, in one alphabetical sequence—cost $7.50. Direct orders and queries to: The Secretary, Technical Services Division, Hennepin County Library, 7009 York Ave. S., Edina, MN 55435.

2. HCL practices, enunciated over the past six years in bimonthly issues of the *HCL Cataloging Bulletin*, were finally codified in May 1979 into a six-page document, *Hennepin County Library Cataloging and Classification Policy*. Send copy requests, accompanied by a self-addressed, stamped envelope, to the Head Cataloger, Hennepin County Library, 7009 York Ave. S., Edina, MN 55435.

3. For probably the best critique of ISBD from the twin standpoints of cataloging theory and user effect, see Seymour Lubetzky's "The Traditional Ideals of Cataloging and the New Revision," in *The Nature and Future of the Catalog* (Phoenix: Oryx Press, 1979), especially pp. 155–9 and 162–4. Also pertinent in the same volume are Marvin Scilken's "The Catalog as a Public Service Tool" (pp. 89–101) and Sanford Berman's "Cataloging for Public Libraries" (pp. 225–39). Additional criticism and citations have appeared in the *HCL Cataloging Bulletin*: e.g., "Descriptive Cataloging: ISBD-M," no. 4 (November 21, 1973): 10–1; "ISBD: SRRT Action Council Opposes 'Total Implementation,' " nos. 6–7 (April 5, 1974): 16; and Marvin Scilken's letter in no. 27 (April 1, 1977): 3.

4. "Rules for Cataloging Audio-Visual Materials at Hennepin County Library," first published in *The Unabashed Librarian* (Spring 1973): 6–8, was later reprinted in Deirdre Boyle's *Expanding Media* (Phoenix: Oryx Press, 1977), pp. 265–72.

5. From the May 1979 HCL code: "Assign added entries for prime titles; titles of novellas and full-length dramas; illustrators (when the graphic element is clearly important, as in children's picture books); up to a total of 3 joint authors; significant agencies and presses; and distinctive, likely-to-be-sought subtitles and catch-titles." See also

"Little Press Access," *HCL Cataloging Bulletin,* nos. 11–13 (March 15, 1975): 7–8.

6. The "background articles and reports" included the whole *Cataloging Service Bulletin,* no. 2 (Fall 1978); "*AACR2*: Background and Summary," *LC Information Bulletin,* (October 20, 1978): 640–52; Robert M. Hiatt's "*AACR2*: Implementation Plans," *LC Information Bulletin* (November 17, 1978): 710–2; and from the *HCL Cataloging Bulletin*: "1980 and All That: A Symposium," no. 34 (May/June 1978): 19–25; Ben R. Tucker's "*Anglo-American Cataloguing Rules—Second Edition,*" no. 36 (September/October 1978): 1–12, with comment by the editor on pp. 35–6; Michael Gorman's "Virginia's Cataloging Lesson," no. 37 (November/December 1978): 29–31; Sanford Berman's "Proposed: *AACR2* Options and Addenda for School and Public Libraries," no. 38 (January/February 1979): 24–6; Berman's "Living amid Closed Catalogs," no. 39 (March/April 1979): 6–10; and Arlene Taylor Dowell's "Staying Open in 1981," no. 39 (March/April 1979): 11–5.

Such a background packet would now also contain Gorman's "The *Anglo-American Cataloguing Rules,* Second Edition," *Library Resources & Technical Services,* v. 22, no. 3 (Summer 1978): 209–26; Wesley Simonton's "An Introduction to *AACR2,*" *LRTS,* v. 23, no. 3 (Summer 1979): 321–39; Ben R. Tucker's "*AACR2* Options Proposed by the Library of Congress, Chapters 2–11," *LC Information Bulletin* (August 10, 1979): 307–16; and the entire *Cataloging Service Bulletin,* no 6 (Fall 1979).

7. See, for instance, Nancy Williamson's *Cataloguing and Bibliography: A Comparative Study of Their Interrelationships as Seen Through Their Principles and Practices* (Ann Arbor: University Microfilms International, 1977), quoted and cited by Phyllis A. Richmond, "The *AACR,* Second Edition, What Next?," in *the Nature and Future of the Catalog* (Phoenix: Oryx Press, 1979), pp. 192–3, 196.

8. As an extra-library precedent: the December 1978 Minneapolis telephone directory enters the J.C. Penney Company under "Penney J C Co. Inc." and the University of Minnesota under *U.* See the *1979 White Pages,* pp. 991, 1300.

9. This also happens to be the way most people address envelopes.

10. "The Mystery of lps and Mono; Or, Do Students Understand AV Card Catalog Terms?," *Wisconsin Library Bulletin* (November/December 1973): 381–3, reprinted in Boyle's *Expanding Media,* pp. 273–5.

11. For the full report, see "Sure, They Save Space, but Who Knows What They Mean?" *HCL Cataloging Bulletin,* no. 40 (May/June 1979): 24–9.

PERIODICALS

Paradoxically, cataloging periodicals can be both an extremely painful *and* hugely satisfying experience. "HCL Rules" presents a workable, low-cost, satisfying way not only to control a system-wide magazine collection, but to maximize access to its 1,400-plus titles. The critical, expense-saving omission of exact holdings data is made possible by HCL's annual publication of a main-entry *Periodicals List* that *does* indicate the precise holdings at each of the system's 24 agencies.

"From Sea to Shining Sea" somewhat lightheartedly reflects the painful aspect of periodicals cataloging: incessant (and often infernal) title changes. And "If There Were a *Sex Index* . . ." seeks to foment, by example, better and more widespread attention to an important, but underappreciated, kind of serial: the sex magazine.

HCL Rules

1. Determine essential data (e.g., title, publisher, frequency) from latest issue. New periodicals are to be cataloged from the *first* issue received on a "rush" basis. Follow the basic rules and forms in *AACR* Chapter 7, "Serials," except as amended by these guidelines (e.g., Rule 163, "Holdings," will not apply). Secure additional data (e.g., suspensions and absorbed publications, as well as prior titles, editors, and frequencies) from earlier issues and such secondary sources as Ulrich, Katz, ULS, NST, and MULS.

2. Enter generic, nondistinctive titles (e.g., *Annual Report, Bulletin, Circular, Journal, Proceedings, Review, Transactions*) under the responsible corporate body; e.g.,

---

American Association of University Professors.
Bulletin.
Minneapolis Institute of Arts.
Bulletin.

---

3. Make added entries for variant and popular forms of title; e.g.,

---

Library journal.   Publishers weekly.
I. Title: LJ.   I. Title: PW.

---

4. Record title changes prior to initial cataloging in a "Title varies" note (see *AACR*, p. 238) and trace. When a cataloged periodical undergoes a major title change, the former title will be closed out and the new one cataloged as another, independent entry with connecting "historical notes"; e.g.,

---

American libraries.   Z magazine.
Supersedes ALA bulletin.   Supersedes Nshila and Zambia.

---

5. Southdale Information Services will report cessations, suspensions, and cancellations, totally discarded titles to be withdrawn

Reprinted from *HCL Cataloging Bulletin*, nos. 14–15 (June 1, 1975): 20–5.

from the catalog and the entries for ceased or suspended—but still retained—titles updated with an appropriate note; e.g.,

> Ceased publication with May 1975 issue.
> Suspended publication with volume 11, number 2 (January 1975).

6. Cite sponsoring bodies, editors, etc., only if sufficiently important to merit tracing; e.g.,

> Unabashed librarian.
>   Editor: M.H. Scilken.
>   I. Scilken, Marvin H., 1926- editor.

7. Trace all small and alternative publishers listed in *HCL Cataloging Bulletin*, nos. 11–13, pp. 7–8, *Alternatives in Print*, or the *International Directory of Little Magazines and Small Presses*, together with any other publishers that are substantially responsible for a periodical's content or for which the periodical functions as an official organ; e.g.,

> American libraries. A.L.A.
>   I. American Library Association.

8. Call number for all unclassed periodicals, except URMs and GOV DOCs, is PER.

9. Final note on *all* entries:

> For HCL holdings and location, see Librarian.

10. Conclude subject tracings with —PERIODICALS subhead; e.g.,

> ENGINEERING—PERIODICALS   JAZZ MUSIC—PERIODICALS
>   SEWING—PERIODICALS

11. Sample formats:

> PER   Dollars & sense; a monthly bulletin of economic affairs.
>
>   "Sponsored by the Union for Radical Political Economics."
>   For HCL holdings and location, see Librarian.
>
>   1. Economic policy—Periodicals. 2. United States—
>   Economic conditions—Periodicals. 3. Alternative economics—
>   Periodicals. I. Union for Radical Political Economics. II. Title:
>   A monthly bulletin of economic affairs. [NOTE: Frequency
>   omitted from collation line since it appears in subtitle.]

PER   North country anvil. North Country Alternatives.

bimonthly.

Began publication 1972.
Frequently cited as Anvil.
Editor: Jack Miller.
For HCL holdings and location, see Librarian.

1. Minnesota—Periodicals. 2. Counter-culture—Periodicals. 3. Radicalism—Periodicals. 4. Cooperatives—Minnesota—Periodicals. I. North Country Alternatives. II. Miller, Jack, editor. III. Title: Anvil.

PER   Booklegger magazine. Booklegger Press.

bimonthly
Began publication 1973.
"Published by/for library workers."
For HCL holdings and location, see Librarian.

1. Libraries—Periodicals. 2. Libraries and the counter-culture—Periodicals. 3. Radicalism—Bibliography—Periodicals. 4. Counter-culture—Bibliography—Periodicals. 5. Libraries and Society—Periodicals. 6. Radical librarians—Periodicals. 7. Alternative press—Periodicals. I. Booklegger Press.

PER   Catalogue & Index. Library Association Cataloguing & Indexing Group

quarterly

For HCL holdings and location, see Librarian.

1. Cataloging—Periodicals. I. Library Association. Cataloguing & Indexing Group.

PER   International cataloguing; quarterly bulletin of the IFLA Committee on Cataloging. Longman Group.

Supersedes the Committee's Newsletter.
For HCL holdings and location, see Librarian.

1. Cataloging—Periodicals. I. International Federation of Library Associations. Committee on Cataloguing. [NOTE: Frequency omitted from collation line since it appears in subtitle.]

PER   Title varies. Librarians United To Fight Costly, Silly, Unnecessary Serial Title Changes.

bimonthly.

Began publication 1973.
Frequently cited as TV.
For HCL holdings and location, see Librarian.

1. Cataloging of serial publications—Periodicals. I. Librarians United To Fight Costly, Silly, Unnecessary Serial Title Changes. II. Title: TV (Periodical).

PER   Music cataloging bulletin; a monthly publication of the
       Music Library Assn.

       For HCL holdings and location, see Librarian.

       1. Cataloging of music—Periodicals. I. Music Library
       Association.

PER   Sipapu.

       semiannual

       Began publication 1970.
       "A newsletter for librarians, editors, collectors and others
       interested in Third World Studies, the counter-culture, the
       alternative formerly underground & independent (also called
       small) presses."
       Editor: N. Peattie.
       For HCL holdings and location, see Librarian.

       1. Libraries and the counter-culture—Periodicals. 2. Eth-
       nic Studies—Periodicals. 3. Alternative press—Periodicals.
       4. Small presses—Periodicals. 5. Libraries and minorities—
       Periodicals. I. Peattie, Noel, 1932- editor.

PER   The Unabashed librarian; the "how I run my library good" letter.

       quarterly.

       Began publication 1971.
       Frequently cited as U*L.
       Editor: M.H. Scilken.
       For HCL holdings and location, see Librarian.

       1. Libraries—Periodicals. 2. Cataloging—Periodicals. 3.
       Library service—Periodicals. 4. Public libraries—Periodi-
       cals. I. Scilken, Marvin H., 1926- editor. II. Title: The "How I
       run my library good" letter. III. Title: U*L.

PER   Library of Congress. Processing Dept.
          Cataloging service bulletin
       irregular.

       For HCL holdings and location, see Librarian.

       1. Cataloging—Periodicals. I. Title.

PER   WIN: peace and freedom thru nonviolent action.

       44 numbers yearly.

       "Published . . . with the support of the War Resisters
       League."
       Issued 1965–Oct. 2, 1967 by the Committee for Nonvio-
       lent Action and New York Workshop in Nonviolence.
       For HCL holdings and location, see Librarian.

       1. Radicalism—Periodicals. 2. Counter-culture—Periodi-
       cals. 3. Pacifism—Periodicals. 4. Peace Movement—Peri-
       odicals. 5. Repression, Political—Periodicals. 6. Nonvio-
       lence—Periodicals. I. War Resisters League. II. Committee
       for Nonviolent Action. III. New York Workshop in Nonvio-
       lence. IV. Title: Peace and freedom thru nonviolent action.

PER   Wilson library bulletin. H.W. Wilson.

monthly (except July and August).

Continues Wilson bulletin with volume 13, number 11 (1939).
Issued Sept. 1943–June 1956 in two sections.
Editor: W.R. Eshelman.
Frequently cited as WLB.
For HCL holdings and location, see Librarian.

1. Libraries—Periodicals. 2. Reference books—Reviews—Periodicals. I. Eshelman, William Robert, 1921- editor. II. Title: WLB. III. Title: Wilson bulletin.

PER   Young adult alternative newsletter.

irregular.

Began publication 1973.
Editor: C. Starr.
Frequently cited as YAAN.
For HCL holdings and location, see Librarian.

1. Libraries and youth—Periodicals. I. Starr, Carol, editor. II. Title: YAAN. III. Title: Y.A.A.N.

PER   The Washington monthly.
Began publication 1969.
For HCL holdings and location, see Librarian.

1. United States—Politics and government—1969—Periodicals. 2. Government and the press—United States—Periodicals. 3. Journalism, Political—Periodicals. 4. Investigative journalism—Periodicals.

PER   Woman's day. Fawcett.

monthly.

For HCL holdings and location, see Librarian.

1. Home economics—Periodicals. 2. Cooking—Periodicals. 3. Fashion—Periodicals. 4. Beauty care—Periodicals. 5. Sewing—Periodicals. 6. Women—Periodicals. 7. Women's clothing—Periodicals. 8. Women's periodicals.

PER   womenSports.

monthly.

Editor: R.M. Wright
For HCL holdings and location, see Librarian.

1. Women athletes—Periodicals. 2. Women's sports—Periodicals. 3. Women's periodicals. I. Wright, Rosalie Muller, editor. II. Title: Women sports

PER   Yachting: power and sail.

monthly

"Founded 1907."
Subtitle varies.
For HCL holdings and location, see Librarian.

1. Yachts and yachting—Periodicals. 2. Yacht racing—Periodicals. 3. Sailing—Periodicals. 4. Boats and boating—Periodicals. 5. Regattas—Periodicals. 6. Sailboat racing—Periodicals.

PER   RT; a journal of radical therapy. Radical Therapist.

bimonthly.

Previous titles: Radical therapist, Rough times.
Tabloid format.
For HCL holdings and location, see Librarian.

1. Antipsychiatry—Periodicals. 2. Mental Patients' Liberation Movement—Periodicals. 3. Mentally ill—Rights—Periodicals. 4. Psychiatric reform—Periodicals. 5. Psychiatric hospitals—Periodicals. I. Title: Journal of radical therapy. II. Title: Radical therapist. III. Title: Rough times.

PER   Synthesis: an anti-authoritarian newsletter for citizen-worker self-management ideas and activities. League for Economic Democracy/Philadelphia Solidarity.

quarterly.

Absorbed Solidarity newsletter.
Issues include directories of anti-authoritarian groups, magazines, bookstores, and presses.
For HCL holdings and location, see Librarian.

1. Workers' control—Periodicals. 2. Anarchism and anarchists—Periodicals. 3. Libertarianism—Periodicals. 4. Radical organizations—Directories. 5. Labor solidarity—Periodicals. I. League for Economic Democracy. II. Philadelphia Solidarity. III. Title: Solidarity newsletter. IV. Title: Anti-authoritarian newsletter for citizen-worker self-management ideas and activities. V. Title: Self-management ideas and activities newsletter.

PER   The freeman; a monthly journal of ideas on liberty. Foundation for Economic Education.
For HCL holdings and location, see Librarian.

1. Conservatism—Periodicals. 2. Free enterprise—Periodicals. I. Foundation for Economic Education.

From Sea to Shining Sea . . .
to Inland Sea . . .
to Sea Combined with
Rudder . . . to Sea for the
Inland Boatman . . . to Sea,
Inland Edition . . .

On February 8, 1979, the head cataloger wrote this letter to the publisher of *Sea*(?):

You probably don't *mean* to, but the fact is that you *are* driving me crazy. And probably a hundred other catalogers and serials librarians, too. Why? Because it is simply impossible to determine whether the monthly periodical you produce and we subscribe to is titled *Sea*. Or *Sea Magazine*. Or *Sea Combined with Rudder*. Or *Sea for the Inland Boatman*. Or *Sea: Inland Edition*. Or *Inland Sea*. Every one of those "titles" appears— somewhere—in your December 1978 issue: *Inland Sea* on the spine, *Sea for the Inland Boatman* and *Sea: Inland Edition* on the cover, *Sea Combined with Rudder* on pages 3 and 4, *Sea Magazine* on page 4, and just plain *Sea* on pages 2, 4, 15, and 112, not to mention the tear-out "Reader Service Card."

Well, what *is* it? We can't afford to recatalog the mag every month. We can't shelve a single copy in six different places. And it's clearly wasteful to maintain six distinct check-in cards for *one* periodical. So please pick a title. Any title. And for the next ten years (at least), don't even *think* about changing it. Not a letter. Not a word. Not a punctuation mark. Nothing.

Reprinted from *HCL Cataloging Bulletin*, no. 40 (May/June 1979): 5—7.

Harry Monahan, executive editor, replied on February 27:

In reply to your letter of February 8, you have my sympathies about the cataloging difficulties with our magazine. But you are dealing with only 25 percent of the problem. There actually are FOUR magazines named *Sea*. But that's getting ahead of the story.

My suggestion is that you identify the magazine that you are filing as *Sea, Inland Edition*. If you had an earlier file on *Rudder* magazine, I would suggest a notation to the effect that *Rudder* was succeeded by *Sea* as of July 1977. There were no editions of *Rudder* for April, May and June of 1977. The last edition of the old *Rudder* magazine was March 1977.

When *Sea* acquired *Rudder*, the new, combined publication was identified as *Sea Combined With Rudder* in order for us to retain our claim to the name *Rudder*. We have since dropped the *Combined With Rudder* phrase from the cover in the interests of brevity and graphic impact. The long title is used elsewhere in the magazine to protect that name claim. The combined magazine is produced in four regional editions. however, Eastern, Western, Southern and Inland (Midwest). Originally, those regional designations were used on the covers to identify each edition. But we encountered a conflict with a publication titled *Inland Seas*, so we dropped that marking in favor of the mottos beneath the logo: "For the Inland (Eastern, Southern, Western) Boatman," to serve the same identification purpose.

Now we have dropped the mottos in favor of the cleaner cover look. But through all of this the magazine still is best identified simply as *Sea*. Your library, obviously, is getting the Inland edition, so your catalog would need to reflect that designation.

For clarification, I am enclosing copies of all four regional editions of the February issue of *Sea*. About 50 percent of each of these has exactly the same editorial material; but the other 50 percent is different, being filled with regionally oriented editorial material.

And if you think it is confusing cataloging this gem, think what it must be like to produce it.

If you have any further questions or problems, please contact me.

So this is now the way HCL has cataloged Mr. M.'s "gem":

PER   Sea. Inland edition. CBS Publications.
           monthly.

           Began publication 1908.
           Absorbed Rudder with July 1977 issue.
           Variant titles: Inland Sea; Sea for the inland boatman; Sea combined with Rudder; Sea magazine. Inland edition.
           For HCL holdings and location, see Librarian.

           1. Boats and boating—Periodicals. 2. Boats and boating—Middle West (United States)—Periodicals. 3. Sports—Periodicals. I. Title: Sea combined with Rudder. II. Title: Rudder. III. Title: Inland sea. IV. Title: Sea for the inland boatman. V. Title: Sea magazine. Inland edition.

If There Were a *Sex Index* . . .

There isn't one, of course. Because erotic, Gay, and sexologic materials—"dirty," "deviant" books and magazines—have traditionally embarrassed librarians. Even scared them. But The Sixties and the Sexual Revolution have undermined much of that Victorian tradition, producing a real impetus to now actively collect and access that vast, long-neglected, and ever-growing literature of sensuality. So if H.W. Wilson, SIECUS, or Haworth Press *did* produce a *Sex Index* to belatedly complement the *Art Index, Business Index, Education Index*, etc., it should look something like this:

Fetish T Fetish Times. B & D Company. P.O.B. 7109, Van Nuys, CA 91409. monthly. $18 p.a.; single issues @ $1.50.

Gay Insurg Gay Insurgent: Journal of Gay Liberation Research, Reviews, and News. "Formerly Midwest Gay Academic Journal." P.O.B. 2337, Philadelphia, PA 19103. 3 nos. yearly. $5 p.a.

Gay Sun Gay Sunshine: a Journal of Gay Liberation. P.O.B. 40397, San Francisco, CA 94140. 8 nos. yearly. $8 p.a.

Hum Dig Human Digest: the Sexual Behavior Journal. Thomaston Publications, 380 Madison Ave., New York, NY 10017. 10 nos. yearly. $10 p.a.; single issues @ $1.25.

J Homo Journal of Homosexuality. Haworth Press, 149 Fifth Ave., New York, NY 10010. quarterly. Institutions: $40 p.a.; individuals: $24.

Pillow T Pillow Talk: the Monthly Journal of Sexual Fulfillment. Carla Publishing, 208 E. 43d St., New York, NY 10017. $12 p.a.; single issues @ $1.25.

Resp Response: the New Sexuality. Can-Am Media, P.O.B. 909, Fairfield, CT 06430. monthly. $15 p.a.

Indexed Periodicals

Reprinted with permission from *Sex Magazines in the Library Collection: A Scholarly Study of Sex in Serials and Periodicals*, a monographic supplement to *The Serials Librarian* (Peter Gellatly, editor). © 1980 by The Haworth Press, Inc.

Screw Screw: the Sex Review. Milky Way Productions, P.O.B. 432, Old Chelsea Station, New York, NY 10011. 10 nos. yearly. $9.95 p.a.; single issues @ $1.50.

Sexol Sexology. Medi-Media Publications, 313 W. 53d St., New York, NY 10019. monthly. $15 p.a.; single issues @ $1.25.

Sex L Rptr Sexual Law Reporter. 1800 Highland Ave. (Suite 106), Los Angeles, CA 90028. quarterly. $30 p.a.

SYOL So's Your Old Lady: a Lesbian/Feminist Journal. 3149 Fremont Ave. S., Minneapolis, MN 55408. bimonthly. $7.50 p.a.; single issues @ $1.25.

Var Variations: For Liberated Lovers. Variations Publishing International, 909 Third Ave., New York, NY 10022. bimonthly, beginning Sept. 1979. Special issues @ $2.25.

Sample Entry

RELAXATION

Altman, Carole
   Too tense for love? Try these relaxation techniques that work! Sexol 46—2: 39—43 Oct 79

   An article on the subject of relaxation, written by Carole Altman and titled "Too tense for love? Try these relaxation techniques that work!," appears in *Sexology*, volume 46, number 2 (October 1979), on pages 39—43.

Abbott, Keith
   Rhino Ritz.
      Review (Michael Perkins): Screw 548:21 Sep 3, 79

Abbott, Steve
   Wrecked hearts; raw poetry.
      Review (R. Daniel Evans): Gay Sun 40/41:35 Sum/Fall 79

ACTORS, FILM. *See* EROTIC FILM ACTORS.

ADOLESCENT SEXUALITY. *See* TEENAGERS' SEXUALITY.

ADULT BOOKSHOPS. *See* SEX SHOPS.

ADULT—CHILD RELATIONS. *See* BOY LOVE; CHILD MOLESTING; FATHER—DAUGHTER INCEST; MOTHER—SON INCEST; PEDOPHILIA.

ADVERTISEMENTS, PERSONAL. *See* PERSONAL ADVERTISEMENTS.

AFTERPLAY—PERSONAL ACCOUNTS
   Cordially yours [letter]. Sexol 46-2:63 Oct 79

AIDS, SEX. *See* SEX AIDS.

AIRPLANE SEX—PERSONAL ACCOUNTS
   Joy stick [letter]. Var spec 5:94-5 Mid-Spr 79

ALCOHOLIC LESBIANS. *See* LESBIAN ALCOHOLICS.

ALTERNATIVE PRESS DISTRIBUTORS
   Tsang, Daniel
      Radical distribution. Gay Insurg 4/5:12-13 Spr 79

Altman, Carole
   Too tense for love? Try these relaxation techniques that work! Sexol 46-2:39-43 Oct 79

AMPUTEES
   The amateur surgeon: "permanent public bondage" the roots of amputee love. Fetish T 64:16-17
   One-legged [letter]. Hum Dig 3-1:57-9 Jan 79

ANAL SEX
   Anal fear [letter]. Hum Dig 3-1:89-90 Jan 79

ANAL SEX—PERSONAL ACCOUNTS
   Anal love [letter]. Var spec 5:161-2 Mid-Spr 79
   Delectable delirium [letter]. Var spec 5:162 Mid-Spr 79
   Lawrence, Adele
      A virgin doesn't have to say no. Var spec 5:105-11 Mid-Spr 79

Andrews, Martha
   Brief resolution [poem]. SYOL 21:14 Oct 79

ANDROGYNY
   Bernard, Larry Craig
      Androgyny scores of matched homosexual and heterosexual males. By Larry Craig Bernard and David J. Epstein. J Homo 4-2:169-78 Win 78

ANILINGUS
   Miller, Kate
      Anilingus: something special for your lover. Hum Dig 3-1:32-4 Jan 79

ANIMAL LOVE. *See* BESTIALITY.

ANTI—GAY PREJUDICE. *See* HOMOPHOBIA.

Antler
Poems. Gay Sun 40/41:36 Sum/Fall 79

ARCHIVES, GAY. *See* GAY ARCHIVES.

ARCHIVES, LESBIAN—FEMINIST. *See* LESBIAN—FEMINIST ARCHIVES.

ARMPIT HAIR
Passion pit [letter]. Sexol 46-2:62-3 Oct 79

Arrizabalaga y Prado, Leonardo de
Song without words [poem]. Gay Sun 40/41:35 Sum/Fall 79

"ASS—FUCKING." *See* ANAL SEX.

Austen, Roger
Playing the game: the homosexual novel in America. 1977. Review (Byrne R.S. Fone): J Homo 4-2:195-200 Win 78

AUTOEROTICISM. *See* MASTURBATION.

B/D. *See* BONDAGE AND DISCIPLINE.

BACCHANALIA
Brock, Paul
Pompeii: the first city of sexual freedom. A look at the true meaning of Bacchanalia. Sexol. 46-2:19-22 Oct 79.

BALDNESS FETISH
Bald is bawdy! [letter]. Fetish T 64:10

BALLS, BEN—WA. *See* BEN—WA BALLS.

Bataille, Georges
Blue of noon.
Review (Michael Perkins): Screw 548:21 Sep 3, 79

BEACHES, NUDE. *See* NUDE BEACHES.

Beame, Jeffery
Tonight desire has a man in it [poem]. Gay Sun 40/41:37 Sum/Fall 79

Beckley, Tim
Sex at the roller disco. Pillow T 3-6:62-6 Sep 79

BEN—WA BALLS
Delectable delirium [letter]. Var spec 5:162 Mid-Spr 79
Phillips, Kate
Ben Wa balls: a woman's secret delight. Var spec 5:96-9 Mid-Spr 79

Bentley, Caryl B.
A both/and song for the crones: dedicated to Mary Daly [poem]. SYOL 21:5 Oct 78

Berman, Sanford
Gay access: new approaches in cataloging. Gay Insurg 4/5:14-15 Spr 79

Bernard, Larry Craig
Androgyny scores of matched homosexual and heterosexual males. By Larry Craig Bernard and David J. Epstein. J Homo 4-2:169-78 Win 78

BESTIALITY
Witomsky, T.R.
Oh, you big brute, you. Pillow T 3-6:12-15 Sep 79

BESTIALITY—PERSONAL ACCOUNTS
Doggie-do [letter]. Resp 6-9:26-6 Oct 79

BIG BROTHERS, INC.
Sexual preference of Big Brothers may be subject to scrutiny. Sex L Rptr 4-4:74 Oct/Dec 78

BIRTH CONTROL—LAWS AND REGULATIONS
Distribution of contraceptives to minors may violate parents' Constitutional rights. Sex L Rptr 4-4:63 Oct/Dec 78

BISEXUALS
See also Swinging
Threesomes

BISEXUALS—PERSONAL ACCOUNTS
Bisexual husband [letter]. Var spec 5:28-8 Mid-Spr 79
Bisexual swingers [letter]. Var spec 5:52-4 Mid-Spr 79
Bisexual threesome [letter]. Var spec 5:29 Mid-Spr 79
Bisexual wife [letter]. Var spec 5:28 Mid-Spr 79
Fellatio fan [letter]. Var spec 5:29-30 Mid-Spr 79
Friends and lovers [letter]. Var spec 5:83-4 Mid-Spr 79
Kempler, Jana
A couple takes a chance. Var spec 5:70-81 Mid-Spr 79
Unforgettable melody [letter]. Var spec 5:84-5 Mid-Spr 79
A yacht to learn [letter]. Var spec 5:82 Mid-Spr 79

Blakeston, Oswell
The graveyard [poem]. Gay Sun 40/41:37 Sum/Fall 79

Bliss, K.D.
Beating the short time Charlie blues. Resp. 6-9:27-31 Oct 79

"BLOW JOBS." *See* FELLATIO.

BONDAGE AND DISCIPLINE
See also Eunuchs
Sadomasochism
The amateur surgeon: "permanent public bondage" the roots of amputee love. Fetish T 64:16-17
Bisexual wife [letter]. Var spec 5:28 Mid-Spr 79
Prolong the agony! [letter]. Fetish T 64:9
Stryker, Rod
On the rack. Fetish T 64:12-13
Von Eckmann, Erika
A eunuch in every garage [letter], Fetish T 64:9-10

BONDAGE AND DISCIPLINE FANTASIES
The captured maiden [letter]. Var spec 5:42-3 Mid-Spr 79
A rebellious wench [letter]. Var spec 5:41-2 Mid-Spr 79

BONDAGE AND DISCIPLINE IN TELEVISION
Park, R.L.
Bondage on the boob tube. Fetish T 64:11

BONDAGE AND DISCIPLINE—PERSONAL ACCOUNTS
Christie's book: a life in bondage. Hum Dig 3-1:35-6 Jan 79
Friendly, Suzanne
I can be very friendly. Pillow T 3-6:8-10 Sep 79
White slave [letter]. Hum Dig 3-1:63-6 Jan 79

Bonner, T. Peter
Playing the personals. Resp 6-9:32-8 Oct 79

BOOK REVIEWS

Abbott, Keith
Rhino Ritz.
Review (Michael Perkins): Screw 548:21 Sep 3, 79

Abbott, Steve
Wrecked hearts; raw poetry.
Review (R. Daniel Evans): Gay Sun 40/41:35 Sum/Fall 79

Austen, Roger
Playing the game: the homosexual novel in America. 1977.
Review (Byrne R.S. Fone): J Homo 4-2:195-200 Win 78

Bataille, Georges
Blue of noon.
Review (Michael Perkins): Screw 548:21 Sep 3, 79

Bullough, Vern L.
An annotated bibliography of homosexuality. 1976.
Review (A.P.M. Coxon): Gay Insurg 4/5:49 Spr 79
Review (William Parker): J Homo 4-2:185-92 Win 78

Burroughs, William S.
Blade runner: a movie.
Review (Michael Perkins): Screw 548:21 Sep 3, 79

Christian, Paula
Edge of twilight. 1959.
This side of love. 1963.
Reviews (S.C.): SYOL 21:22 Oct 78

Crew, Louie
The Gay academic. 1978.
Review (Jim Monahan): Gay Insurg 4/5:43-7 Spr 79

Curzon, Daniel
Among the carnivores. 1979.
Review (Scott Jones): Gay Sun 40/41:32 Sum/Fall 79

Dover, Kenneth J.
Greek homosexuality. 1978.
Review (Arthur William Rudolph): Gay Sun 40/41:33-4 Sum/Fall 79

Evans, Arthur.
Witchcraft and the Gay counterculture. 1978.
Review (Will Inman): Gay Sun 40/41:31-2 Sum/Fall 79

Fisher, Pete
Special teachers/special boys. 1979.
Review (Scott Jones): Gay Sun 40/41:32 Sum/Fall 79

Friedman, Leslie
Sex role stereotyping in the mass media: an annotated bibliography. 1974.
Review (Scott C. McDonald): J Homo 4-2:192-4 Win 78

Gay Theory Work Group of the Movement for a New Society
Gay oppression and liberation or, Homophobia: its causes and cure. 1977.
Review (Marc Killinger): Gay Insurg 4/5:37-42 Spr 79

Gibson, E. Lawrence
Get off my ship. 1978.
Review (Daniel Tsang): Gay Insurg 4/5:47 Spr 79

Ginsberg, Allen
To Eberhart from Ginsberg; a letter about HOWL. 1976.
Allen Ginsberg journals; early Fifties early Sixties. Edited by Gordon Ball. 1977.
Mind breaths; poems 1972-1977. 1977.
As ever; the collected correspondence of Allen Ginsberg and Neal Cassady. Edited by Barry Gifford. 1977.
Reviews (David Chura): Gay Sun 40/41:15-16 Sum/Fall 79

Hamilton, Wallace
David at Olivet. 1979.
Review (Scott Jones): Gay Sun 40/41:32 Sum/Fall 79

Kelly, Dennis
Chicken; boy love poems. 1979.
Review (Charley Shively): Gay Sun 40/41:9 Sum/Fall 79

Kirmani, Awhaduddin
Heart's witness; the Sufi quatrains of Awhaduddin Kirmani. Translated by Bernd Manuel Weischer & Peter Lamborn Wilson. 1978.
Review (Winston Leyland): Gay Sun 40/41:33 Sum/Fall 79

Kramer, Larry
Faggots. 1978.
Review (Larry Puchall): Gay Sun 40/41:34 Sum/Fall 79

Leyland, Winston
Now the volcano: an anthology of Latin American Gay literature. 1979.
Review (E.A. Lacey): Gay Sun 40/41:26-31 Sum/Fall 79

Mariah, Paul
This light will spread: selected poems 1960-1975. 1978.
Review (Steve Abbott): Gay Sun 40/41:34 Sum/Fall 79

Morin, Stephen F.
"The Gay movement and the rights of children." J of Social Issues. 1978.
Review (Daniel Tsang): Gay Insurg 4/5:48 Spr 79

Orlovsky, Peter
Clean asshole poems & smiling vegetable songs. 1978.
Review (Charles Shively): Gay Sun 40/41:15 Sum/Fall 79

Parker, William
Homosexuality bibliography: Supplement, 1970-1975. 1977.
Review (Daniel Tsang): Gay Insurg 4/5:49 Spr 79

Rimbaud, Arthur
Rimbaud/Verlaine: a lover's cock. 1979.
Review (Arthur William Rudolph): Gay Sun 40/41:38 Sum/Fall 79

Ronan, Richard
Flowers; poems. 1978.
Review (E.A. Lacey): Gay Sun 40/41:32 Sum/Fall 79

Satin, Mark
New Age politics, healing self and society; the emerging new alternative to Marxism and Liberalism. 1978.
Review (Mitch Walker): Gay Sun 40/41:35 Sum/Fall 79

Tiktin, Carl
Ron. 1979.
Review (Scott Jones): Gay Sun 40/41:32 Sum/Fall 79

Watmough, David
No more into the garden. 1978.
Review (Scott Jones): Gay Sun 40/41:32 Sum/Fall 79

White, Edmund
Nocturnes for the King of Naples. 1978.
Review (Scott Jones): Gay Sun 40/41:32 Sum/Fall 79

Borchette, Suzanne
A night in Central Park.
Var spec 5:86-91 Mid-Spr 79

Boston/Boise Committee
Suggestions for media on handling alleged sex "crimes" involving Gay men. Gay Insurg 4/5:56-9 Spr 79

BOY LOVE
Nichols, D.W.
A boy lover's perspective: D.W. Nichols interviewed by Daniel Tsang, Part II. Gay Insurg 4/5:25-36 Spr 79

BOY LOVE—PERSONAL ACCOUNTS
Pedophiliac [letter]. Hum Dig 3-1:92 Jan 79

BOY LOVE—POETRY—REVIEWS
Kelly, Dennis
Chicken; boy love poems. 1979.
Review (Charles Shively): Gay Sun 40/41:9 Sum/Fall 79
Kirmani, Awhaduddin
Heart's witness: the Sufi quatrains of Awhaduddin Kirmani. Translated by Bernd Manuel Weischer & Peter Lamborn Wilson. 1978.
Review (Winston Leyland): Gay Sun 40/41:33 Sum/Fall 79

BOY PROSTITUTES. See CHILD PROSTITUTES; MALE PROSTITUTES.

BREAST FEEDING
Breast-feeding [letter]. Hum Dig 3-1:91-2 Jan 79

BREAST PLAY
Hodges, Parker
That misunderstood erogenous zone; the nipple—a powerful source of erotic pleasure in both men and women—is largely unexplored. Sexol 46-2:30-4 Oct 79

BREAST SIZE
A big bust [letter]. Sexol 46-2:61-2 Oct 79

BREASTS
Doolittle, Arch
A global view of breasts. Resp 6-9:40-5 Oct 79

Brock, Paul
Pompeii: the first city of sexual freedom. A look at the true meaning of Bacchanalia. Sexol 46-2:19-22 Oct 79

BROTHER—SISTER INCEST—PERSONAL ACCOUNTS
Incestuous seeker [letter]. Hum Dig 3-1:81-3 Jan 79

Bullough, Vern L.
An annotated bibliography of homosexuality. 1976.
Review (William Parker): J Homo 4-2:185-92 Win 78
Review (A.P.M.Coxon): Gay Insurg 4/5:49 Spr 79

Burleson, Tom
Sensual mind control [story]. Var spec 5:32-7 Mid-Spr 79

BURLESQUE SHOWS
Wife depressed over sex shows [letter]. Sexol 46-2:73-5 Oct 79

Burroughs, William S.
Blade runner: a movie.
Review (Michael Perkins): Screw 548:21 Sep 3, 79

CAB SEX. See TAXICAB SEX.

Califia, Pat
Pleasure/pain and power—a Lesbian's view. Var spec 5:56-65 Mid-Spr 79

CALL GIRLS. See FEMALE PROSTITUTES.

CAREER WOMEN
Deni, Laura
Why nice girls finish last. Pillow T 3-6:16-21+ Sep 79

CARRIAGE SEX—PERSONAL ACCOUNTS
Borchette, Suzanne
A night in Central Park. Var spec 5:86-91 Mid-Spr 79

CARRIER PIGEON (FIRM)
Tsang, Daniel
Radical distribution. Gay Insurg 4/5:12-13 Spr 79

CARTOONS
Jordon, Flash.
Dildonuts [cartoon]. Screw 548:24-5 Sep 3, 79
Moon, Little
Doping it out [illustrated limericks]. Screw 548:9-11 Sep 3, 79

CASTRATION
Von Eckmann, Erika
A eunuch in every garage [letter]. Fetish T 64:9-10

CATALOGING OF GAY MATERIALS
Berman, Sanford
Gay access: new approaches in cataloging. Gay Insurg 4/5:14-15 Spr 79

Catherine, Eleanor
It happened on a train. Var spec 5:116-20 Mid-Spr 79

Chadwick, Jerah
Making it new [poem]. Gay Sun 40/41:35 Sum/Fall 79

CHILD—ADULT RELATIONS. See BOY LOVE; CHILD MOLESTING; FATHER—DAUGHTER INCEST; MOTHER—SON INCEST; PEDOPHILIA.

CHILD MOLESTING—LAWS AND REGULATIONS
Age mistake is defense to child molestation. Sex L Rptr 4-4:69 Oct/Dec 78

CHILD "PORNOGRAPHY"
Nichols, D.W.
A boy lover's perspective: D.W. Nichols interviewed by Daniel Tsang, Part II. Gay Insurg 4/5:25-36 Spr 79
Youth Liberation
Children and sex: a Youth Liberation view. Gay Insurg 4/5:22-4 Spr 79

CHILD PROSTITUTES
See also Boy love
Urban tragedy [letter]. Sexol 46-2:61 Oct 79
Youth Liberation
Children and sex: a Youth Liberation view. Gay Insurg 4/5:44-2 Spr 79

CHILDREN, GAY. See GAY CHILDREN.

CHILDREN'S RIGHTS
Distribution of contraceptives to minors may violate parents' Constitutional rights. Sex L Rptr 4-4:63 Oct/Dec 78
Youth Liberation
Children and sex: a Youth Liberation view. Gay Insurg 4/5:22-4 Spr 79

CHILDREN'S SEXUALITY
See also Boy love
Child "pornography"
Child prostitutes
Gay children
Incest
Pedophilia
Youth Liberation
Children and sex: a Youth Liberation view. Gay Insurg 4/5:22-4 Spr 79

CHILDREN'S SEXUALITY—
PERSONAL ACCOUNTS
Chalking it up [letter]. Var spec 5:159-60 Mid-Spr 79
Childhood erotic memories [letter]. Var spec 5:150-6 Mid-Spr 79

Christian, Paula
Edge of twilight. 1959.
This side of love. 1963.
Reviews (S.C.): SYOL 21:22 Oct 78

CHROMOTHERAPY
Jackson, Martin A.
How color affects your life and love. Pillow T 3-6:77-81+ Sep 79

CIRCUMCISION—PERSONAL ACCOUNTS
A satisfied reader [letter]. Sexol 46-2:63 Oct 79

CLUBS, SWINGERS'. See SWINGERS' CLUBS.

COITAL POSITIONS
See also
Heterosexual intercourse
Homosexual intercourse
Karlen, Arno
Who's on top? The sexual conflict people don't talk about. Sexol 46-2:24-9 Oct 79

COITUS. See HETEROSEXUAL INTERCOURSE; HOMOSEXUAL INTERCOURSE.

Colebrook, Val
Inside out [poem]. SYOL 21:24 Oct 78
Strange songs (dreams) [poem]. SYOL 21:15 Oct 78

COLOR PSYCHOLOGY
Jackson, Martin A.
How color affects your life and love. Pillow T 3-6:77-81+ Sep 79

CONSUMER GUIDES. See BOOK REVIEWS; ENCYCLOPEDIA EVALUATION; EROTIC FILMS—REVIEWS; GAY FILMS—REVIEWS; SEX AIDS—EVALUATION.

Cooperstock, David
The joys of sex without an erection. Var spec 5:12-17 Mid-Spr 79

COPROPHILIA
Witomski, T.R.
Beyond the last taboo. Var spec 5:136-40 Mid-Spr 79

Corinne, Tee
The lady who loved horses [graphic]. SYOL 21:24 Oct 78

COUNSELING, SEX. See SEX COUNSELING AND THERAPY.

Cozad, William
Cruisin' the Bay Area. Resp 6-9:52-6 Oct 79

Crew, Louie
The Gay academic. 1978.
Review (Jim Monahan): Gay Insurg 4/5:43-7 Spr 79

Crown, Sandra
Female sexual fulfillment, what it really means. Hum Dig 3-1:39-45 Jan 79

Cruikshank, Peg
Notes on two films: Julia and Word is out. SYOL 21:11 Oct 78

CUNNILINGUS
Small, Larry
Hot licks: a guide to cunnilingus. Resp 6-9:46-50 Oct 79

CUNNILINGUS—PERSONAL ACCOUNTS
A fellow traveler [letter]. Sexol 46-2:55 Oct 79
Home help [letter]. Var spec 5:100-1 Mid-Spr 79
Lawrence, Adele
A virgin doesn't have to say no. Var spec 5:105-11 Mid-Spr 79
Little Miss Muffet [letter]. Var spec 5:157-8 Mid-Spr 79

"CUNT SHAVING." See PUBIS SHAVING.

"CUNT SUCKING." See CUNNILINGUS.

Curzon, Daniel
Among the carnivores. 1979.
Review (Scott Jones): Gay Sun 40/41:32 Sum/Fall 79

Dailey, Jan
Women and orgasm: how to achieve it no matter what. Sexol 46-2:10-18 Oct 79

DANGER SEX. See AIRPLANE SEX; BONDAGE AND DISCIPLINE; CARRIAGE SEX; ELEVATOR SEX; EXHIBITIONISM; MUSEUM SEX; OFFICE SEX; RESTAURANT SEX; ROLLER-COASTER SEX; SADOMASOCHISM; SAUNA SEX; STORE SEX; TAXICAB SEX; THEATER SEX; TRAIN SEX.

DATING
Smith, Belle
Sexual myths. Hum Dig 3-1:46-9 Jan 79

Dean, Charles
Reflections of a rapist. Sexol 46-2:44-5 Oct 79

Deni, Laura
Why nice girls finish last. Pillow T 3-6:16-21+ Sep 79

Diamond, Deborah L.
Alcohol abuse among Lesbians: a descriptive study. J Homo 4-2:123-42 Win 78

DIAPER FETISH—PERSONAL ACCOUNTS
Diaper lover [letter]. Var spec 5:160-1 Mid-Spr 79

DILDOS
Double dong [letter]. Var spec 5:101-2 Mid-Spr 79
Little Miss Muffet [letter]. Var spec 5:157-8 Mid-Spr 79

DILDOS—CARTOONS
Jordon, Flash
Dildonuts [cartoon]. Screw 548:24-5 Sep 3, 79

DISCIPLINE. See BONDAGE AND DISCIPLINE.

DISCO SKATING
     Beckley, Tim
          Sex at the roller disco. Pillow T 3-6:62-6 Sep 79

DISCRIMINATION AGAINST GAYS. *See* HOMOPHOBIA.

DOLLS, SEX. *See* SEX DOLLS.

DOMINATION. *See* BONDAGE AND DISCIPLINE.

Doolittle, Arch
     A global view of breasts. Resp 6-9:40-5 Oct 79

Dover, Kenneth J.
     Greek homosexuality. 1978.
          Review (Arthur William Rudolph): Gay Sun 40/41:33-4
          Sum/Fall 79

DRUGS AND SEX
     Moon, Little
          Doping it out [illustrated limericks]. Screw 548:9-11 Sep
          3, 79

Duncan, Robert
     Interview. Gay Sun 40/41:1-8 Sum/Fall 79

ELDERLY PEOPLE'S SEXUALITY. *See* SENIORS'
     SEXUALITY.

ELECTRIC HAIRDRYERS. *See* HAIRDRYERS.

ELEVATOR SEX—PERSONAL ACCOUNTS
     Elevated sex [letter]. Var spec 5:92 Mid-Spr 79

ENCYCLOPEDIA EVALUATION
     SantaVicca, Edmund F.
          Evaluating encyclopedias: a framework summary. Gay
          Insurg 4/5:15-17 Spr 79

ENEMA FILMS—CATALOGS
     Film fare [advertisement]. Fetish T 64:15

"ENGLISH CULTURE." *See* BONDAGE AND DISCIPLINE.

Epstein, David J.
     Androgyny scores of matched homosexual and heterosex-
     ual males. By Larry Craig Bernard and David J. Epstein. J.
     Homo 4-2:169-78 Win 78

ERECTIONS
     See also Impotence
                    Penis size
     Cooperstock, David
          The joys of sex without an erection. Var spec 5:12-17
          Mid-Spr 79

EROTIC BOOKS
     See also Erotic fiction
     Stryker, Rod
          On the rack. Fetish T 64:12-13

EROTIC FICTION—REVIEWS
     Bataille, Georges.
          Blue of Noon.
               Review (Michael Perkins): Screw 548:21 Sep 3, 79
     Burroughs, William S.
          Blade runner: a movie.
               Review (Michael Perkins): Screw 548:21 Sep 3, 79

EROTIC FILM ACTORS—INTERVIEWS
     Hoffman, Lisa
          A bisexual wedding; interview and photos. Porn film star
          Marc Stevens married transsexual model Jill Monro. Var
          spec 5:18-27 Mid-Spr 79

EROTIC FILMS
     Gersten, Leon
          "The fantasy game." Pillow T 3-6: 91-3 Sep 79
     Helping hand [letter]. Hum Dig 3-1:73-4 Jan 79

EROTIC FILMS—CATALOGS
     Your favorite XXX full-length movies are now on video
          tapes! [advertisement]. Screw 548:8 Sep 3, 79

EROTIC FILMS—REVIEWS
     Neuhaus, Manny
          Kennel ration raunch [review of Fulfilling young cups].
          Screw 548:23 Sep 3, 79
     Perkowski, Donald
          A flesh start: video vice. Screw 548:17 Sep 3, 79

EROTIC PERIODICALS—REVIEWS
     Easy to be hard-core; Screw reviews issue no. 4 of the
          graphic glossy gash mag Puritan. Screw 548:4-7 Sep 3,
          79

ETHICS, SEXUAL. *See* SEXUAL ETHICS.

EUNUCHS
     Von Eckmann, Erika
          A eunuch in every garage [letter]. Fetish T 64:9-10

Evans, Arthur
     Witchcraft and the Gay counterculture. 1978.
          Review (Will Inman): Gay Sun 40/41:31-2 Sum/Fall 79

EXERCISE
     Altman, Carole
          Too tense for love? Try these relaxation techniques that
          work! Sexol 46-2:39-43 Oct 79

EXERCISE FOR WOMEN
     Large vagina [letter]. Hum Dig 3-1:80-1 Jan 79

EXHIBITIONISM
     See also Nude beaches

EXHIBITIONISM—PERSONAL ACCOUNTS
     The balcony [letter]. Var spec 5:121-2 Mid-Spr 79
     Catherine, Eleanor
          It happened on a train. Var spec 5:116-20 Mid-Spr 79
     Chasing the commuter blues [letter]. Var spec 5:123-4
          Mid-Spr 79

EXTRAMARITAL RELATIONS
     See also Brother-sister incest
                    Father-daughter incest
                    Homosexuality
                    Mate-swapping
                    Mother-son incest
                    Swinging

EXTRAMARITAL RELATIONS—
     PERSONAL ACCOUNTS
     Fighting VD [letter]. Hum Dig 3-1:97 Jan 79
     A glorious discovery [letter]. Sexol 46-2:57-9 Oct 79
     Sexual freedom [letter]. Hum Dig 3-1:67-8 Jan 79
     Uptight hubby [letter]. Hum Dig 3-1:86-7 Jan 79

FANTASIES
See also
Bondage and discipline
fantasies
Rape fantasies
Sadomasochist fantasies
Gersten, Leon
"The fantasy game." Pillow T 3-6:91-3 Sep 79

FANTASIES—FICTION
Burleson, Tom
Sensual mind control [story]. Var spec 5:32-7 Mid-Spr 79

FANTASIES—PERSONAL ACCOUNTS
Califia, Pat
Pleasure/pain and power—a Lesbian's view. Var spec
5:56-65 Mid-Spr 79
The captured squaw [letter]. Var spec 5:39-40 Mid-Spr 79
Cold comfort [letter]. Var spec 5:103 Mid-Spr 79
Female fantasy [letter]. Var spec 5:40 Mid-Spr 79
Rape fantasy [letter]. Var spec 5:38 Mid-Spr 79
Scenes [letter]. Var spec 5:40-1 Mid-Spr 79

FATHER—DAUGHTER INCEST—PERSONAL ACCOUNTS
Father knows best [letter]. Resp 6-9:19-23 Oct 79

FATHERS, GAY. See GAY FATHERS.

FELLATIO—PERSONAL ACCOUNTS
Bedpost fun [letter]. Var spec 5:102-3 Mid-Spr 79
A daring debut [letter]. Var spec 5:114-15 Mid-Spr 79
Fellatio fan [letter]. Var spec 5:29-30 Mid-Spr 79
Furtive fellatio [letter]. Var spec 5:92-3 Mid-Spr 79
Lawrence, Adele
A virgin doesn't have to say no. Var spec 5:105-11 Mid-
Spr 79
Scuba sex [letter]. Var spec 5:157 Mid-Spr 79

FEMALE MASTURBATION
See also Ben-Wa Balls
Dildos
Hairdryers
Shower sprays
Vibrators

FEMALE MASTURBATION—PERSONAL ACCOUNTS
Bedpost fun [letter]. Var spec 5:102-3 Mid-spr 79
Cold comfort [letter]. Var spec 5:103 Mid-Spr 79
Phillips, Kate
Ben Wa balls: a woman's secret delight. Var spec 5:96-9
Mid-Spr 79
Virgin by choice [letter]. Var spec 5:112 Mid-Spring 79

FEMALE ORGASM
Crown, Sandra
Female sexual fulfillment: what it really means. Hum Dig
3-1:39-45 Jan 79
Dailey, Jan
Women and orgasm: how to achieve it no matter what.
Sexol 46-2:10-18 Oct 79
Holaday, Robert
Frigidity: the causes & the cures. Hum Dig 3-1:23-7 Jan .
79

FEMALE ORGASM—PERSONAL ACCOUNTS
Can't reach climax [letter]. Sexol 46-2:72-3 Oct 79

FEMALE PROSTITUTES—PERSONAL ACCOUNTS
Finley, Theresa
Transsexual call girl. Var spec 5:127-31 Mid-Spr 79

FEMINIST—LESBIAN ARCHIVES. See LESBIAN—FEMINIST
ARCHIVES.

FETISHES. See BALDNESS FETISH; DIAPER FETISH; PANTY
FETISH; PILLOW FETISH; RUBBER FETISH.

FICTION. See EROTIC FICTION; GAY FICTION; SHORT
STORIES.

FILM ACTORS. See EROTIC FILM ACTORS.

FILM REVIEWS. See EROTIC FILMS—REVIEWS; GAY
FILMS—REVIEWS.

FILMS, ENEMA. See ENEMA FILMS.

FILMS, EROTIC. See EROTIC FILMS.

FILMS, GAY. See GAY FILMS.

Finley, Theresa
Transsexual call girl. Var spec 5:127-31 Mid-Spr 79

Fisher, Pete
Special teachers/special boys. 1979.
Review (Scott Jones): Gay Sun 40/41:32 Sum/Fall 79

FIST—FUCKING—PERSONAL ACCOUNTS
Califia, Pat
Pleasure/pain and power—a Lesbian's view. Var spec
5:56-65 Mid-Spr 79

Fletcher, Sheila
Quarry [poem]. SYOL 21:10 Oct 78

FLYING SEX. See AIRPLANE SEX.

FOURSOMES. See MATE-SWAPPING; SWINGING.

Friedman, Leslie
Sex role stereotyping in the mass media: an annotated
bibliography. 1974.
Review (Scott C. McDonald): J Homo 4-2:192-4 Win 78

Friel, T.
Transvestite marriage: hubby was wigged-out on women's
clothes. Fetish T 64:4-6+

Friendly, Suzanne
I can be very friendly. Pillow T 3-6:8-10 Sep 79

FRIGIDITY
See also Impotence
Holaday, Robert
Frigidity: the causes & the cures. Hum Dig 3-1:23-7 Jan
79

"FUCKING." See ANAL SEX; BESTIALITY; HETEROSEXUAL
INTERCOURSE; HOMOSEXUAL INTERCOURSE.

FULFILLING YOUNG CUPS (FILM).
Neuhaus, Manny
Kennel ration raunch [review of Fulfilling young cups].
Screw 548:23 Sep 3, 79

Gambill, Sue
Opening, a short story. SYOL 21:7-8 Oct 78

GAY ARCHIVES
See also Lesbian-Feminist archives
Monahan, Jim
Considerations in the organization of Gay archives. Gay Insurg 4/5:8-10 Spr 79

GAY CHILDREN
Morin, Stephen F.
"The Gay movement and the rights of children." J of Social Issues. 1978.
Review (Daniel Tsang): Gay Insurg 4/5:48 Spr 79

GAY FATHERS—PERSONAL ACCOUNTS
Latham, Jack Purdom
Tender mornings: progress of a faggot father. Gay Sun 40/41:10-12 Sum/Fall 79

GAY FICTION
Gambill, Sue
Opening, a short story. SYOL 21:7-8 Oct 78

GAY FICTION—BIBLIOGRAPHY
McDonnell, Linda
Bibliography: 20th Century American Lesbian novels. SYOL 21:16 Oct 78

GAY FICTION—HISTORY AND CRITICISM—REVIEWS
Austen, Roger
Playing the game: the homosexual novel in America. 1977.
Review (Byrne R.S. Fone): J Homo 4-2: 195-200 Win 78

GAY FICTION—REVIEWS
Christian, Paula
Edge of twilight. 1959.
This side of love. 1963.
Reviews (S.C.): SYOL 21:22 Oct 78

Curzon, Daniel
Among the carnivores. 1979.
Review (Scott Jones): Gay Sun 40/41:32 Sum/Fall 79
Fisher, Pete
Special teachers/special boys. 1979.
Review (Scott Jones): Gay Sun 40/41:32 Sum/Fall 79
Hamilton, Wallace
David at Olivet. 1979.
Review (Scott Jones): Gay Sun 40/41:32 Sum/Fall 79
Kramer, Larry
Faggots. 1978.
Review (Larry Puchall): Gay Sun 40/41:34 Sum/Fall 79
Tiktin, Carl
Ron. 1979.
Review (Scott Jones): Gay Sun 40/41:32 Sum/Fall 79
Watmough, David
No more into the garden. 1978.
Review (Scott Jones): Gay Sun 40/41:32 Sum/Fall 79
White, Edmund
Nocturnes for the King of Naples. 1978.
Review (Scott Jones): Gay Sun 40/41:32 Sum/Fall 79

GAY FILMS—REVIEWS
Cruikshank, Peg
Notes on two films: Julia and Word is out. SYOL 21:11 Oct 78

GAY LIBERATION MOVEMENT—BIBLIOGRAPHY
Katz, Jonathan
Gay men, Lesbians, and Socialism: a bibliography of some relevant books, pamphlets, essays, periodicals, and news items. Gay Insurg 4/5:51-6 Spr 79

GAY LIBERATION MOVEMENT—BOOK REVIEWS
Crew, Louie
The Gay academic. 1978.
Review (Jim Monahan): Gay Insurg 4/5:43-7 Spr 79
Gay Theory Work Group of the Movement for a New Society
Gay oppression and liberation or. Homophobia: its causes and cure. 1977.
Review (Marc Killinger) Gay Insurg 4/5:37-42 Spr 79

GAY LIBERATION MOVEMENT—LIBRARY RESOURCES
Tsang, Daniel
The Gay press. Gay Insurg 4/5:18-21 Spr 79

GAY LITERATURE
See also Gay fiction
Gay poetry

GAY LITERATURE—HISTORY AND CRITICISM—BOOK REVIEWS
Leyland, Winston
Now the volcano: an anthology of Latin American Gay literature. 1979.
Review (E.A. Lacey): Gay Sun 40/41:26-31 Sum/Fall 79

GAY LITERATURE—REVIEWS
Ginsberg, Allen
To Eberhart from Ginsberg; a letter about HOWL. 1976.
Allen Ginsberg journals; early Fifties early Sixties. 1977.
As ever; the collected correspondence of Allen Ginsberg and Neal Cassady. 1977.
Mind breaths; poems 1972-1977. 1977.
Reviews (David Chura): Gay Sun 40/41:15-16 Sum/Fall 79

GAY MEN
See also Gays
Homosexuality

GAY MEN—IDENTITY
Weinberg, Thomas S.
On "doing" and "being" Gay: sexual behavior and homosexual male self-identity. J Homo 4-2: 143-56 Win 78

GAY MEN IN NEWS MEDIA
Boston/Boise Committee
Suggestions for media on handling alleged sex "crimes" involving Gay men. Gay Insurg 4/ 5:56-9 Spr 79

GAY MEN—PSYCHOLOGY
Bernard, Larry Craig
Androgyny scores of matched homosexual and heterosexual males. J Homo 4-2: 169-78 Win 78
Ross, Michael W.
The relationship of perceived societal hostility, conformity, and psychological adjustment in homosexual males. J Homo 4-2: 157-68 Win 78
Weinberg, Thomas S.
On "doing" and "being" Gay: sexual behavior and homosexual male self-identity. J Homo 4-2: 143-56 Win 78

GAY MEN—SEXUALITY
See also Anal sex
   Anilingus
   Boy love
   Fellatio
   Fist-fucking
   Homosexuality
   Male prostitutes
Witomski, T.R.
   Beyond the last taboo. Var spec 5:136-40 Mid-Spr 79

GAY PACIFISTS
Mager, Don
   Dr. Magnus Hirschfeld as socialist pacifist thinker. Gay Insurg 4/5:2-8 Spr 79

GAY PERIODICALS—BIBLIOGRAPHY—UNION LISTS
Tsang, Daniel.
   The Gay press. Gay Insurg 4/5:18-21 Spr 79

GAY POETRY
Antler
   Poems. Gay Sun 40/41:36 Summer/Fall 79
Arrizabalaga y Prado, Leonardo de
   Song without words [poem]. Gay Sun 40/41:35 Sum/Fall 79
Beame, Jeffery
   Tonight desire has a man in it [poem]. Gay Sun 40/41:37 Sum/Fall 79
Blakeston, Oswell
   The graveyard [poem]. Gay Sun 40/41:37 Sum/Fall 79
Chadwick, Jerah
   Making it new [poem]. Gay Sun 40/41:35 Sum/Fall 79
Goldberg, Arleen
   Bow/river: Banff 1977 [poem]. SYOL 21:9 Oct 78
Hawley, Ellen
   The repeal of the St. Paul Gay Rights Ordinance/A variation on the repeal of the St. Paul Gay Rights Ordinance [poems]. SYOL 21:2 Oct 78
Peterson, Marcia A.
   Today [poem]. SYOL 21:12 Oct 78
Reith, Kimi
   Being a dyke [poem]. SYOL 21:2 Oct 78
Shurin, Aaron
   Return to Delphi [poem]. Gay Sun 40/41:40 Sum/Fall 79
Stein, Diane
   Let's just let it go at that [poem]. SYOL 21:3 Oct 78

   When it hit the fan [poem]. SYOL 21:3 Oct 78

   Why I get fired again again [poem]. SYOL 21:3 Oct 78
Trifonov, Gennady
   Three poems. Gay Sun 40/41:12 Sum/Fall 79
Wallner, S.
   Kathleen [poem]. SYOL 21:10 Oct 78

GAY POETRY—REVIEWS
Abbott, Steve
   Wrecked hearts; raw poetry
      Review (R. Daniel Evans): Gay Sun 40/41:35 Sum/Fall 79
Kelly, Dennis
   Chicken; boy love poems. 1979.
      Review (Charley Shively): Gay Sun 40/41:9 Sum/Fall 79

Kirmani, Awhaduddin
   Heart's witness. 1978.
      Review (Winston Leyland): Gay Sun 40/41:33 Sum/Fall 79
Mariah, Paul
   This light will spread: selected poems 1960-1975. 1978.
      Review (Steve Abbott): Gay Sun 40/41:34 Sum/Fall 79
Orlovsky, Peter
   Clean asshole poems & smiling vegetable songs. 1978.
      Review (Charles Shively): Gay Sun 40/41:15 Sum/Fall 79
Rimbaud, Arthur
   Rimbaud/Verlaine: a lover's cock. 1979.
      Review (Arthur William Rudolph). Gay Sun 40/41:38 Sum/Fall 79.
Ronan, Richard
   Flowers; poems. 1978.
      Review (E.A. Lacey): Gay Sun 40/41:32 Sum/Fall 79

GAY POETS—INTERVIEWS
Duncan, Robert.
   Interview. Gay Sun 40/41:1-8 Sum/Fall 79

GAY PRISONERS—PERSONAL ACCOUNTS
Williams, Dalton Lloyd
   Prison sex at age 16; County Jail: a true incident. Gay Sun 40/41:14 Sum/Fall 79

GAY RESEARCH—BOOK REVIEWS
Crew, Louie
   The Gay academic. 1978.
      Review (Jim Monahan): Gay Insurg 4/5:43-7 Spr 79

GAY RIGHTS
Sullivan, Timothy J.
   Attempted repeals of Gay Rights ordinances: the facts. Sex L Rptr 4-4: 61+ Oct/Dec 78

GAY RIGHTS—POETRY
Hawley, Ellen
   The repeal of the St. Paul Gay Rights Ordinance/A variation on the repeal of the St. Paul Gay Rights Ordinance [poems]. SYOL 21:2 Oct 78

GAY SOCIALISM— BIBLIOGRAPHY
Katz, Jonathan
   Gay men, Lesbians, and Socialism: a bibliography of some relevant books, pamphlets, essays, periodicals, and news items. Gay Insurg 4/5:51-6 Spr 79

GAY SOCIALISTS
Mager, Don
   Dr. Magnus Hirschfeld as socialist pacifist thinker. Gay Insurg 4/5:2-8 Spr 79

GAY SOLDIERS—BOOK REVIEWS
Gibson, E. Lawrence
   Get off my ship. 1978.
      Review (Daniel Tsang): Gay Insurg 4/5:47 Spr 79

Gay Theory Work Group of the Movement for a New Society
   Gay oppression and liberation or, Homophobia: its causes and cure. 1977.
      Review (Marc Killinger): Gay Insurg 4/5:37-42 Spr 79

GAY WOMEN. *See* LESBIANS.

GAYS—BIBLIOGRAPHY—REVIEWS
Bullough, Vern L.
An annotated bibliography of homosexuality. 1976.
Review (A.P.M. Coxon): Gay Insurg 4/5:49 Spr 79
Parker, William
Homosexuality bibliography: Supplement, 1970-1975.
1977.
Review (Daniel Tsang): Gay Insurg 4/5:49 Spr 79

GAYS—HISTORY
See also Homosexuality-History

GAYS—HISTORY—BOOK REVIEWS
Evans, Arthur
Witchcraft and the Gay counterculture. 1978.
Review (Will Inman): Gay Sun 40/41:31-2 Sum/Fall 79

GAYS IN ENCYCLOPEDIAS
SantaVicca, Edmund F.
Evaluating encyclopedias: a framework summary. Gay
Insurg 4/5:15-17 Spr 79

GAYS—LANGUAGE—BIBLIOGRAPHY
Hayes, Joseph J.
Language and language behavior of Lesbian women
and Gay men: a selected bibliography (Part 1). J Homo
4-2:201-12 Win 78

GAYS—LATIN AMERICA
Lacey, E.A.
Latin America: myths and realities. Gay Sun 40/41:22-6
Sum/Fall 79

GAYS—LEGAL STATUS, LAWS, ETC.
See also Gay rights
Sodomy law
Appellate court again declares Ohio solicitation law uncon-
stitutional. Sex L Rptr 4-4:64-8 Oct/Dec 78
Sexual preference of Big Brothers may be subject to
scrutiny. Sex L Rptr 4-4:74 Oct/Dec 78
Sullivan, Timothy J.
Attempted repeals of Gay Rights ordinances: the facts.
Sex L Rptr 4-4:61+ Oct/Dec 78

GAYS—SUBJECT HEADINGS. *See* SUBJECT HEADINGS—
GAYS.

Gersten, Leon
"The fantasy game." Pillow T 3-6:91-3 Sep 79

Gibson, E. Lawrence
Get off my ship. 1978.
Review (Daniel Tsang): Gay Insurg 4/5: 47 Spr 79

Ginsberg, Allen
To Eberhart from Ginsberg; a letter about HOWL. 1976.
Allen Ginsberg journals; early Fifties early Sixties. 1977.
Mind breaths; poems 1972-1977. 1977.
As ever; the collected correspondence of Allen Ginsberg
and Neal Cassady. 1977.
Reviews (David Chura): Gay Sun 40/41:15-16 Sum/Fall
79

Goldberg, Arleen
Bow/river: Banff 1977 [poem]. SYOL 21:9 Oct 78
A well kept secret [poem]. SYOL 21:21 Oct 78

"GREEK CULTURE." *See* ANAL SEX.

GROUP SEX. *See* SWINGING; THREESOMES.

HAIR, ARMPIT. *See* ARMPIT HAIR.

HAIRDRYERS
Home help [letter]. Var spec 5:100-1 Mid-Spr 79

Hamilton, Jack
The Redcoats are coming. Screw 548:18-19 Sep 3, 79

Hamilton, Wallace
David at Olivet. 1979.
Review (Scott Jones): Gay Sun 40/41:32 Sum/Fall 79

HAND—FUCKING. *See* FIST—FUCKING.

HAND HAIRDRYERS. *See* HAIRDRYERS.

HAND VIBRATORS. *See* VIBRATORS.

Hawley, Ellen
The repeal of the St. Paul Gay Rights Ordinance/A variation
on the repeal of the St. Paul Gay Rights Ordinance [poems].
SYOL 21:2 Oct 78

Hayes, Joseph J.
Language and language behavior of Lesbian women and
Gay men: a selected bibliography (Part 1). J Homo 4-2:201-
12 Win 78

Hellander, Martha
On edge [poem]. SYOL 21:12 Oct 78

HETEROSEXUAL INTERCOURSE
See also Afterplay
Anal sex
Coital positions
Erections
Bliss, K.D.
Beating the short time Charlie blues. Resp 6-9:27-31 Oct
79
Karlen, Arno
Who's on top? The sexual conflict people don't talk ab-
out. Sexol 46-2:24-9 Oct 79
Shore, Jeannie
How to cope with those first-night jitters. Hum Dig 3-1:9-
12 Jan 79
That size question [letter]. Hum Dig 3-1:66-7 Jan 79

HETEROSEXUAL INTERCOURSE—PERSONAL ACCOUNTS
Borchette, Suzanne
A night in Central Park. Var spec 5:86-91 Mid-Spr 79
Cooperstock, David
The joys of sex without an erection. Var spec 5:12-17
Mid-Spr 79
Crown, Sandra
Female sexual fulfillment: what it really means. Hum Dig
3-1:39-45 Jan 79
Delectable delirium [letter]. Var spec 5:162 Mid-Spr 79
Jingle balls [letter]. Var spec 5:159 Mid-Spr 79
Joy stick [letter]. Var spec 5:94-5 Mid-Spr 79
One-legged [letter]. Hum Dig 3-1:57-9 Jan 79
A rare virgin [letter]. Var spec 5:114 Mid-Spr 79
Snow games [letter]. Var spec 5:94 Mid-Spr 79
Stahl, Jerry
A way to find ecstasy; after a week of yoga, fasting and
silence, a man and a woman experience supreme bliss
at the edge of a precipice. Var spec 5:6-11 Mid-Spr 79

HETEROSEXUAL MEN—PSYCHOLOGY
  Bernard, Larry Craig
    Androgyny scores of matched homosexual and hetero-
    sexual males. J Homo 4-2:169-78 Win 78

HETEROSEXUALITY
  Deni, Laura
    Why nice girls finish last. Pillow T 3-6:16-21+ Sep 79
  Pomeroy, Wardell B.
    What heterosexuals can learn from homosexuals. Sexol
    46-2:36-8 Oct 79

HIRSCHFELD, MAGNUS
  Mager, Don
    Dr. Magnus Hirschfeld as socialist pacifist thinker. Gay
    Insurg 4/5:2-8 Spr 79

Hodges, Parker
  That misunderstood erogenous zone; the nipple—a powerful source of erotic pleasure in both men and women—is
  largely unexplored. Sexol. 46-2:30-4 Oct 79

Hoffman, Lisa
  A bisexual wedding; interview and photos. Porn film star
  Marc Stevens marries transsexual model Jill Monro. Var
  spec 5:18-27 Mid-Spr 79

Hoffman, Susan
  A meditation on Adrienne Rich's Splittings [poem]. SYOL
  21:5 Oct 78

Holaday, Robert
  Frigidity: the causes & the cures. Hum Dig 3-1:23-7 Jan 79

Holt, Miranda
  Part-time marriage: a new way to have your cake and eat it
  too. Hum Dig 3-1:19-22 Jan 79

HOMOPHOBIA—BOOK REVIEWS
  Gay Theory Work Group of the Movement For A New Soci-
    ety Gay oppression and liberation or, Homophobia: its
    causes and cure. 1977.
      Review (Marc Killinger): Gay Insurg 4/5:37-42 Spr 79

HOMOPHOBIA IN LIBRARIANSHIP
  Berman, Sanford
    Gay access: new approaches in cataloging. Gay Insurg
    4/5:14-15 Spr 79

HOMOPHOBIA IN NEWS MEDIA
  Boston/Boise Committee
    Suggestions for media on handling alleged sex "crimes"
    involving Gay men. Gay Insurg 4/5:56-9 Spr 79

HOMOPHOBIA IN THE ARMED FORCES—BOOK REVIEWS
  Gibson, E. Lawrence
    Get off my ship. 1978.
      Review (Daniel Tsang): Gay Insurg 4/5:47 Spr 79

HOMOSEXUAL CHILDREN. See GAY CHILDREN.

HOMOSEXUAL INTERCOURSE
  See also Afterplay
          Anal sex
          Coital positions
          Erections
          Fist-fucking

HOMOSEXUAL INTERCOURSE—PERSONAL ACCOUNTS
  Bisexual husband [letter]. Var spec 5:28-9 Mid-Spr 79

HOMOSEXUAL MEN. See GAY MEN.

HOMOSEXUAL WOMEN. See LESBIANS.

HOMOSEXUALITY
  See also Bisexuals
          Boy love
          Gay men
          Gays
          Homosexual   intercourse
          Lesbians
  Pomeroy, Wardell B.
    What heterosexuals can learn from homosexuals. Sexol
    46-2:36-8 Oct 79

HOMOSEXUALITY—BIBLIOGRAPHY—REVIEWS
  Bullough, Vern L.
    An annotated bibliography of homosexuality. 1976.
      Review (A.P.M. Coxon): Gay Insurg 4/5:49 Spr 79
      Review (William Parker): J Homo 4-2:185-92 Win 78
  Parker, William
    Homosexuality bibliography: Supplement, 1970-1975.
    1977.
      Review (Daniel Tsang): Gay Insurg 4/5:49 Spr 79

HOMOSEXUALITY—HISTORY
  See also Gays—History

Kennedy, Hubert C.
  The case for James Mills Peirce. J Homo 4-2:79-84 Win 78

HOMOSEXUALITY—HISTORY—BOOK REVIEWS
  Dover, Kenneth J.
    Greek homosexuality. 1978.
      Review (Arthur William Rudolph): Gay Sun 40/41:33-4
      Sum/Fall 79

HOMOSEXUALITY IN ENCYCLOPEDIAS
  SantaVicca, Edmund F.
    Evaluating encyclopedias: a framework summary. Gay
    Insurg 4/5:15-17 Spr 79

HOMOSEXUALS. See GAYS

"HOOKERS." See FEMALE PROSTITUTES; MALE
  PROSTITUTES.

HUMILIATION. See BONDAGE AND DISCIPLINE; SADO-
  MASOCHISM.

HYGIENE, SEXUAL. See SEXUAL HYGIENE.

IMPOTENCE
  Potency problem [letter]. Hum Dig 3-1:83-4 Jan 79

INCEST
  See also Brother-sister incest
          Father-daughter incest
          Mother-son incest
  Love thy mother [letter]. Hum Dig 3-1:62 Jan 79

INCEST—PERSONAL ACCOUNTS
  Secret lovers [letter]. Hum Dig 3-1:59-60 Jan 79

INFERTILITY
  Romeo, Sherry
    Infertility. Sexol 46-2:8-9 Oct 79

INTERCOURSE. See ANAL SEX; BESTIALITY; HETEROSEX-
  UAL INTERCOURSE; HOMOSEXUAL INTERCOURSE.

Jackson, Damaris
Dancers in the studio [poem]. SYOL 21:4 Oct 78
To the Winter solstice [poem]. SYOL 21:24 Oct 78

Jackson, Martin A.
How color affects your life and love. Pillow T 3-6:77-81+ Sept 79

Jardine, Jack Owen
Oh, you beautiful doll! Var spec 5:142-7 Mid-Spr 79

"JERKING OFF." See MALE MASTURBATION.

Jolly, Lara
A time of reaping [poem]. SYOL 21:22 Oct 78

Jordon, Flash
Dildonuts [cartoon]. Screw 548:24-5 Sep 3, 79

JULIA (FILM)
Cruikshank, Peg
Notes on two films: Julia and Word is out. SYOL 21:11 Oct 78

Karlen, Arno
Who's on top? The sexual conflict people don't talk about. Sexol 46-2:24-9 Oct 79

Katz, Jonathan
Gay men, Lesbians, and Socialism: a bibliography of some relevant books, pamphlets, essays, periodicals, and news items. Gay Insurg 4/5:51-6 Spr 79

Kelly, Dennis
Chicken; boy love poems. 1979.
Review (Charley Shively): Gay Sun 40/41:9 Sum/Fall 79

Kempler, Jana
A couple takes a chance. Var spec 5:70-81 Mid-Spr 79

Kennedy, Hubert C.
The case for James Mills Peirce. J Homo 4-2:179-84 Win 78

Kirmani, Awhaduddin
Heart's witness; the Sufi quatrains of Awhaduddin Kirmani. 1978.
Review (Winston Leyland): Gay Sun 40/41:33 Sum/Fall 79

Klaskin, Ronnie
The difference between making love and getting fucked. Pillow T 3-6:67-71 Sep 79

Klein, Art
Hello, I am Joe's penis. Pillow T 3-6:82-8 Sep 79

Kramer, Larry
Faggots. 1978.
Review (Larry Puchall): Gay Sun 40/41:34 Sum/Fall 79

Krause, Donna M.
Playing tough [poem]. SYOL 21:24 Oct 78

Lacey, E.A.
Latin America: myths and realities. Gay Sun 40/41:22-6 Sum/Fall 79

LATEX FETISH. See RUBBER FETISH.

Latham, Jack Purdom
Tender mornings: progress of a faggot father. Gay Sun 40/41:10-12 Sum/Fall 79

LATIN AMERICA
Lacey, E.A.
Latin America: myths and realities. Gay Sun 40/41:22-6 Sum/Fall 79

LATIN AMERICA—BOOK REVIEWS
Leyland, Winston
Now the volcano: an anthology of Latin American Gay literature. 1979.
Review (E.A. Lacey): Gay Sun 40/41:26-31 Sum/Fall 79

Lawrence, Adele
A virgin doesn't have to say no. Var spec 5:105-11 Mid-Spr 79

LAWS, SEX. See SEX LAWS.

LeBlanc, Maryjean
Leaving [story]. SYOL 21:13-14 Oct 78

LESBIAN ALCOHOLICS
Diamond, Deborah L.
Alcohol abuse among Lesbians: a descriptive study. J Homo 4-2:123-42 Win 78

LESBIAN—FEMINIST ARCHIVES
Nestle, Joan
Radical archiving: a Lesbian Feminist perspective. Gay Insurg 4/5:10-12 Spr 79

LESBIAN HERSTORY ARCHIVES
Nestle, Joan
Radical archiving: a Lesbian Feminist perspective. Gay Insurg 4/5:10-12 Spr 79

LESBIAN MOTHERS—FICTION
Gambill, Sue
Opening, a short story. SYOL 21:7-8 Oct 78

LESBIANS
See also Gays
Homosexuality
Women's sexuality

LESBIANS—DIARIES
McNaron, Toni
Excerpts from a New York journal, April 1978. SYOL 21:18-20 Oct 78

LESBIANS—FICTION—BIBLIOG-
RAPHY
McDonnell, Linda
Bibliography: 20th Century American Lesbian novels. SYOL 21:16 Oct 78

LESBIANS—IDENTITY
Coming out [letter]. Hum Dig 3-1:68-70 Jan 79

LESBIANS IN FICTION
Christian, Pauls
Edge of twilight. 1959.
This side of love. 1963.
Reviews (S.C.): SYOL 21:22 Oct 78

LESBIANS—PERSONAL ACCOUNTS
Califia, Pat
Pleasure/pain and power—a Lesbian's view. Var spec 5:56-65 Mid-Spr 79

Catherine, Eleanor
It happened on a train. Var special 5:116-20 Mid-Spr 79
Coming out [letter]. Hum Dig 3-1:68-70 Jan 79
Craves punishment [letter]. Var spec 5:68 Mid-Spr 79
Double dong [letter]. Var spec 5:101-2 Mid-Spr 79
Spanking lovers [letter]. Var spec 5:66-8 Mid-Spr 79

LESBIANS—POETRY
Goldberg, Arleen
Bow/river: Banff 1977 [poem]. SYOL 21:9 Oct 78
Peterson, Marcia A.
Today [poem]. SYOL 21:12 Oct 78
Reith, Kimi
Being a dyke [poem]. SYOL 21:2 Oct 78
Stein, Diane
Let's just let it go at that [poem]. SYOL 21:3 Oct 78
When it hit the fan [poem]. SYOL 21:3 Oct 78
Why I get fired again again [poem]. SYOL 21:3 Oct 78
Wallner, S.
Kathleen [poem]. SYOL 21:10 Oct 78

LESBIANS—PSYCHOLOGY
Diamond, Deborah L.
Alcohol abuse among Lesbians: a descriptive study. J Homo 4-2: 123-42 Win 78
Leyland, Winston
Now the volcano: an anthology of Latin American Gay literature. 1979.
Review (E.A. Lacey): Gay Sun 40/41:26-31 Sum/Fall 79

LIBRARY HOMOPHOBIA. See HOMOPHOBIA IN LIBRARIANSHIP.

LIMERICKS
Moon, Little
Doping it out [illustrated limericks]. Screw 548:9-11 Sep 3, 79

LINGERIE FETISH. See PANTY FETISH.

LUBRICATION, VAGINAL. See VAGINAL LUBRICATION.

McCartney, Nora
How to beat those "not tonight dear, I've got a headache" blues. Hum Dig 3-1:28-31 Jan 79

McDonnell, Linda
Angling [poem]. SYOL 21:9 Oct 78
Bibliography: 20th Century American Lesbian novels. SYOL 21:16 Oct 78

McGregor, Michelle
Viva vibrators! A complete rundown on all the latest vibrators and sex aids. A consumer report for the truly sensual woman. Hum Dig 3-1:50-4 Jan 79

McNaron, Toni
Excerpts from a New York journal, April 1978. SYOL 21:18-20 Oct 78

Mager, Don
Dr. Magnus Hirschfeld as socialist pacifist thinker. Gay Insurg 4/5:2-8 Spr 79

MALE IMPOTENCE. See IMPOTENCE.

MALE MASTURBATION.
See also Hairdryers
Sex dolls
Shower sprays
Vibrators

MALE MASTURBATION—PERSONAL ACCOUNTS.
An endless source of pleasure [letter]. Var spec 5:148-9 Mid-Spr 79
Glove love [letter]. Var spec 5:149 Mid-Spr 79
Helping hand [letter]. Hum Dig 3-1:73-4 Jan 79
Light my fire [letter]. Var spec 5:158-9 Mid-Spr 79
Man's ingenuity [letter]. Var spec 5:156-7 Mid-Spr 79

MALE PROSTITUTES
Male prostitutes [letter]. Var spec 5:133-4 Mid-Spr 79
Urban tragedy [letter]. Sexol 46-2:61 Oct 79

MALE PROSTITUTES—PERSONAL ACCOUNTS
Advice from a male prostitute [letter]. Var spec 5:132-5 Mid-Spr 79

MAN/BOY LOVE. See BOY LOVE.

Mariah, Paul
This light will spread: selected poems 1960-1975. 1978.
Review (Steve Abbott): Gay Sun 40/41:34 Sum/Fall 79

MARRIAGE
See also Extramarital relations
Mate-swapping
Part-time marriage
Hoffman, Lisa
A bisexual wedding; interview and photos. Porn film star Marc Stevens marries transsexual model Jill Monro. Var spec 5:18-27 Mid-Spr 79

MARRIAGE—FICTION
LeBlanc, Maryjean
Leaving [story]. SYOL 21:13-14 Oct 78

MARRIAGE, PART—TIME. See PART—TIME MARRIAGE.

Marshall, Thurgood
Mr. Justice Marshall on sexual privacy rights. Sex L Rptr 4-4:75-7 Oct/Dec 78

MASOCHISM. See SADOMASOCHISM.

MASSAGE
Altman, Carole
Too tense for love? Try these relaxation techniques that work! Sexol 46-2:39-43 Oct 79

MASSAGE—PERSONAL ACCOUNTS
Facing it [letter]. Sexol 46-2:57 Oct 79

MASTURBATION
See also Female masturbation
Male masturbation
Mutual masturbation
Sex aids

MASTURBATION—PERSONAL ACCOUNTS
Catherine, Eleanor
It happened on a train. Var spec 5:116-20 Mid-Spr 79
Masturbation hints [letter]. Hum Dig 3-1:56 Jan 79

MATE—SWAPPING
  See also Swinging

MATE—SWAPPING—PERSONAL ACCOUNTS
  Anal fear [letter]. Hum Dig 3-1:89-90 Jan 79
  Bisexual swingers [letter]. Var spec 5:52-4 Mid-Spr 79
  Hamilton, Jack
    The Redcoats are coming. Screw 548:18-19 Sep 3, 79
  Swappers' life style [letter]. Var spec 5:51-2 Mid-Spring 79

MEN, GAY. *See* GAY MEN.

MEN, HETEROSEXUAL. *See* HETEROSEXUAL MEN.

MEN PROSTITUTES. *See* MALE PROSTITUTES.

MENAGE A TROIS. *See* THREESOMES.

MEN'S MASTURBATION. *See* MALE MASTURBATION.

MEN'S SEXUALITY. *See* ERECTIONS; GAY MEN; HETERO-
  SEXUAL INTERCOURSE; HETEROSEXUAL MEN; HOMO-
  SEXUAL INTERCOURSE; IMPOTENCE; MALE MASTUR-
  BATION; MALE PROSTITUTES; MIDDLE-AGED MEN'S
  SEXUALITY; PENIS; PENIS SIZE; PREMATURE EJACULA-
  TION; SENIOR MEN'S SEXUALITY; TRANSSEXUALS;
  TRANSVESTITES.

MIDDLE—AGED MEN'S SEXUALITY
  Thistle, Frank
    Are dirty old men really dirty? Pillow T 3-6:28-33 Sep 79

Miller, Kate
  Analingus: something special for your lover. Hum Dig
  3-1:32-4 Jan 79

Milton, John
  Mail order madness. Screw 548:32 Sep 3, 79

MISCONCEPTIONS
  Smith, Belle
    Sexual myths. Hum Dig 3-1:46-9 Jan 79

Monahan, Jim
  Considerations in the organization of Gay archives. Gay
  Insurg 4/5:8-10 Spr 79

MONRO, JILL
  Hoffman, Lisa
    A bisexual wedding; interview and photos. Porn film star
    Marc Stevens marries transsexual model Jill Monro. Var
    spec 5:18-27 Mid-Spr 79

Moon, Little
  Doping it out [illustrated limericks]. Screw 548:9-11 Sep 3,
  79

Moos, Kate
  Eggs, for Janis [poem]. SYOL 21:12 Oct 78
  The seer [poem]. SYOL 21:12 Oct 78
  To Joseph [poem]. SYOL 21:10 Oct 78

Morin, Stephen F.
  "The Gay movement and the rights of children." J of Social
  Issues. 1978.
    Review (Daniel Tsang): Gay Insurg 4/5:48 Spr 79

MOTHER—SON INCEST
  Love thy mother [letter]. Hum Dig 3-1:62 Jan 79

MOUTH PLAY—PERSONAL ACCOUNTS
  Facing it [letter]. Sexol 46-2:57 Oct 79

MOVIE ACTORS. *See* EROTIC FILM ACTORS.

MUSEUM SEX—PERSONAL ACCOUNTS
  The balcony [letter]. Var spec 5:121-2 Mid-Spr 79

MUTUAL MASTURBATION—PERSONAL ACCOUNTS
  The first time [letter]. Var spec 5:112-13 Mid-Spr 79

Nestle, Joan
  Radical archiving: a Lesbian Feminist perspective. Gay
  Insurg 4/5:10-12 Spr 79

Neuhaus, Manny
  Bare facts. Screw 548:13 Sep 3, 79
  Kennel ration raunch [review of Fulfilling young cups].
  Screw 548:23 Sep 3, 79

NEW AGE—BOOK REVIEWS
  Satin, Mark
    New Age politics, healing self and society; the emerging
    new alternative to Marxism and Liberalism. 1978.
      Review (Mitch Walker): Gay Sun 40/41:35 Sum/Fall 79

NEWS MEDIA GUIDELINES
  Boston/Boise Committee
    Suggestions for media on handling alleged sex "crimes"
    involving Gay men. Gay Insurg 4/5:56-9 Spr 79

Nichols, D.W.
  A boy lover's perspective; D.W. Nichols interviewed by
  Daniel Tsang, Part II. Gay Insurg 4/5:25-36 Spr 79

NIPPLE PLAY
  Hodges, Parker
    That misunderstood erogenous zone; the nipple—a
    powerful source of erotic pleasure in both men and
    women—is largely unexplored. Sexol 46-2:30-4 Oct 79

NUDE BEACHES
  A day at the (nude) beach. Var spec 5:122-3 Mid-Spr 79
  Neuhaus, Manny
    Bare facts. Screw 548:13 Sep 3, 79

OBSCENITY LAW
  Buffalo anti-obscenity ordinance is voided. Sex L Rptr 4-
  4:63 Oct/Dec 78
  'The Finger' is not an obscene gesture. Sex L Rptr 4-4:77
  Oct/Dec 78
  Obscenity 'Scienter Test' is subject of dispute. Sex L Rptr
  4-4:80 Oct/Dec 78
  Supreme Court rules broadcasters' use of indecent
  language may be regulated. Sex L Rptr 4-4:62-3 Oct/
  Dec 78

OFFICE SEX
  Gersten, Leon
    "The fantasy game." Pillow T 3-6:91-3 Sep 79

OLD PEOPLE'S SEXUALITY. *See* SENIORS' SEXUALITY.

ORAL SEX. *See* ANILINGUS; CUNNILINGUS; FELLATIO;
  MOUTH PLAY.

ORGASM, FEMALE. *See* FEMALE ORGASM.

"ORIENTAL" LOVE BALLS. *See* BEN-WA BALLS.

Orlovsky, Peter
    Clean asshole poems & smiling vegetable songs. 1978.
        Review (Charles Shively): Gay Sun 40/41:15 Sum/Fall 79

OVER—60 SEXUALITY. *See* SENIORS' SEXUALITY.

PACIFISTS, GAY. *See* GAY PACIFISTS.

PAGE, BETTY
    Stryker, Rod
        On the rack. Fetish T 64:12-13

PANTY FETISH—PERSONAL ACCOUNTS
    Kinky craftsmanship [letter]. Fetish T 64:9
    Light my fire [letter]. Var spec 5:158-9 Mid-Spr 79

PARENTING
    Turnabout [letter]. Sexol 46-2:53-4 Oct 79

Park, R.L.
    Bondage on the boob tube. Fetish T 64:11

Parker, William
    Homosexuality bibliography: Supplement, 1970-1975.
    1977.
        Review (Daniel Tsang): Gay Insurg 4/5:49 Spr 79

PART—TIME MARRIAGE
    Holt, Miriam
        Part-time marriage: a new way to have your cake and eat
        it too. Hum Dig 3-1:19-22 Jan 79

PEDERASTY. *See* BOY LOVE.

PEDOPHILIA.
    See also Boy love
    Incestuous seeker [letter]. Hum Dig 3-1:81-3 Jan 79

PEIRCE, JAMES MILLS
    Kennedy, Hubert C.
        The case for James Mills Peirce. J Homo 4-2:179-84 Win
        78

PENIS
    See also Circumcision
             Erections
             Impotence
             Premature ejaculation

PENIS—ANECDOTES, SATIRE
    Klein, Art
        Hello, I am Joe's penis. Pillow T 3-6:82-8 Sep 79

PENIS SIZE
    Hoffman, Lisa
        A bisexual wedding; interview and photos. Porn film star
        Marc Stevens marries transsexual model Jill Monro. Var
        spec 5:18-27 Mid-Spr 79
    It's not the size [letter]. Sexol 46-2:59-60 Oct 79
    That size question [letter]. Hum Dig 3-1:66-7 Jan 79

PERIODICALS, EROTIC. *See* EROTIC PERIODICALS.

PERIODICALS, GAY. *See* GAY PERIODICALS.

Perkowski, Donald
    A flesh start: video vice. Screw 548:17 Sep 3, 79

PERSONAL ADVERTISEMENTS
    Bonner, T. Pete
        Playing the personals. Resp 6-9:32-8 Oct 79

Peterson, Marcia A.
    Today [poem]. SYOL 21:12 Oct 78

Phillips, Kate
    Ben Wa balls: a woman's secret delight. Var spec 5:96-9
    Mid-Spr 79

PILLOW FETISH
    Pillow talk [letter]. Var spec 5:156 Spr 79

POETRY. *See* GAY POETRY; LIMERICKS; WOMEN'S
    POETRY.

Pomeroy, Wardell B.
    What heterosexuals can learn from homosexuals. Sexol
    46-2:36-8 Oct 79

POMPEII
    Brock, Paul
        Pompeii: the first city of sexual freedom. A look at the true
        meaning of Bacchanalia. Sexol 46-2:19-22 Oct 79

Poole, Tom
    How to turn on a reluctant lover. Pillow T 3-6:72-5 Sep 79

"PORN" FILM ACTORS. *See* EROTIC FILM ACTORS.

"PORN" FILMS. *See* EROTIC FILMS.

"PORN" MAGAZINES. *See* EROTIC PERIODICALS.

"PORNOGRAPHY," CHILD. *See* CHILD "PORNOGRAPHY."

POSITIONS, COITAL. *See* COITAL POSITIONS.

PREJUDICE AGAINST GAYS. *See* HOMOPHOBIA.

PREMATURE EJACULATION
    Bliss, K.D.
        Beating the short time Charlie blues. Resp 6-9:27-31 Oct
        79

Prendergast, William E.
    The sex offender: how to spot him before it's too late. Sexol
    46-2:46-51 Oct 79

PRISON SEX—PERSONAL ACCOUNTS
    Williams, Dalton Lloyd
        Prison sex at age 16; County Jail: a true incident. Gay Sun
        40/41:14 Sum/Fall 79

PRIVACY RIGHTS. *See* SEXUAL PRIVACY RIGHTS.

PROSTITUTES, CHILD. *See* CHILD PROSTITUTES.

PROSTITUTES, FEMALE. *See* FEMALE PROSTITUTES.

PROSTITUTES, MALE. *See* MALE PROSTITUTES.

PSYCHOLOGY OF GAY MEN. *See* GAY MEN—
    PSYCHOLOGY.

PSYCHOLOGY OF HETEROSEXUAL MEN. *See* HETERO-
    SEXUAL MEN—PSYCHOLOGY.

PSYCHOLOGY OF LESBIANS. *See* LESBIANS—
    PSYCHOLOGY.

PSYCHOLOGY OF SEX. *See* SEXUAL PSYCHOLOGY.

PSYCHOLOGY, SEXUAL. *See* SEXUAL PSYCHOLOGY.

PUBIS SHAVING
    Double dong [letter]. Var spec 5:101-2 Mid-Spr 79

PUBLIC SEX. *See* AIRPLANE SEX; BACCHANALIA; CARRIAGE SEX; ELEVATOR SEX; EXHIBITIONISM; MUSEUM SEX; OFFICE SEX; RESTAURANT SEX; ROLLER-COASTER SEX; SAUNA SEX; STORE SEX; TAXICAB SEX; THEATER SEX; TRAIN SEX.

PUNISHMENT. *See* BONDAGE AND DISCIPLINE; SADO-MASOCHISM.

PURITAN (PERIODICAL)
Easy to be hard-core; Screw reviews issue no. 4 of the graphic glossy gash mag Puritan. Screw 548:4-7 Sep 3, 79

"PUSSY—EATING." *See* CUNNILINGUS.

"PUSSY SHAVING." *See* PUBIS SHAVING.

Radtke, Janel
Consider the possibilities [poem]. SYOL 21:15 Oct 78

RAPE FANTASIES
Female fantasy [letter]. Var spec 5:40 Mid-Spr 79
Rape fantasy [letter]. Var spec 5:38 Mid-Spr 79

RAPISTS
See also Sex offenders

RAPISTS—PERSONAL ACCOUNTS
Dean, Charles
Reflections of a rapist. Sexol 46-2:44-5 Oct 79
Reith, Kimi
Being a dyke [poem]. SYOL 21:2 Oct 78

RELAXATION
Altman, Carole
Too tense for love? Try these relaxation techniques that work! Sexol 46-2:39-43 Oct 79
McCartney, Nora
How to beat those 'not tonight dear, I've got a headache' blues. Hum Dig 3-1:28-31 Jan 79

RESTAURANT SEX—PERSONAL ACCOUNTS
Furtive fellatio [letter]. Var spec 5:92-3 Mid-Spr 79

RIGHTS OF CHILDREN. *See* CHILDREN'S RIGHTS.

RIGHTS OF GAYS. *See* GAY RIGHTS.

RIGHTS OF SEXUAL PRIVACY. *See* SEXUAL PRIVACY RIGHTS.

Rimbaud, Arthur
Rimbaud/Verlaine: a lover's cock. 1979.
Review (Arthur William Rudolph): Gay Sun 40/41:38 Sum/Fall 79

"RIMMING." *See* ANALINGUS.

RIN—NO—TAMA BALLS. *See* BEN—WA BALLS.

ROLLER—COASTER SEX—PERSONAL ACCOUNTS.
Roller-coaster riders [letter]. Var spec 5:93-4 Mid-Spr 79

ROLLER DISCO. *See* DISCO SKATING.

Romeo, Sherry
Infertility. Sexol 46-2:8-9 Oct 79

Ronan, Richard
Flowers; poems. 1978.
Review (E.A. Lacey): Gay Sun 40/41:32 Sum/Fall 79

Ross, Michael W.
The relationship of perceived societal hostility, conformity, and psychological adjustment in homosexual males. J Homo 4-2:157-68 Win 78

RUBBER FETISH
Stryker, Rod
On the rack. Fetish T 64:12-13

S/M. *See* SADOMASOCHISM.

STD. *See* VENEREAL DISEASE.

SADISM. *See* SADOMASOCHISM.

SADOMASOCHISM
See also Bondage and discipline
Fist-fucking
Spanking
Whipping

SADOMASOCHISM—PERSONAL ACCOUNTS
Califia, Pat
Pleasure/pain and power—a Lesbian's view. Var spec 5:56-65 Mid-Spr 79
Friendly, Suzanne
I can be very friendly. Pillow T 3-6:8-10 Sep 79
White slave [letter]. Hum Dig 3-1:63-6 Jan 79

SADOMASOCHIST FANTASIES
The captured squaw [letter]. Var spec 5:39-40 Mid-Spr 79

SAN FRANCISCO BAY AREA
Cozad, William
Cruisin' the Bay Area. Resp 6-9:52-6 Oct 79

SantaVicca, Edmund F.
Evaluating encyclopedias: a framework summary. Gay Insurg 4/5:15-17 Spr 79

Satin, Mark
New Age politics, healing self and society; the emerging new alternative to Marxism and Liberalism. 1978.
Review (Mitch Walker): Gay Sun 40/41:35 Sum/Fall 79

SAUNA SEX
The sauna the better [letter]. Sexol 46-2:55-6 Oct 79

"SCAT." *See* COPROPHILIA.

SCHALLER, JON—INTERVIEWS
Tsang, Daniel
Radical distribution. Gay Insurg 4/5:12-13 Spr 79

"SCREWING." *See* ANAL SEX; BESTIALITY; HETEROSEX-UAL INTERCOURSE; HOMOSEXUAL INTERCOURSE.

SEDUCTION
Poole, Tom
How to turn on a reluctant lover. Pillow T 3-6:72-5 Sep 79

SENIOR MEN'S SEXUALITY
Thistle, Frank
Are dirty old men really dirty? Pillow T 3-6:28-33 Sep 79

SENIORS' SEXUALITY
Man's ingenuity [letter]. Var spec 5:156-7 Mid-Spr 79

SEX AIDS
See also Ben-Wa balls
Dildos
Hairdryers
Sex dolls
Sex shops
Shower sprays
Vibrators
Chalking it up [letter]. Var spec 5:159-60. Mid-Spr 79
An endless source of pleasure [letter]. Var spec 5:148-9
Mid-Spr 79
Glove love [letter]. Var spec 5:149 Mid-Spr 79
Jingle balls [letter]. Var spec 5:159 Mid-Spr 79
Little Miss Muffet [letter]. Var spec 5:157-8 Mid-Spr 79

SEX AIDS—CATALOGS
Stryker, Rod
On the rack. Fetish T 64:12-13

SEX AIDS—EVALUATION
Milton, John
Mail order madness. Screw 548:32 Sep 3, 79

SEX AND LAW. *See* SEX LAWS.

SEX AND URINATION. *See* "WET" SEX.

SEX COUNSELING AND THERAPY
Bliss, K.D.
Beating the short time Charlie blues. Resp 6-9:27-31 Oct
79
Dailey, Jan
Women and orgasm: how to achieve it no matter what.
Sexol 46-2:10-18 Oct 79
Holaday, Robert
Frigidity: the causes & the cures. Hum Dig 3-1:23-7 Jan
79

SEX CRIMES IN NEWS MEDIA
Boston/Boise Committee
Suggestions for media on handling alleged sex "crimes"
involving Gay men. Gay Insurg 4/5:56-9 Spr 79

SEX DOLLS
Jardine, Jack Owen.
Oh, you beautiful doll! Var spec 5:142-7 Mid-Spr 79

SEX FILMS. *See* EROTIC FILMS.

SEX HYGIENE. *See* SEXUAL HYGIENE.

SEX IN AIRPLANES. *See* AIRPLANE SEX.

SEX IN CABS. *See* TAXICAB SEX.

SEX IN CARRIAGES. *See* CARRIAGE SEX.

SEX IN ELEVATORS. *See* ELEVATOR SEX.

SEX IN MUSEUMS. *See* MUSEUM SEX.

SEX IN OFFICES. *See* OFFICE SEX.

SEX IN PRISON. *See* PRISON SEX.

SEX IN RESTAURANTS. *See* RESTAURANT SEX.

SEX IN RETAIL STORES. *See* STORE SEX.

SEX IN SAUNAS. *See* SAUNA SEX.

SEX IN STORES. *See* STORE SEX.

SEX IN TAXICABS. *See* TAXICAB SEX.

SEX IN THE SNOW. *See* SNOW SEX.

SEX IN THEATERS. *See* THEATER SEX.

SEX IN TRAINS. *See* TRAIN SEX.

SEX IN WATER. *See* UNDERWATER SEX.

SEX LAWS
See also Birth control—Laws and regulations
Child molesting—Laws and regulations
Gays—Legal status, laws, etc.
Obscenity law
Sexual privacy rights
Sodomy law
Solicitation law
Youth Liberation
Children and sex: a Youth Liberation view. Gay Insurg
4/5:22-4 Spr 79

SEX OFFENDERS
See also Rapists
Prendergast, William E.
The sex offender: how to spot him before it's too late.
Sexol 46-2:46-51 Oct 79

SEX ON ELEVATORS. *See* ELEVATOR SEX.

SEX ON ROLLER—COASTERS. *See* ROLLER—COASTER
SEX.

SEX ON TRAINS. *See* TRAIN SEX.

SEX PERIODICALS. *See* EROTIC PERIODICALS.

SEX PSYCHOLOGY. *See* SEXUAL PSYCHOLOGY.

SEX ROLE IN MASS MEDIA—BIBLIOGRAPHY—REVIEWS
Friedman, Leslie
Sex role stereotyping in the mass media: an annotated
bibliography. 1974.
Review (Scott C. McDonald): J Homo 4-2:192-4 Win 78

SEX SHOPS
Double dong [letter]. Var spec 5:101-2 Mid-Spr 79

SEX SHOWS
See also Burlesque shows
Erotic films
Friendly, Suzanne
I can be very friendly. Pillow T 3-6:8-10 Sep 79

SEX THERAPY. *See* SEX COUNSELING AND THERAPY.

SEX TOYS. *See* SEX DOLLS.

SEX UNDER WATER. *See* UNDERWATER SEX.

SEX WITH ANIMALS. *See* BESTIALITY.

SEXISM IN MASS MEDIA—BIBLIOGRAPHY—REVIEWS
Friedman, Leslie
Sex role stereotyping in the mass media: an annotated
bibliography. 1974.
Review (Scott C. McDonald): J Homo 4-2:192-4 Win 78

SEXUAL AIDS. *See* SEX AIDS.

Stryker, Rod
    On the rack. Fetish T 64:12-13

SUBJECT HEADINGS—GAYS
    Berman, Sanford
        Gay access: new approaches in cataloging. Gay Insurg
        4/5:14-15 Spr 79

"SUCKING CUNT." See CUNNILINGUS.

"SUCKING OFF." See FELLATIO.

Sullivan, Timothy J.
    Attempted repeals of Gay Rights ordinances: the facts. Sex
    L Rptr 4-4:61+ Oct/Dec 78

SWAPPING MATES. See MATESWAPPING.

SWINGERS' CLUBS
    Swinging roundup: the West Coast, the Midwest, the East
        Coast. Var spec 5:44-50 Mid-Spr 79

SWINGING
        See also Mate-swapping
                 Part-time marriage
                 Threesomes
    Swinging roundup: the West Coast, the Midwest, the East
        Coast. Var spec 5:44-50 Mid-Spr 79
    Watson, Tom
        The swinging life. Pillow T 3-6:95-6 Sep 79

SWINGING—PERSONAL ACCOUNTS
    A date with eight [letter]. Var spec 5:55 Mid-Spr 79
    Here comes the bride [letter]. Var spec 5:54-5 Mid-Spr 79

TAXICAB SEX—PERSONAL ACCOUNTS
    Sex on wheels [letter]. Var spec 5:123 Mid-Spr 79

TEENAGERS' SEXUALITY
    Accentuate the positive [letter]. Sexol 46-2:54 Oct 79
    Adolescent anxieties [letter]. Hum Dig 3-1:77-8 Jan 79
    Not quite ready [letter]. HumDig 3-1:79-80 Jan 79
    Turnabout [letter]. Sexol 46-2:53-4 Oct 79

TELEVISION BONDAGE AND DISCIPLINE. See BONDAGE
    AND DISCIPLINE IN TELEVISION.

TEMPLE UNIVERSITY LIBRARY
    Tsang, Daniel
        The Gay press. Gay Insurg 4/5:18-21 Spr 79

THEATER SEX
    "The fantasy game." Pillow T 3-6:91-3 Sep 79

THERAPY, SEX. See SEX COUNSELING AND THERAPY.

Thistle, Frank
    Are dirty old men really dirty? Pillow T 3-6:28-33 Sep 79

THREESOMES
    Friel, T.
        Transvestite marriage: hubby was wigged-out on
        women's clothes. Fetish T 64:4-6+

THREESOMES—PERSONAL ACCOUNTS
    Bisexual threesome [letter]. Var spec 5:29 Mid-spr 79
    Crown, Sandra
        Female sexual fulfillment: what it really means. Hum Dig
        3-1:39-45 Jan 79
    Friends and lovers [letter]. Var spec 5:83-4 Mid-Spr 79

Kempler, Jana
    A couple takes a chance. Var spec 5:70-81 Mid-Spr 79
    Unforgettable melody [letter]. Var spec 5:84-5 Mid-Spr 79
    A yacht to learn [letter]. Var spec 5:82 Mid-Spr 79

Tiktin, Carl
    Ron. 1979.
        Review (Scott Jones): Gay Sun 40/41:32 Sum/Fall 79

TOYS, SEX. See SEX DOLLS.

TRAIN SEX
    Gersten, Leon
        "The fantasy game." Pillow T 3-6:91-3 Sep 79

TRAIN SEX—PERSONAL ACCOUNTS
    Catherine, Eleanor
        It happened on a train. Var spec 5:116-20 Mid-Spr 79
    Chasing the commuter blues [letter]. Var spec 5:123-4
        Mid-Spr 79

TRANSSEXUALS—INTERVIEWS
    Hoffman, Lisa
        A bisexual wedding; interview and photos. Porn film star
        Marc Stevens marries transsexual model Jill Monro. Var
        spec 5:18-27 Mid-Spr 79

TRANSSEXUALS—PERSONAL ACCOUNTS
    Finley, Theresa
        Transsexual callgirl. Var spec 5:127-31 Mid-Spr 79

TRANSVESTITES
    Friel, T.
        Transvestite marriage: hubby was wigged-out on
        women's clothes. Fetish T 64:4-6+

TRANSVESTITES—PERSONAL ACCOUNTS
    Shopping tip [letter]. Hum Dig 3-1:74. Jan 79

Trifonov, Gennady
    Three poems. Gay Sun 40/41:12 Sum/Fall 79

Tsang, Daniel
    The Gay press. Gay Insurg 4/5:18-21 Spr 79
    Radical distribution. Gay Insurg 4/5:12-13 Spr 79

UNDERWATER SEX—PERSONAL ACCOUNTS
    Scuba sex [letter]. Var spec 5:157 Mid-Spr 79

URINATION AND SEX. See "WET" SEX.

VD. See VENEREAL DISEASE.

VAGINA SIZE
    Large vagina [letter]. Hum Dig 3-1:80-1 Jan 79

VAGINAL LUBRICATION
        See also Cunnilingus
    Too dry [letter]. Hum Dig 3-1:94 Jan 79

VENEREAL DISEASE
    Fighting VD [letter]. Hum Dig 3-1:97 Jan 79

VIBRATORS
    Good vibrations [letter]. Var spec 5:100 Mid-Spr 79
    McGregor, Michelle
        Viva vibrators! A complete rundown on all the latest vib-
        rators and sex aids. A consumer report for the truly
        sensual woman. Hum Dig 3-1:50-4 Jan 79

Phillips, Kate
Ben Wa balls: a woman's secret delight. Var spec 5:96-9 Mid-Spr 79

VIDEOTAPE CATALOGS
Your favorite XXX full-length movies are now on video tapes! [advertisement]. Screw 548:8 Sep 3, 79

VIDEOTAPE REVIEWS
Perkowski, Donald
A flesh start: video vice. Screw 548:17 Sep 3, 79

VIRGINITY
Not quite ready [letter]. Hum Dig 3-1:79-80 Jan 79
The power of virginity [letter]. Sexol 46-2:53 Oct 79

VIRGINITY—PERSONAL ACCOUNTS
A daring debut [letter]. Var spec 5:114-15 Mid-Spr 79
The first time [letter]. Var spec 5:112-13 Mid-Spr 79
Lawrence, Adele
A virgin doesn't have to say no. Var spec 5:105-11 Mid-Spr 79
A rare virgin [letter]. Var spec 5:114 Mid-Spr 79
Virgin by choice [letter]. Var spec 5:112 Mid-Spr 79

Von Eckmann, Erika
A eunuch in every garage [letter]. Fetish T 64:9-10

Wallner, S.
Kathleen [poem]. SYOL 21:10 Oct 78

"WATER SPORTS." See "WET" SEX.

WATERPIK SPRAYS. See SHOWER SPRAYS.

Watmough, David
No more into the garden. 1978.
Review (Scott Jones): Gay Sun 40/41:32 Sum/Fall 79

Watson, Tom
The swinging life. Pillow T 3-6:95-6 Sep 79

Weinberg, Thomas S.
On "doing" and "being" Gay: sexual behavior and homosexual male self-identity. J Homo 4-2:143-56 Win 78

"WET" SEX.
Urinating into the vagina [letter]. Sexol 46-2:76-8 Oct 79

WHIPPING—PERSONAL ACCOUNTS
Kinky craftsmanship [letter]. Fetish T 64:9

White, Edmund
Nocturnes for the King of Naples. 1978.
Review (Scott Jones): Gay Sun 40/41:32 Sum/Fall 79

Williams, Dalton Lloyd
Prison sex at age 16; County Jail: a true incident. Gay Sun 40/41:14 Sum/Fall 79

WINTER SEX. See SNOW SEX.

Wiseman, Sarah
Solstice poem. SYOL 21:24 Oct 78

Witomski, T.R.
Beyond the last taboo. Var spec 5:136-40 Mid-Spr 79
Oh, you big brute, you. Pillow T 3-6:12-15 Sep 79

WOMEN, GAY. See LESBIANS.

WOMEN PROSTITUTES. See FEMALE PROSTITUTES.

WOMEN'S ART
Corinne, Tee
The lady who loved horses [graphic]. SYOL 21:24 Oct 78

WOMEN'S EXERCISE. See EXERCISE FOR WOMEN.

WOMEN'S MASTURBATION. See FEMALE MASTURBATION.

WOMEN'S MOVEMENT
Women's Lib 10 years later: is there sex after liberation? [discussion]. Hum Dig 3-1:13-17 Jan 79

WOMEN'S POETRY
See also Lesbians—Poetry
Andrews, Martha
Brief resolution [poem]. SYOL 21:14 Oct 78
Bentley, Caryl B.
A both/and song for the crones [poem]. SYOL 21:5 Oct 78
Colebrook, Val
Inside out [poem]. SYOL 21:24 Oct 78
Strange songs (dreams) [poem]. SYOL 21:15 Oct 78
Fletcher, Sheila
Quarry [poem]. SYOL 21:10 Oct 78
Goldberg, Arleen
A well kept secret [poem]. SYOL 21:21 Oct 78
Hellander, Martha
On edge [poem]. SYOL 21:12 Oct 78
Hoffman, Susan
A meditation on Adrienne Rich's Splittings [poem]. SYOL 21:5 Oct 78
Jackson, Damaris
Dancers in the studio [poem]. SYOL 21:4 Oct 78
To the winter solstice [poem]. SYOL 21:24 Oct 78
Jolly, Lara
A time of reaping [poem]. SYOL 21:22 Oct 78
Krause, Donna M.
Playing tough [poem]. SYOL 21:24 Oct 78
McDonnell, Linda
Angling [poem]. SYOL 21:9 Oct 78
Moos, Kate
Eggs, for Janis [poem]. SYOL 21:12 Oct 78
The seer [poem]. SYOL 21:12 Oct 78
To Joseph [poem]. SYOL 21:10 Oct 78
Radtke, Janel
Consider the possibilities [poem]. SYOL 21:15 Oct 78
Stifter, Catherine M.
Abduction/seduction [poem]. SYOL 21:22 Oct 78
Wiseman, Sarah
Solstice poem. SYOL 21:24 Oct 78

WOMEN'S SEXUALITY
See also Breast feeding
Breasts
Exercise for women
Female masturbation
Female orgasm
Frigidity
Heterosexual intercourse

Women's Sexuality (cont'd)
        Homosexual intercourse
        Lesbians
        Transsexuals
        Vagina size
        Vaginal lubrication
    Crown, Sandra
        Female sexual fulfillment: what it really means. Hum Dig
        3-1:39-45 Jan 79
    Deni, Laura
        Why nice girls finish last. Pillow T 3-6: 16-21 + Sep 79
    Shore, Jeannie
        How to cope with those first-night jitters. Hum Dig 3-1:9-
        12 Jan 79
    Women's Lib 10 years later: is there sex after liberation?
        [discussion]. Hum Dig 3-1:13-17 Jan 79

WORD IS OUT (FILM)
    Cruikshank, Peg
        Notes on two films: Julia and Word is out. SYOL 21:11
        Oct 78

WORLD WAR I-BOOK REVIEWS
    Mager, Don
        Dr. Magnus Hirschfeld as socialist pacifist thinker. Gay
        Insurg 4/5:2-8 Spr 79

X-RATED FILMS. *See* EROTIC FILMS.

YOGA
    Stahl, Jerry
        A way to find ecstasy; after a week of yoga, fasting and
        silence, a man and a woman experience supreme bliss
        at the edge of a precipice. Var spec 5:6-11 Mid-Spr 79

Youth Liberation
    Children and sex: A Youth Liberation view. Gay Insurg
    4/5:22-4 Spr 79

ZOOPHILIA. *See* BESTIALITY.

Note: This model index consists of author and subject entries derived from single issues of 12 periodicals. A full-scale *Sex Index* would cover at least three or four times as many titles on a quarterly or semiannual basis.

Since standard subject-heading schemes—like that developed by the Library of Congress—are, to put it charitably, almost *asexual,* a special thesaurus rooted in the material itself must necessarily be devised to fairly and usefully represent sexologic topics. BONDAGE AND DISCIPLINE, for example, while a common term in sexuality literature, doesn't even appear as a cross-reference in the LC scheme. And the same is (incredibly) true for HOMOPHOBIA, ANILINGUS, SEXUAL FANTASIES, DILDOS, SEXUAL FREEDOM, HETEROSEXUALITY, GAY RIGHTS, GAY POETS, GAY COUPLES, LESBIAN MOTHERS, SEXUAL REVOLUTION, PREMATURE EJACULATION, SEX AIDS, THREESOMES, COPROPHILIA, MATE-SWAPPING, NUDE BEACHES, SEX SHOPS, and the various fetishes. By contrast, the LC list *does* "validate" the judgmental—indeed, puritanical—descriptor, SEXUAL DEVIATION, which it unsurprisingly cross-references from "Sexual Perversion"!

Headings employed for the model:

● Mainly reflect the language actually and preponderantly found in the indexed magazines, augmented by a few primary forms and cross-references derived from sources like Erwin J. Haeberle's *Sex Atlas* (Seabury Press, 1978), Bernhardt J. Hurwood's *Whole Sex Catalogue* (Pinnacle Books, 1975), Joan K. Marshall's *On Equal Terms: A Thesaurus for Nonsexist Indexing and Cataloging* (Neal-Schuman, 1977), the *Hennepin County Library Authority File,* and *Sexual Nomenclature: A Thesaurus* (G.K. Hall, 1976), compiled by JoAnn Brooks and Helen C. Hofer at the Indiana University Institute for Sex Research Library.

- Follow natural word order both to ensure consistency and avoid awkward constructions like EJACULATION PREMATURE or BEACHES NUDE.

- Represent unbiased terminology, excluding "loaded" nomenclature like "deviance," "perversion" and "pornography," but favoring self-declared group names (e.g. GAYS instead of HOMO-SEXUALS).

- Embody popular rather than clinical or academic terms (e.g. TEENAGERS' SEXUALITY instead of ADOLESCENT SEXUALITY) and include slang or "street" cross-references (e.g., from "Fucking" and "Cunt shaving") in order to promote access by the greatest possible range of users, not merely specialists or researchers.

ACCESS/EQUITY

These 20 pieces all relate to two simply stated questions:

- How can library materials be made easier to find through the catalog?
- How can the language of the catalog, especially the subject vocabulary, be made more accurate, precise, and nonjudgmental?

"Chauvinistic Headings" triggered what subsequently became a chain reaction: publication of *Prejudices and Antipathies* in 1971; the MISR subject heading list a year later; a mounting number of letters and articles in the library press on biased and inadequate nomenclature; and vastly increased debate and dialogue in professional forums, highlighted by packed hearings on racist and sexist LC headings conducted in 1974 and 1975 by ALA's Subject Analysis Committee. [For a sampling of contemporary reports and eruptions, see "Random Notes on Subject Cataloging," MISR Library *Accessions List/Bulletin* (September 1972):22-4; "Poverty of Thinking," *Race Today*, v. 5, no. 10 (October/November 1973):301-3; Suzanne LeBarron, "ALA/LC 'Sweetheart Pact,'" *SRRT Newsletter,* no. 30 (March 1974):12-3; "WASH–SRRT Joins in Assailing Merriam's 'Jap' Definition," *ibid.*, pp. 13-4; "Sexist/Racist Subject Heads under Fire," *SRRT Newsletter*, no. 31 (May 1974):14; "'Negroes' and 'Orientals' in A/V Program: Cohen Objects, Schloat Agrees," *ibid.*, pp. 16-7; "Conference Kaleidoscope," *SRRT Newsletter*, no. 32 (August 1974):4-6; "SRRT Task Force Launches Offensive against 'Homosexuality,'" *HCL Cataloging Bulletin*, nos. 8-10 (September 1, 1974):33-4; "SAC Acts," *ibid.*, pp. 34-5; "RRIC Seminar Thumps LC Racism, Stereotypes/Mumford Responds," *HCL Cataloging Bulletin*, no. 11-13 (March 15, 1975):80-2; "SAC Notes," *ibid.*, p. 82; William Eshelman, "A Wary-eye View of ALA/NY," *Wilson Library Bulletin* (September 1974):67; Edward J. Blume and Treva Turner, "RTSD/CCS Subject Analysis Committee," *LC Information Bulletin* (August 17, 1973):A159-60; Edward J. Blume, "RTSD CCS Subject Analysis Committee and Subcommittee on Subject Headings for Correctional Materials," *LC InformationBulletin* (August 9, 1974):A174.]

However, despite the weighty, accumulated evidence as well as the demands and suggestions articulated by concerned groups like SRRT's Women and Gay Liberation Task Forces, ALA's Black

Caucus, the Jewish Librarians' Caucus, and Southern California R.C.I.A. Unions Retirees Clubs, the national leadership in Chicago and Washington alike has reacted slowly, grudgingly, and often wrong-headedly to the demonstrated problems and defects of standard subject cataloging vocabulary and praxis. For example, the defamatory and inauthentic headings, BUSHMEN and HOTTEN-TOTS, had been publicly and persuasively assailed in the early 1970s. [See, for instance, "Miscellanea," MISR Library *Accessions List/Bulletin* (December 1971):18-21; "Editorial III," *ibid.* (January 1972):18; "Random Notes on Subject Cataloging (Continued)," *ibid.* (May 1972):10; and "The Trouble with 'Bushmen' and 'Hottentots.' "] Yet it was not until *after* preparation of the "African Ethnonyms" statement in 1977 and its endorsement by the African Studies Association that the Library of Congress acted, at last rectifying those two mistakes. As the direct result of women's pressure, LC belatedly introduced the term, FEMINISM, in the mid-1970s, but simultaneously —and for no good reason—cancelled the perfectly valid, previously *active* form, WOMEN'S LIBERATION MOVEMENT! [See the 1974-1976 LCSH Supplement, pp. 247 and 755.] It eventually—again, sluggishly—replaced FIREMEN with FIREFIGHTERS, but never substituted the androgynous term, HUMANS, for the macho MAN! It has slightly reduced the Christocentrism that otherwise permeates its subject heading scheme by establishing complementary, even-handed rubrics like CHRISTIAN SAINTS, JAINA SAINTS, BUDDHIST SAINTS, SIKH SAINTS, and HINDU SAINTS; however, it has done little to similarly equalize the treatment of dozens of other religious topics, beginning with GOD.

Even though one after another "authority"—most recently, the National Library of Canada—has declared "Inuit" to be the correct, self-preferred name for the northern people mistakenly known for decades as "Eskimos," as of late 1979 the LCSH heading perversely continues to be ESKIMOS. [For a potpourri of Inuit data, see "The Columbus Legacy and Native Americans/the 'Eurindian Question'/'Eskimos' or 'Inuit'?" *HCL Cataloging Bulletin*, nos. 6/7 (April 5, 1974):21-3, 42; "Feedback," *ibid.*, nos. 8-10 (September 1, 1974):2-7; *Sears List of Subject Headings: Canadian Companion* (H.W. Wilson, 1978), p. v, 32; and *Canadian Subject Headings* (National Library of Canada, 1978), p. xiv, 117-21.] And as though oblivious to the manifold complaints, proofs, and recommendations from both within and outside the profession, JEWISH QUESTION and YELLOW PERIL and MAMMIES and AGED and a multitude of PRIMITIVE forms are still "acceptable," still "approved," while KWANZA and KIBBUTZ and THIRD WORLD and AGEISM and RED POWER are not. Likewise, apart from some notable improvement lately in legitimizing certain musical topics (e.g., STEELBAND, REGGAE, SOUL, DISCO) *before* the genre or style declines or wholly vanishes, most genuinely "alternative" and pioneering concepts, together with many contemporary movements and trends, either go totally unnoticed or become misleading cross-references to impossibly large and unlikely descriptors (e.g., "Counter culture. *See* Collective settlements; Conflict of generations; Conformity; Drugs and youth; Hippies; Radicalism; Sex customs; Social history—1945- ; Subculture; Underground press . . .").

An observation from the April 1972 MISR Library *Accessions List/Bulletin* (p. 28) remains basically, if unfortunately, true:

> The sensibilities of White Westerners have been more highly valued and accorded greater deference by subject-catalogers than those of the rest of humankind. Similarly, and quite independent of the literature itself, men have been exalted, women denigrated, management favored over labor, sex consigned to the waterfront penny-arcade, children abused, "radicals" uniquely associated with a variety of nasty mischief, and Christians (especially Protestants) allotted a place nearer to Heaven than any other believers. Beyond that, the innovation of headings to encompass relatively recent or contemporary ideas and social phenomena like national Liberation Movements, Workers' Control, and Free Schools have been extraordinarily tardy, if done at all.

But while there's abundant cause for bitterness and dismay, there's also a basis for hope and even elation inasmuch as the obstinate brontosaurus in Washington *has* been compelled to *move*; scores of colleagues have joined the campaign for modern, humanized cataloging; and a number of institutions, from Wellesley, Massachusetts to Waterloo, Iowa, have independently—without divine sanction from ALA or LC—enhanced both access and equity through local reforms and innovations.

To conclude on a note of sheer frivolity, the open invitation for more x-refs to BUTTOCKS ("Bringing Up the Rear") spawned two imaginative replies: Steve Marquardt offered "cush" (a "corrupted abbreviation of cushion"); Phyllis Yaffe and Sherrill Cheda jointly contributed "rump"; and all three agreed on "cheeks," with Yaffe and Cheda invoking Monty Python as their semantic "authority."

Chauvinistic Headings

After three weeks of using the LC subject heading list at the University of Zambia Library, what I long suspected has now been disgustingly confirmed: Western chauvinism permeates the scheme (and *Sears,* too). Presuming that American libraries, democratic and equalitarian in spirit, do not wish their card catalogs to enshrine and perpetuate a racist/colonial bias, I propose that:

1. The New Round Table on the Social Responsibilities of Libraries undertakes a comprehensive study of the extent to which our major cataloging and classification schemes are White-, imperialist-, and Christian-oriented, with concrete suggestions for improvement.

2. Some immediate corrections be made by libraries sensitive to the history and achievements—indeed, the integrity—of both the Third World and our own ethnic minorities, e.g.,

a. "Native Races" as a subdivision could be replaced simply by "Peoples." "Races" is clearly an anachronism, no longer sound anthropologically, while "Native" is the sort of word employed by an outsider, a European or American, not an African or Asian. Much the same objection may be lodged against "Native Clergy," "Native Labor," and "Native Races"—all primary headings. Possible substitutes: "Local Clergy," "Colonies—Labor and Laboring Classes," "Colonized Peoples."

b. "Race Question," as a subdivision (e.g., under "United States" and "Africa, South"), smacks of White supremacy (it is surely no mere "question," no leisurely abstraction, to American and South African Blacks). "Race Relations" would be more neutral and objective.

c. The heading "Negroes in Africa" (together with its permutations, e.g., "Negroes in Africa, West") is utterly absurd (just as "Orientals in Asia" or "Caucasian Race in Europe" would be). It should be stricken from subject lists. And the same might be done with "Negroes in South Africa," which wrongfully suggests they are a minority in their own country.

Also, the accuracy and worth of that long-standing subdivision, "Discovery and Exploration," need to be reexamined. "Africa—Discovery and Exploration" and "North America—Discovery and Exploration," for example, are colossal pieces of ethnocentrism.

Letter reprinted from *Library Journal* (February 15, 1969): 695. Published by R.R. Bowker Co. (a Xerox company). Copyright © 1969 by Xerox Corporation.

Cortez no more discovered Mexico for the Aztecs than Livingstone did Victoria Falls for the Leya people, who much earlier had named it "Nsyungu Namutitima." If not scrapped altogether, the subhead should, at the very least, be employed only with a further qualification indicating *who* did the discovering and exploring (e.g., French, European, American, English). Unqualified, "Discovery and Exploration" represents an insult to the many peoples and lands which, so it appears in our library catalogs, didn't really exist until White men happened to notice them.

And a corollary matter: how quaint and self-righteous that the United States does not now (and never did) have "colonies" (not a nice word), but only "territories and possessions"! In other words, Cubans, Guamians, Filipinos, Okinawans, Puerto Ricans, Midway and Virgin Islanders, Hawaiians, Samoans, and Indians, unlike their less fortunate brothers and sisters in Africa, Asia, and South America, were spared a "colonial" experience.

What then, was (or is) it? Can't we bear to call a thing by its right name? Certainly, no disinterested scheme for the arrangement of books and knowledge ought to employ such a transparent double standard and self-serving euphemisms.

Counter-Cataloging

Professor Seymour Lubetzky's review of *Prejudices and Antipathies* (LJ [February 15, 1972]: 658–9) is most welcome as a solid start toward the very "dialogue and action" projected in the book's introduction.

That so illustrious a cataloger himself finds that the "headings cited incontestably reflect a pervasive bias and bigotry" appears to confirm the "tract's" central thesis. Many of his remarks, however, raise or imply certain crucial issues and problems that require comment:

1. *Whose* bias and prejudice?" he repeatedly asks, explaining that "a list of subject headings is not a social treatise reflecting its author's philosophy or point of view. It is," he holds, "merely a list of the subjects with which the materials in the library's collections are concerned, and any imbalance in the character of these materials will naturally be reflected in the headings." Yes, any subject scheme relates to a library's actual holdings, but does not necessarily mirror those holdings faithfully nor fully. Rather, it reflects the catalogers' perception of the holdings. "To arbitrate political questions . . . is a novel, but scarcely tenable, concept of the function of the subject cataloger" sounds eminently objective and admirably modest, but it just isn't the case. Catalogers "arbitrate" regularly.

In terms of "perception," Lubetzky admits that material on "Heroines" has been consistently subsumed under "Heroes." That is, "heroines" have not been perceived as entities in their own right, despite the fact of holdings on heroines. (Parenthetically, it's a trifle naive to argue that "male chauvinism" can't account for misogynist subject forms since "cataloging departments at LC and elsewhere have traditionally been dominated by women." Plantation-owners found some slaves willing to wield the whip over their brothers. The South African security service includes African agents. And the Nazis enlisted some Jews to help exterminate their fellows. "Uncle-Tomism" knows no bounds of sex, race, or ethnicity. Within an institutional or societal context of male chauvinism," some women will function as male chauvinists.) As the book indicates, there was good authority available prior to LC's first edition for selecting "Muslims" and "Islam" over "Mohammedans" and "Mohammedanism." LC chose the latter, offensive forms, only rectifying that misperception some 50 years later. To deliberately belabor the point: Those initial forms sprang not from the holdings, but from the catalogers' approach to the holdings.

Concerning "imbalance," it's a virtual certainty that collections as immense as LC's do contain, e.g., material on other kinds of Communists, bankers, capitalists, and criminals than solely Jews, Blacks, or Catholics. If not whole works, then undoubtedly chapters, whose contents—providing the cataloger notices them—may be disclosed through subject analytics. It's instructive here to note that when the "Criminals" question first arose in the literature (see *Prejudices*, pp. 35–8), an LC respondent didn't defend the adjectival forms on the same basis as Lubetzky. He did not assert that LC had no books on, say, Italian or Italian-American criminals, but rather lamely maintained that these were adequately covered by geographical subdivisions like —ITALY. Perception again. The blame for "pervasive bias and bigotry" can't be laid exclusively on a hatefully obsessed "community" or slanted publishing practices. A cataloger confronted by four titles on the same topic in which one author writes of "Negroes," another of "Blacks," the third "Afro-Americans," and the fourth "niggers" must choose one heading to embrace them all (even if the ultimate choice necessitates revision of an established, standard head). Similarly, he or she must make both a political and intellectual decision on whether to prefer "Hottentots" or "Khoi-Khoin," "Kafirs" or "Xhosa," the former rubric in both instances being a White supermacist tab while the other represents what the people calls itself. Again, catalogers have opted for the racists' or subjugators' terms. Another example: A multitude of works deal with the comparatively less industralized, poorer, essentially agricultural countries of Asia, Africa, and Latin America. Such works could be cataloged under "Backward areas," "Underdeveloped areas," "Developing countries," or "Third World." LC *picked* the negatively charged "Underdeveloped areas" instead of the relatively "value-free," commonly used, and equally serviceable "Third World." The total *holdings* on "Anarchism" no more dictate its association with "Terrorism" than those on "Socialism" demand a cross-reference to "Sabotage." And only a slight effort should suffice to find works to which the proposed "balancing" head, LABOR RIGHTS, could be applied [e.g., "Human Rights in the Economic World," Chapter 14 in G.A. Johnston's *International Labour Organisation* (London: Europa, 1970); as well as C.W. Jenks' *Human Rights and International Labour Standards* (London: Stevens, 1960) and *International Protection of Trade Union Freedom* (London: Stevens, 1957)]. The problem is less one of *holdings* than of *will*. Books, to enunciate a pertinent truism, don't catalog themselves.

2. JEWISH QUESTION. Of course it appears in the literature, in many languages. Jews themselves have employed it. Jews have also worn yellow stars and been regaled with lovely epithets like "Kikes" and "Judsau." *Use,* in short, doesn't alone validate "Jewish

Question" any more than it does yellow stars, "Kikes," or "Judsau." Since the phrase encompasses material on the usually unequal and often deadly relationship between Jews and their "host" communities or governments, all the proffered active "substitutes" (see *Prejudices*, pp. 25–6) would no less accurately cover the material. An extra refinement, however—e.g., under JEWS IN EUROPE— might be to introduce subheads like —GOVERNMENT RELATIONS (as is done for Amerindians) and —RELATIONS WITH GENTILES [or NON-JEWS]. If Lubetzky agrees that " 'Jewish Question' is a 'most odious' example of 'outright racism,' " then why not agree to the same "relegation to oblivion" that he heartily and rightly recommends for that "most conspicuous racist heading 'Yellow Peril,' " a "vestige of an earlier and darker age" which could easily be replaced by "current terminology"?

3. COLONIES VS. TERRITORIES AND POSSESSIONS. A judgment is involved and can't be escaped. If, as Lubetzky implies, official designations should be automatically honored, then pre-independence Algeria was, indeed, a French "Department"; Mozambique, Angola, and Guinea-Bissau are not Portuguese "overseas provinces" (although LC, contrary to the Lubetzky-principle, continues entering omnibus material on them under "Portugal—Colonies," e.g., J.D. Gerhard's 1969 *Grundzuege der Geschichte Portugals und seiner Uebersee-Provinzen*); Southwest Africa constitutes an integral part of the Republic of South Africa, being its "fifth province"; and Micronesia is merely an American "Trust Territory." If, however, a cataloger recognizes that "colonialism" signifies "control by one power over a *dependent* area or people" (Webster; emphasis added), and additionally, that such "control" is exercised without the freely given consent of that "area or people," it becomes obvious that official rubrics like "Department," "Overseas Province," or "Territory" qualify as self-justifying mystifications. Even beyond the strictly semantic dimension, abundant evidence illustrates how the subject peoples themselves regard their status. The long-rebelling Algerians hardly considered themselves "French" nor "departmental"; the Congress of Micronesia has unequivocally protested the "present [US] quasi-colonial system"; the fruits of being a Portuguese "province" have so overwhelmed PAIGC that it's presently removing the last third of "Portuguese" Guinea from Portuguese dominion; and the United Nations and International Court of Justice have explicitly denied South African authority to govern, much less annex, Namibia (i.e., Southwest Africa), while SWAPO activity in the Caprivi Strip and the recent, massive strike of Ovambo miners strongly suggest that majority Black Namibians have not "consented" to Pretoria-overrule, just as the Mama and Herero in the early 1900s militantly refused German overrule. The cataloger who blindly accepts the "master's" nomenclature, the conqueror's terminology (e.g., "Native races," "Territories and possessions," "Primitive," "Negroes," "Bushmen," "Pagen"), allies him- or herself with master and conqueror, as well as abdicating responsibility (and opportunity) of independent, creative, people-responsive judgment.

Daily, catalogers make "political" judgments. Hopefully, the book demonstrates that many of those judgments can be improved, furnishing bountiful citations to document that, e.g., "Territories and possessions" is not "generally so referred to in the literature on the subject" (unless, of course, Lubetzky restricts "literature" in this sphere entirely to what governments and their apologists produce). Frankly, no such "judgments" will be "universally shared." But they might command greater respect if more firmly rooted in both reality and compassion.

4. LITERATURE, IMMORAL. The text unfortunately invites misinterpretation, as Lubetzky well reveals. Unquestionably, the rubric is not applied, nor is it intended to apply, to an "erotic novel or volume of poetry." That would be "labelling," not cataloging. But the contested heading is no *less* a form of labelling. In practice, it is assigned to works on erotica or the sociolegal aspects of "obscenity" and "pornography," for which far more specific headings abound. A study on the particularly moral aspects or effects of literature, whether pro or con in temper, can be conveniently placed under LITERATURE AND MORALS (LCSH, p. 751) or assigned totally new constructions like EROTICA—MORAL [SOCIAL, POLITICAL] ASPECTS. What the book contends is that "Literature, immoral" and "Art, immoral" are wholly gratuitous, unnecessary, and puritanically inspired forms, linking sex *per se* with "immorality," regardless of whether the cataloged authors (e.g., Ginzburg and Miller) themselves do so. Moreover, definitionally, "Literature, Immoral" cannot be fully equated— as the x's currently do—with either "Obscene literature" or "Pornography." E.g., pornography—more precisely: sexually explicit material—is not *ipso facto* "immoral." Even a cursory reading of the Commission on Obscenity and Pornography's *Report* should cement that conclusion.

5. LYNCHING. The text does not, as Lubetzky states, propound a cross-reference from NEGROES—SOCIAL CONDITIONS, but rather from and to AFRO-AMERICANS—PERSECUTIONS.

Finally, not all "cataloging questions" are pristinely "technical." To have rendered Biafra (Black) invisible while "Confederate States of America" (White) enjoys "two full columns of primary and subordinate headings"—a ponderous precedent for an analogous situation—bespeaks something of what the system is all about. And "technical" doesn't quite describe it.

The Trouble with "Bushmen" & "Hottentots"

On April 2, 1974, the head cataloger directed this letter to the *Africana Library Journal:*

Nancy J. Schmidt's critical approach toward children's books about "the Bushmen and the Bantu" (*ALJ*, IV, 4) deserves applause from everyone concerned about the variously patronizing, ethnocentric, racist, stereotyped, and plainly inaccurate treatment of African peoples in much juvenile literature. However, in this instance, Ms. Schmidt's consistent use of the name "Bushmen" seriously undermines the intended impact of her otherwise sympathetic and fair-minded survey. For there are *no* peoples—in Africa or elsewhere—whose *own*, authentic name is "Bushmen" or (though not mentioned, but surely germane here) "Hottentots."

A "cosmic observation" seems appropriate at this point: European or Western chauvinism often dictates or suffuses the very names by which Third World peoples become generally known. Obviously, the Apache and Choctaw never called *themselves* "Indians." The label clearly derives from Columbus' navigational naiveté. Similarly, the South African groups commonly known as "Bushmen" and "Hottentots" bear monickers assigned them by the Dutch-speaking Boer immigrants.

The *Shorter Oxford English Dictionary* on p. 238 indicates that "Bushman" originated in about 1785, adding "app. after Du. *boschjesman*, as used in S. Africa." On the next page it records an early, pejorative quality attributed to the name itself: "Stunted representatives of humanity, under the name of Bushmen 1845." Under "Hottentot" (p. 926), which dates from at least 1677, appears the etymological explanation: "Du. *Hottentot*, said by Dapper to mean 'stutterer' or 'stammerer.'" By 1726, the term had already acquired the extra meaning of "A person of inferior intellect or culture." Such degrading, arrogant rubrics—it might be argued—are necessary in the absence of any authoritative substitutes. But what could be *more* authoritative than what a people calls itself? According to I. Schapera, relying on L. Schultze's *Zur Kenntnis der Koerpers der Hottentoten und Buschmaenner* (1928, p. 211), the "Hottentots" term themselves *Khoi-Khoin* and call the "Bushmen" *San*. Indeed, it is from these two *indigenous* names that the linguistic classification, "Khoisan," has been compounded, encompassing all South African "click" languages. [See Schapera's *Khoisan Peoples of South Africa; Bushmen and Hottentots* (London: G. Routledge & Sons, 1930), pp. 5, 31; Joseph Greenberg, *Studies in African*

Reprinted from *HCL Cataloging Bulletin*, nos. 8–10 (September 1, 1974): 31–2.

Linguistic Classification (New Haven, CT: Compass Books, 1955), p. 80; and Hermann Baumann, "Les Khoi-Sans," as well as Diedrich Westermann, "Les langues Khoisanes," in their *Peuples et les civilisations de l'Afrique*, tr. by L. Homburger (Paris: Payot, 1957), pp. 92-110, 447-8.]

Perhaps the most clear-cut, enlightened, and damning statement with respect to the nomenclature imposed by Western chauvinists upon the earliest inhabitants of South Africa comes from Endre Sik: "Literature," he writes, "generally calls the Khoi-Khoi 'Hottentots' and the Saan 'Bushmen.' Both denominations are derogatory, abusive nicknames given to those peoples by their first 'civilized' abusers, and are therefore inadmissible." [See his *History of Black Africa*, 7th ed., tr. by Sandor Simon (Budapest: Akademiai Kiado, c1970), v. 1, p. 16.] Sik himself employs "Khoi-Khoi" and "Saan" in his ethnological discussion on pp. 78-80. Labelling it "derisory," Brian Bunting similarly eschews the term "Hottentots." Instead he refers to the "Khoi-Khoin." [See *Rise of the South African Reich* (Harmondsworth, Middlesex: Penguin Books, 1964), p. 13.] Basil Davidson, too, abjures "Hottentots" in favor of "Khoi." [See *The Africans; An Entry to Cultural History* (London: Longmans, Green, 1969), p. 29.]

Another powerful endorsement of the view that "Bushmen" and "Hottentots" alike are inapplicable, on both ethnological and ethical grounds, to the peoples so tabbed appeared in the first 1972 issue of the *Journal of African History* (v. 13, no. 1). On pp. 55-80, Shula Marks traces the history of "Khoisan resistance to the Dutch in the Seventeenth and Eighteenth centuries," definitely preferring the terms *Khoikhoi* and *San*, while largely enclosing "Hottentots" and "Bushmen" in quotation marks. Her opening paragraph declares:

> The Khoisan peoples of South Africa, or, as they are usually called in the literature, the Bushmen and Hottentots, have on the whole had a bad press from historians, as indeed they had from most of their 17th- and 18th-century European contemporaries. To this day, the *Shorter Oxford Dictionary* has as one of the definitions of "Hottentot" "a person of inferior intellect and culture," and illustrates its use with the sentence: "The most I can do for him is to consider him a respectable Hottentot." Jan van Riebeeck, the first commander of the Dutch East India Company's settlement at the Cape, was neither the first nor the last to refer to the Hottentots as "a dull, stupid, lazy, stinking nation"—who were, at the same time, "bold, thievish and not to be trusted." Stereotypes of the San or Bushmen as "incorrigible banditti," "ineducable," and "unassimilable" also abound in the literature of South Africa.

Marks later cites further examples of clichéd stereotypes and on p. 55 incidentally underpins an editorial contention in the March 1972 MISR Library *Accessions List/Bulletin*—"It's a commonplace that the history of 'conquered' or 'subject' peoples is written by the 'conquerors' or 'subjugators' themselves"—with the observation that

> History tends to be the history of the successful, and the Khoikhoi herders and San hunter-gatherers, whom Europeans encountered when they first rounded the African continent, have all but disappeared from 20th-century South Africa, at least in their earlier guise.

Returning to the "cosmic" plane: If we deliberately and regularly accepted the "outsider principle" in naming peoples, then Americans might well appear in scholarly literature and library subject-heading lists as "Gringos," Britons as "Limeys," the French as "Frogs," Germans as "Krauts" or "Huns," etc. The possibilities are endless, for nearly every people has been branded with one or more debasing nicknames. To sensitive Westerners these appellations seem rightly offensive. How then, can anyone defend calling a non-Western people "Stammerers," "Stutterers," or the simplistic, manifestly condescending and inauthentic "Bushmen," once—if not still—connoting "stunted representatives of humanity"? Yet HOTTENTOT LANGUAGE and HOTTENTOTS jointly appear in boldface on p. 603 of the Library of Congess subject heading scheme (7th ed., 1966), and BUSHMAN LANGUAGE, in tandem with BUSHMEN, on p. 170, while Ms. Schmidt unqualifiedly mentions "Bushmen" or "Bushman" no less than 50 times in the space of three pages!

"In designating an ethnic group," say Tamotsu Shibutani and Kian M. Kwan, "we have tried to use the name preferred by the people themselves." [See their *Ethnic Stratification; A Comparative Approach* (New York: Macmillan, 1965), p. vii.] And F.E. Auerbach—on p. 50 of his *ABC of Race* (Johannesburg: South African Institute of Race Relations, 1970)—suggests avoiding "all group names which are disliked by the people of whom we use them." This seems altogether wise practice and advice. Which, if followed by Ms. Schmidt, would have resulted in 50 instructive, wholly unobjectionable references to "San." For reasons of both intellectual honesty and human decency, let's banish "Bushmen" and "Hottentots" from our lexicons and catalogs. Except, perhaps, as examples of bygone chauvinist slang or—library-wise—as quote-marked cross-references to these peoples' *real* names.

A P.S. followed on April 11th:

Noteworthy in the contents table for v. 4 of *Africa South of the Sahara; Index to Periodical Literature, 1900-1970* (Boston: G.K. Hall, 1971) is an absolute preference among the citations under "South West Africa" for KHOI PEOPLE and KHOISAN PEOPLE over the Boer-gestated "Hottentots" and "Bushmen." So assiduously, in fact, has LC's African Section—which compiled the 4-volume index—pursued the excellent policy of assigning to African peoples their *own* names that "Bushmen" and "Hottentots" *nowhere* figure in the table of contents. May this creditable practice soon "spill over" into LC's Subject Cataloging Division, as well as children's book publishing and academic literature.

African Ethnonyms: A Brief on Library of Congress Headings

All of the active name forms shown below are variously alien, inauthentic, and outdated. Most are also abusive and defamatory. Therefore, pursuant to the *Principles for Establishing Subject Headings Relating to People and Peoples* endorsed by both the ALA/RTSD Subject Analysis Committee and Library of Congress Subject Cataloging Division in mid-1975, as well as the July 1976 ALA "Resolution on Racism and Sexism Awareness," which mandated "the reform of cataloging practices that now perpetuate racism . . .," these descriptors should be totally and speedily replaced.

---

1. LCSH Forms

BOER STUDENTS
 Citation: 8th ed., p. 205

x Students, Boer
 Citation: 8th ed., p. 205

BOERS

x Africanders
 Afrikaanders
 Afrikanders

BOERS IN THE ARGENTINE
 REPUBLIC [THE NETHER-
 LANDS, etc.]
 Citation: 8th ed., p. 205

Proposed Substitutes

AFRIKANER STUDENTS

x Boer students
 Students, Afrikaner
 Students, Boer

AFRIKANERS

 Here are entered works on the
 Dutch-descended, Afrikaans-
 speaking people of South
 Africa who have also been
 known as Boers.

x Africanders
 Afrikaanders
 Afrikanders
 Boers

AFRIKANERS IN THE ARGEN-
 TINE REPUBLIC [THE
 NETHERLANDS, etc.]

Reprinted from *HCL Cataloging Bulletin*, no. 26 (February 1, 1977): 16–23.

Remarks

"Boer" represents an anachronism, now almost completely supplanted by "Afrikaner" in scholarly, popular, and official literature alike.

Precedents/Usage Examples/ Discussions

African Encyclopedia. New York: Oxford University Press, 1974, p. 47.

Allen, P.M., and Segal, A. "Glossary." In their *Traveler's Africa.* New York: Hopkinson & Blake, 1973, p. 903.

American Heritage Dictionary of the English Language. New York: American Heritage/Houghton Mifflin, 1973, p. 23.

Deasy, Michael. "South Africa." In David Wallechinsky and Irving Wallace, *People's Almanac.* New York: Doubleday, 1975, p. 450-1.

HCL Cataloging Bulletin, nos. 6/7 (April 5, 1974):42, 66; no. 16 (August 1, 1975):25.

Hennepin County Library. *Alphabetic Catalog of Materials.* 2d ed. Edina, MN, January 1975, A/B v., p. 51.

"Southern Africa in Brief." *Minneapolis Tribune*, November 28, 1976, p. 10A.

Subject Headings Employed at the Makerere Institute of Social Research Library: A Select List. Kampala, Uganda: Makerere University Library, 1972, pp. 10-1.

"Where It's at in South Africa at This Time." *MACSA* [Madison Area Committee on Southern Africa] *News*, nos. 48/51 (March/June 1975), p. 10.

World Book Dictionary. New York: Doubleday/Field Enterprises Educational Corp., 1974, p. 39.

---

2. LCSH Forms

BUSHMAN LANGUAGES
Citation: 8th ed., p. 242

x San languages

BUSHMEN
Citation: 8th ed., p. 242; 1974/75 supplement, p. 57

x Bosjesmen
    !Kung (African people)
    San (African people)

Proposed Substitutes

SAN LANGUAGES

x "Bushman" languages
    "Click" languages
    Khoisan languages

SAN (AFRICAN PEOPLE)

Here are entered works on the Southern African people who have been popularly but erroneously termed "Bushmen."

x "Bochimans" (African people)
    "Bosiesmans" (African people)
    "Bosjesmans" (African people)
    "Bosmanekens" (African people)
    "Buschleute" (African people)
    "Buschmaenner" (African people)
    Rwa (African people)
    Saan (African people)
    Sane (African people)
    Sarwa (African people)
    Saunqua (African people)
    Sonqua (African people)
    Sunqua (African people)

"Bushman: app. after Du. *boschjesman*, as used in S. Africa . . . Stunted representatives of humanity . . ." *(Shorter Oxford English Dictionary).*

"Literature generally calls the Khoi-Khoi 'Hottentots' and the Saan 'Bushmen.' Both denominations are derogatory . . . nicknames given to those peoples by their first 'civilized' abusers" (Endre Sik).

Remarks

Precedents/Usage Examples/Discussions

African Encyclopedia. New York: Oxford University Press, 1974, p. 443.

Baumann, Hermann. "Les Khoi-Sans." In *Peuples et les civilisations de l'Afrique.* Paris: Payot, 1957, pp. 92-110.

Berman, Sanford. "The Trouble With 'Bushmen' & 'Hottentots.'" *HCL Cataloging Bulletin,* nos. 8-10 (September 1, 1974):31-3.

"Cataloging Notes." *Africana Libraries Newsletter,* no. 3 (November 1975):7-8; no. 4 (February 1976):25-6.

Encyclopedia of Africa. New York: F. Watts, 1976, p. 32.

Greenberg, Joseph. *Studies in African Linguistic Classification.* New Haven, CT: Compass Books, 1955, p. 80.

HCL Cataloging Bulletin, no. 1 (May 3, 1973):5; no. 3 (September 17, 1973):14; nos. 6-7 (April 5, 1974):9, 11-2; nos. 14-15 (June 1, 1975):8-10, 57; nos. 23-24 (September 1, 1976):40, 45.

Hennepin County Library. *Alphabetic Catalog of Materials.* 2d ed. Edina, MN: January 1975, S/T v., p. 22.

Hiernaux, Jean. "The Khoisan Peoples." In his *Peoples of Africa.* London: Weidenfeld and Nicolson, 1975, p. 98.

McCarthy, Cavan. "FID-back." *HCL Cataloging Bulletin,* nos. 11-13 (March 15, 1975):19.

Makerere Institute of Social Research Library. *Accessions List/ Bulletin* (December 1971):18-21; (January 1972):18; (March 1972):20; (April 1972):27.

Marks, Shula. "Khoisan Resistance to the Dutch in the Seventeenth and Eighteenth Centuries." *Journal of African History,* v. 13, no. 1 (1972):55-80.

Moore, Robert B. "'Loaded' Words and Africans." In his *Racism in the English Language.* New York:CIBC, 1976, p. 12.

"Outlining South African History." *Ufahamu,* v. 3, no. 1 (Spring 1972):27.

Schapera, Isaac. *Khoisan Peoples of South Africa: Bushmen and Hottentots.* London: Routledge, 1930, pp. 5, 31.

Sik, Endre. *History of Black Africa.* 7th ed. Budapest: Akademiai Kiado, c1970, v. 1, pp. 16, 78-80.

Stein, Harry. *Southern Africa.* New York: F. Watts, 1975, pp. 13-4, 23.

Subject Headings Employed at the Makerere Institute of Social Research Library: A Select List. Kampala, Uganda: Makerere University Library, 1972, p. 83.

Westermann, Diedrich. *"Les langues Khoisanes."* In *Peuples et les civilisations de l'Afrique.* Paris: Payot, 1957, pp. 447-8.

3. LCSH Forms

GALLA LANGUAGE
Citation: 8th ed., p. 737

x Ilmorna language

GALLAS
Citation: 8th ed., p. 737

x Oromons

Proposed Substitutes

OROMO LANGUAGE

x "Galla" language
Ilma Orma language
Ilmorna language

OROMO (AFRICAN PEOPLE)

x "Galla" (African people)
"Gallaei" (African people)
"Gallani" (African people)

Remarks

" 'Oromo' now replaces 'Galla' as the name for the language both in publications and broadcasts. The name 'Galla,' which is foreign to the Oromo, and of dubious origin, is now regarded as objectionable . . ." *(IAI Bulletin).*

Precedents/Usage/ Examples/Discussions

Africana Libraries Newsletter, no. 6 (June 1976):23.
Subject Headings Employed at the Makerere Institute of Social Research Library: A Select List. Kampala, Uganda: Makerere University Library, 1972, p. 73.

4. LSCH Forms

HOTTENTOT LANGUAGE
Citation: 8th ed., p. 849

HOTTENTOTS
Citation: 8th ed., p. 849;
1974/75 supplement, p. 174

x Khoi-Khoin (African people)

Proposed Substitutes

KHOI LANGUAGE

x "Click" languages
"Hottentot" language
Khoisan languages

KHOI-KHOIN (AFRICAN PEOPLE)

Here are entered works on the Southern African people who have been popularly but erroneously termed "Hottentots."

x Cape "Hottentots"
"Hottentots" (African people)

Remarks

"Du. *Hottentot,* said . . . to mean 'stutterer' or 'stammerer' . . . A person of inferior intellect or culture" *(Shorter Oxford English Dictionary).*

"Africans, called *Hottentots* by the [Dutch] settlers and *Khoi-Khoi* . . . in their own language, were employed as servants to guard cattle and sheep" (Harry Stein).

African Encyclopedia. New York: Oxford University Press, 1974, p. 290.

Baumann, Hermann. "Les Khoi-Sans." In *Peuples et les Civilisations de l'Afrique*. Paris: Payot, 1957, pp. 92-110.

Berman, Sanford. "The Trouble with 'Bushmen' & 'Hottentots.'" *HCL Cataloging Bulletin*, nos. 8-10 (September 1, 1974):31-3.

Bunting, Brian. *Rise of the South African Reich*. New York: Penguin Books, 1964, p. 13.

"Cataloging notes." *Africana Libraries Newsletter*, no. 3 (November 1975):7-8; no. 4 (February 1976):25-6.

Davidson, Basil. *The Africans: An Entry into Cultural History*. London: Longmans, 1969, p. 29.

Encyclopedia of Africa. New York: F. Watts, 1976, p. 32.

Greenberg, Joseph. *Studies in African Linguistic Classification*. New Haven, CT: Compass Books, 1955, p. 80.

HCL Cataloging Bulletin, no. 1 (May 3, 1973):4; no. 3 (September 17, 1973):14; nos. 6-7 (April 5, 1974):9; nos. 11-13 (March 15, 1975):31, 52; nos. 14-15 (June 1, 1975):8-10; nos. 23-24 (September 1, 1976):39-40, 44.

Hennepin County Library. *Alphabetic Catalog of Materials. Supplement*. 2d ed. Edina, MN, August 1976, G/O v., p. 225.

Hiernaux, Jean. "The Khoisan Peoples." In his *Peoples in Africa*. London: Weidenfeld and Nicolson, 1975, p. 98.

Kroenlein, J.G. *Wortschatz der Khoi-Khoin*. Berlin: Deutsche Kolonialgesellschaft, 1889.

McCarthy, Cavan. "FID-back." *HCL Cataloging Bulletin*, nos. 11–13 (March 15, 1975): 19.

Makerere Institute of Social Research Library. *Accessions List/Bulletin* (December 1971):18-21.

Marks, Shula. "Khoisan Resistance to the Dutch in the Seventeenth and Eighteenth Centuries." *Journal of African History*, v. 13, no. 1 (1972):55-80.

Moore, Robert B. "'Loaded' Words and Africans." In his *Racism in the English Language*. New York: CIBC, 1976, p. 12.

Schapera, Isaac. *Khoisan Peoples of South Africa: Bushmen and Hottentots*. London: Routledge, 1930, pp. 5, 31.

Sik, Endre. *History of Black Africa*. 7th ed. Budapest: Akademiai Kiado, c1970, v. 1, pp. 16, 78-80.

Stein, Harry. *Southern Africa*. New York: F. Watts, 1975, p. 23.

Subject Headings Employed at the Makerere Institute of Social Research Library: A Select List. Kampala, Uganda: Makerere University Library, 1972, p. 55.

Westermann, Diedrich. "Les langues Khoisanes." In *Peuples et les Civilisations de l'Afrique*. Paris: Payot, 1957, pp. 447-8.

Precedents/Usage Examples/Discussions

5. LCSH Form

PYGMIES
Citation: 8th ed., p. 1485

sa . . .
  Bambute
  Batwa

  . . .
  x Pigmies

Proposed Substitutes

MBUTI (AFRICAN PEOPLE)

  x Bambute (African people)
  x Batwa (African people)
     Bambuti (African people)
     "Pygmies," Twa
     Efe (African people)
     Ituri "Pygmies"
     "Pygmies," Ituri
     "Pygmies," Mbuti
     Wambuti (African people)

TWA (AFRICAN PEOPLE)
  x Batwa (African people)
     "Pygmies," Twa

Remarks

"It might be impossible to document that 'racists' or 'chauvinists' deliberately manufactured the word 'Pygmy.' Nevertheless, most literate persons—who have at some juncture read or seen phrases like 'intellectual pigmy' or 'moral pygmy'—understand at once the over- and under-tones it conveys. And they are obviously *negative*. Even as a 'scientific' designation, the word slights and obscures the people it ostensibly names. To focus on the 'Pygmies'' stature in our own nomenclature discloses much more about *us* than about *them*. It reveals a circus-side-show obsession with size and exotica, not a sympathetic interest in nor respect for the Mbuti, Twa, and others as *human beings*. The fact of their comparative shortness is a relatively superficial thing, certainly no sound basis for an *ethnic* or *cultural* classification. As a visually distinguishing feature—like color in other places—it may influence their social relationships with neighboring groups, etc., yet is not necessarily a signal determinant of their *internal* social structure and cultural patterns. Some equivalent of 'Pygmies' may be justified as a bio-taxonomic designation—though there doesn't appear to be a correlative term for tall-statured people (Ambrose Bierce once facetiously suggested "Hogmies")—but whether *any* single socio-cultural rubric should be applied to these groups, who inhabit not only portions of the Zaire Republic but also Rwanda and Zambia, as well as the Andaman Islands, Philippines, Malay Peninsula, and New Guinea, and who are *all* often interchangeably dubbed 'Pygmies,' 'Dwarfs,' 'Negritos,' or 'Negrillos' (the latter two diminutives of 'Negroes') solely on the size-plus-'wooly-hair'-criterion, regardless of habitat or ethnic traits, remains questionable" (MISR Library *Accession list/bulletin*).

**Precedents/Usage
Examples/Discussions**

"Cataloging notes." *Africana Libraries Newsletter*, no. 3 (November 1975):7, 9; no. 4 (February 1976):27.

HCL Cataloging Bulletin, no. 4 (November 21, 1973): 18; no. 16 (August 1, 1975): 20.

Hennepin County Library. *Alphabetic Catalog of Materials*. 2d ed. Edina, MN, January 1975, L/M/N v., p. 368; O/P/Q v., p. 395.

Makerere Institute of Social Research Library. *Accessions List/Bulletin* (November 1971): 12-3; (December 1971): 18-21.

Sik, Endre. *History of Black Africa*. 7th ed. Budapest: Akademiai Kiado, c1970, v. 1, p. 80.

Subject Headings Employed at the Makerere Institute of Social Research Library: A Select List. Kampala, Uganda: Makerere University Library, 1972, p. 65.

ALA, Watch Your Language!

This is what appears on page 158 of the University of Chicago Press *Manual of Style* (12th ed., revised, 1969):

NATIONALITIES, TRIBES, AND OTHER GROUPS OF PEOPLE

7.32 The names of racial, linguistic, tribal, religious, and other groupings of mankind are capitalized:

Aryan	Magyar
Asian	Malay
Bushman	Mongol (mongoloid)
Caucasian (caucasoid)	Mormon
Frenchman	Negro (negroid)
Hottentot	Nordic
Indian	Oriental
Indo-European	Protestant
Kaffir	Pygmy

7.33 Designations based on mere color, size, or local usage are cased:

aborigine	colored	red man
black	highlander	redneck
bushman	pygmy	white

On February 23, 1977, the head cataloger sent the following letter to Donald E. Stewart, associate executive director, Publishing Services, American Library Association:

I understand that ALA Publishing edits copy in accordance with the University of Chicago Press style manual. If so, I strongly urge that ALA itself revamp sections 7.32 and 7.33 (12th ed., revised, p. 158) since the captions, text, and examples alike are seriously biased, inaccurate, and dated. Indeed, they should hugely embarrass, if not disturb, any literate, sensitive person. Here is a possible reworking:

Reprinted from *HCL Cataloging Bulletin*, no. 27 (April 1, 1977): 38–40.

NATIONALITIES, FAITHS, ETHNIC GROUPS, AND OTHER
CATEGORIES OF PEOPLE

7.32 The names of ethnic, linguistic, religious, and other human
groups should be authentic, nonsexist, and capitalized:

Afro-American [not "black," "colored," "negro," "Negro"]
Asian [not "Oriental"]
Black American [not "black," "colored," "negro," "Negro"]
Blacks [not "blacks," "coloreds," "negroes," "Negroes"]
Catholic
European [not "Caucasian," "Caucasoid"]
French [not "Frenchman"]
Inuit [not "Eskimo"]
Jew
Khoi-Khoi [not "Hottentot"]
Magyar
Malay
Mormon
Muslim
Native American [not "Indian," "red man"]
Protestant
Saame [not "Lapp"]
San [not "Bushman"]
Xhosa [or "South African," not "Kaffir"]

7.33 [Delete]

Both ALA's Subject Analysis Committee (SAC) and the Library of Congress Subject Cataloging Division have endorsed the enclosed "Principles," which mandate authenticity in "ethnic, national, religious, social, or sexual" nomenclature. Further, ALA more than a year ago declared it would no longer sanction sexist terminology (e.g., "Frenchman," "mankind").

Except in *social* science, "race" is a dubious, even ridiculous concept (see, for example, Ashley Montagu's *Man's Most Dangerous Myth: The Fallacy of Race*).

"Bushman," "Hottentot," "Kaffir," "Negro," and "Oriental" are alien, often derogatory terms, while "Pygmy" is at once ethnocentric and voyeurist (most material on "Pygmies" in fact deals with the *Mbuti* of Zaire, an ethnic group that *happens* to be of relatively short stature and, in any event, has its *own* name).

"Mongol" might be acceptable as an ethnic/national descriptor, but not "mongoloid," which represents poor biology and may be too easily confused with "Mongolism" (properly: Down's Syndrome).

Re "Negro": LC has already begun to replace such subject forms with either "Afro-American" or "Black" constructions. It would therefore be appropriate for ALA to follow suit (especially since the impetus for that change derived from SAC, an ALA body).

Leading anthropologists have totally abandoned "Tribe," an inexact and frequently demeaning term. (The same, of course, holds for "Primitive.")

Finally, with particular respect to the original 7.33, my firm personal opinion is that color-coding people, however well intentioned, reinforces negative, as well as foolish, stereotypes and attitudes. It emphasizes— even sanctifies—purely superficial traits, essentially dehumanizing the subjects by separating them from their ethnic/national matrix. In short, I think it wiser to *avoid* color-coding when possible. (Incidentally, "Colored" can only be used—legitimately—with regard to the so-designated South African group, and even then should appear in quote marks. Further, *if* persons or groups are denoted by "color" terms, simple respect and fairness dictate that those designators be regarded as proper nouns and thus capitalized—e.g., Blacks, Whites, Browns.)

* * *

Encs: University of Chicago Press *Manual of Style* (12th ed., rev.), p. 158.

"Principles for Establishing Subject Headings Relating to People and Places" (1975).

"African Ethnonyms: A Brief on Library of Congress Headings." *HCL Cataloging Bulletin*, no. 26 (February 1, 1977): 16-23.

"'Oriental' Is Demeaning." *Interracial Books for Children Bulletin*, v. 7, nos. 2/3, (1976): 31.

Prejudices and Antipathies (Scarecrow Press, 1971), p. 102-6.

cc: Editors, *Manual of Style* (University of Chicago Press).

Mr. George S. Bobinski, Chairperson, ALA Publishing Committee.

Easy Access vs. Authenticity

"Sure, 'Inuit' may be the right, legitimate name, but most people in the "real world" are still going to look for 'Eskimos' in the catalog. Even if there's a cross-reference, how does that square with the philosophy of making the library's wares as accessible as possible, so people can find them swiftly and without jumping librarian-made hurdles?" The question—a composite of already expressed comment—deserves an answer. In these cases—to lay it all out front—the *easy* route is *not* the *right* one. And so the access consideration necessarily becomes less important than considerations of honesty, correctness, and human respect. To personalize the matter: If someone's name is "Jane" and yet she's persistently called "Henrietta," that doesn't make her Henrietta. She's still *Jane*. And it's not hard to understand her irritation, if not anger, at being tabbed something else. Similarly, Jews *are* sometimes termed *Hebes*, *Yids*, or *Kikes*. In some quarters, unhappily, those epithets may be more *commonly* used than "Jews." But that hardly constitutes "warrant" for employing them in a subject scheme or anywhere else. Most individuals want to be called by their own names. And most of us respect that preference. Most ethnic, religious, or racial groups don't appreciate offensive, frequently alien, labels to describe themselves. So why the reluctance to extend the self-name principle to groups? The access argument is really a red herring in this context. The problem is not one of *access* to material on the Inuit, for instance, but rather of what *kind* of access: i.e., via their *own* name or what somebody else has laid on them? Hopefully, most library users—being relatively intelligent and retentive folk—will only need to jump this access hurdle *once*. Afterwards they'll *know* that "Eskimo" items are listed under INUIT, "Hottentot" titles under KHOI-KHOIN, etc. And that very awareness may be worth a lot.

Reprinted from *HCL Cataloging Bulletin*, nos. 11–13 (March 15, 1975): 87.

Bringing Up the Rear

We've been cracking jokes, drawing funny pictures, and just plain sitting on them for years. But not until the 1973 *Supplement to LC Subject Headings* (Card Division, 1974) did the Library of Congress finally place its distinguished seal of approval on those "two fleshy protuberances forming the lower and back part of the trunk." This, for the record, is how they did it (on page 42):

> BUTTOCKS
>
> x Derriere
>   Gluteal region

Now, the skeptical and impatient may grumble that LC only recognized the obvious. And rather tardily at that. Perhaps. Still, it's a welcome step toward greater body awareness. And another leap into the real world that might help restore catalog credibility. However, even while applauding the new head itself—and admiring the innovators' gutsy, uncompromising professionalism—it's hard to repress some little disappointment, a tinge of disquiet, about the cross-references. Granted, either the Francophile or literate snob will be duly led to the primary form via "Derriere." And the physician or anatomist should nicely—if also unexcitingly—reach it by the "Gluteal" route. But what about everyone else? Why merely *two*, largely arcane x-referents to this truly universal—indeed, omnipresent—topic for which nearly every culture has devised a veritable army of lovely synonyms? Could it be chalked up to genteel propriety? Space limits? Insufficient research? A sudden, massive failure of imagination? Or of will? Whatever the reason, such spartan, gallo-gluteal cross-referencing hardly promotes easy, maximum access by ordinary library users. The deficiency, however, can be

Reprinted from *HCL Cataloging Bulletin*, no. 11–13 (March 15, 1975): 88.

partially corrected by (1) introducing these basic equivalents culled (after a five-minute, frankly inspired, search) from the *Random House Unabridged Dictionary*:

Term	Suggested gloss	Lexical remarks	Page
Ass	(Anatomy)	Slang	89
Behind	(Anatomy)	Slang	135
Bottom	(Anatomy)		173
Bum	(Anatomy)	Chiefly Brit.	196
Butt	(Anatomy)	Slang	202
Heinie	(Anatomy)	Slang	658
Posteriors	(Anatomy)		1123
Rear	(Anatomy)		1196
Rump	(Anatomy)		1252
Seat	(Anatomy)		1287
Tokus		Slang	1491
Tushie		Informal, Babytalk. Also, tushy. [hypocoristic alter. of TOKUS . . .]	1528

and (2) inviting our devilishly clever readers to nominate more bona fide candidates for the x-roster, all submissions to be published in the next issue and then soberly transmitted to LC's Subject Cataloging Division. For shredding.

Let There Be Music
(But Not Too Soon)

LC Form	Date Established	Notes
ROCK MUSIC	May 1972	Term "rock-and-roll" *first used in 1951*; publicly *broadcast* by Cleveland disc jockey, Alan Freed, *in 1954.*

Genre began as "combination of country music with blues, spirituals (gospel songs), folk song, and urban rhythm and blues, played largely on electric guitars with high, amplified sound." Soon called simply "rock," and became *very popular in the late 1950s and early 1960s* in America, England, and elsewhere." Among the leading creators and performers: Elvis Presley, Bill Haley, Little Richard, The Beatles, Rolling Stones, Grateful Dead.

Presley's *Fun in Acapulco* album appeared in 1963, *Spinout* in 1966, and *Double Trouble* in 1967. All three LC cataloged under MOVING-PICTURE MUSIC—EXCERPTS. MUSIC, POPULAR (SONGS, ETC.)—U.S. also assigned to 1967 disc alone.

The Beatles Story (1964), *Beatles '65* (1964), *Beatles VI* (1965), *Early Beatles* (1965), *Revolver* (1966), and *Sgt. Pepper's Lonely Hearts Club Band* (1967) each assigned the sole heading: MUSIC, POPULAR (SONGS, ETC.).

No subject head applied by LC to *Our Own Story,* the Rolling Stones' collective autobiography (1964).

LC subject tracings for *Roots, the Rock and Roll Sounds of Louisiana and Mississippi,* a 1965 Folkways LP: 1. Dance music, American. 2. Music, Popular (Songs, etc.)—U.S. No title added-entry made for "Rock and Roll Sounds of Louisiana and Mississippi."

Sources: Letter, dated October 20, 1975, from Edward J. Blume, chief of LC's Subject Cataloging Division; Albert Goldman, "The Emergence of Rock," in Elie Siegmeister, ed., *New Music Lover's Handbook* (1973), pp. 486–95; Irwin Stambler, "Rock 'n' Roll," in his *Encyclopedia of Popular Music* (1965), p. 200; Melvin Shestack, *The Country Music Encyclopedia* (1974), p. 207; Christine Ammer, *Harper's Dictionary of Music* (1972), pp. 300–1; *Barnhart Dictionary of New English Since 1963* (1973), pp. 408–9; *Library of Congress Catalog: Music and Phonorecords, 1963–1967* (1969), v. 1, pp. 135–6, 452, 472, 553, v. 2, pp., 422, 446, 450, 549, 617.

Reprinted from *HCL Cataloging Bulletin,* nos. 18–19 (December 1, 1975): 41–6.

	Notes	LC Form	Date Established

"A type of American popular music, mostly vocal, that *developed* from old English and Scottish ballads brought to the Appalachian mountain areas *during the late eighteenth century* . . . . Originating in the isolated communities of the mountain areas and kept alive by community social activities . . . , country music began to become *more widespread* (and commercial) with the advent of radio and phonograph music *in the 1920s.* One of the most important factors in its growth was a single radio station, *WSU* in Nashville, Tennessee, which *began broadcasting in 1925* and became the national headquarters for country music with its weekly music program "Grand Ole Opry." The show *attracted the attention of large record companies,* which *during the 1930s* sent their representatives throughout the rural South to record local music."

COUNTRY MUSIC   May 1972

LC subject tracings for *Country Music Who's Who,* a serial that started in *1960:* 1. Music—Almanacs, yearbooks, etc. 2. Hillbilly musicians. And for the *1964* Vanguard LP, *Country Music and Bluegrass at Newport:* 1. Ballads, American. 2. Music, Popular (songs, etc.)—U.S.

Bill C. Malone's *Country Music U.S.A.; a Fifty-year History* issued in 1968. LC's subject treatment: 1. Music—U.S.—History and criticism. 2. Music, Popular (Songs, etc.)—U.S.—History and criticism. 3. Music, Popular (Songs, etc.)—U.S.—Discography.

COUNTRY MUSIC introduced as primary *Music Index* form in 1955.

Sources: Blume letter; Ammer, p. 85; 1963–67 LC music/phonorecord catalog, v. 1, p. 388, and 1968–72 ed., p. 307; 1955 *Music Index Annual Cumulation* (1957), p. 128.

"A type of American dance music that *developed in the nineteenth century* and was *very popular around 1910.*"

RAGTIME MUSIC   August 1972

Stravinsky composed 11-instrument *Ragtime* in 1911 and *Piano Rag-music* in 1920. Dot's 1958 LP, *The Masters Write Jazz,* including 1920 Stravinsky piece, Hindemith's *Ragtime,* and *Three Rag Caprices* by Milhaud, subject-traced soley under PIANO MUSIC (JAZZ).

Subtitle for Portents' mid-1960s recording of Scott Joplin's *Selections from Treemonisha:* "Five Classic Rags." Cataloger's note: "Ragtime opera." LC subject tracings: 1. Operas—Excerpts. 2. Piano music (Jazz). Single heading assigned to Joplin's *Original Ragtime Compositions,* issued in early '60s on Audiophile label: 1. Piano music (Jazz).

They All Played Ragtime, by Rudi Blesh and Harriet Janis (1966), assigned four LC descriptors: 1. Jazz music. 2. Jazz music—Bibliography. 3. Jazz music—Discography. 4. Piano music (Jazz). No title added-entry made for "Ragtime."

LC rubrics applied to *1963* Piedmont LP, *Ragtime—A Recorded Documentary:* 1. Music, Popular (Songs, etc.)—U.S. 2. Instrumental ensembles. 3. Dance-orchestra music.

RAGTIME MUSIC and analogous forms "for specific instruments" added to LC thesaurus in *mid-1972. Great Ragtime Classics,* an RCA Stereo LP, issued in *1974.* Lone LC subject tracing: 2. Piano music (4 hands), Arranged.

RAGTIME an active *Music Index* heading for 27 years.

Sources: Blume letter; Ammer, p. 286; 1963–67 LC music/phonorecord catalog, v. 1, pp. 207, 788, v. 2, pp. 119, 393; January-June 1974 *Library of Congress Catalog—Music: Books on Music and Sound Recordings,* p. 146; 1949 *Music Index Annual Cumulation* (1950), p. 238.

LC Form	Date Established	Notes
GOSPEL MUSIC	April 1975	

"GOSPEL SONG: religious song developed by the Negro *during slavery days* in the southern United States." ·

Cataloger's note for 1964 RCA LP, *A Gospel Jubilee:* "Twelve highlight performances by greats of gospel music selected from top RCA Victor sacred recordings." LC subject tracing: 1. Sacred vocal music.

Gospel Song Styles of 12 Great Artists, a 1967 RCA LP, subject-cataloged under HYMNS, ENGLISH and SONGS, ENGLISH.

Malcolm Stewart's *Now Songs,* 1969 collection of "contemporary gospel songs with guitar chords," assigned one rubric: HYMNS, ENGLISH. And RCA's 1966 disc, *The Grand Old Gospel,* similarly cataloged under a single head: SACRED QUARTETS WITH PiANO.

GOSPEL SINGERS, GOSPEL SINGING, and GOSPEL SONGS major *Music Index* rubrics since 1955.

Sources: Blume letter; *Barnhart Dictionary,* p. 190; Stambler, p. 95; Goldman, pp. 488–9; 1963–67 LC music/phonorecord catalog, v. 1, pp. 601, 609, and 1968–72 ed., p. 290; 1955 *Music Index Annual Cumulation* (1957).

At the very least, these data indicate a profound "musical lag," together with undue reticence in actually assigning appropriate forms *already* in the LCSH arsenal or even making added entries for topical *Schlagwoerter.* The tangible consequence of both the lag and erratic praxis is to severely limit access to thousands of books, scores, records, and tapes in these mainly pop and folk genres. Nor is that lag merely historic. Unfortunately, it did *not* end with the laughably late "innovation" of GOSPEL MUSIC (which the September 1975 *Music Cataloging Bulletin* greeted with infantile gusto). *Still* unrecognized, for instance, are these three categories, all well represented in the literature, widely known, and clearly thriving.

HCL Form	Notes
REGGAE MUSIC	

"Popular music form of Jamaican . . . origin." Was performed by such island stars as Millie Small and Desmond Dekker for occasional hits in Europe and the U.S. *during the 1960s,* but did not receive *major attention outside Jamaica* until the early '70s. By 1972–73 dozens of first-rank U.S. and English artists were going to Jamaica to record songs with reggae flavor or were composing reggae-style songs."

LC subject tracing for 1974 Atlantic stereo LP, *Reggae:* 1. Jazz ensembles.

REGGAE in 1972 became primary *Music Index* descriptor.

Sources: Blume letter; Irwin Stambler, *Encyclopedia of Pop, Rock and Soul* (1974), p. 429; 1974 LC catalog, *Music: Books on Music and Sound Recordings* (1975), p. 592; 1972 *Music Index Subject Heading List* (1973), p. 105; Stephen Davis, "Wailers' Reggae: Serious and Sensual," *Rolling Stone* (April 24, 1975), pp. 52+.

Notes   *HCL Form*

"A style of Afro-American popular music that combines elements of blues and jazz. *Developed* in the United States *after about 1945*, it began mainly as dance music."

RHYTHM AND
BLUES MUSIC

"In *the second half of the '40s* R&B really started coming on strong . . . . By *the early 1950s* R&B had pretty well captured the Black audience. . . ."

From the *December 10, 1966 New Yorker:* "four young Negro men . . . sat down to drums and electric guitars and filled the storefront with almost deafening funky *rhythm-and-blues.*"

LC subject tracings for L.E. McCutcheon's *Rhythm and Blues: an Experience and Adventure in its Origin and Development* (1971): 1. Music, Popular (Songs, etc.)—United States—History and criticism. 2. Blues (Songs, etc.)—History and criticism. And for John Broven's *Walking to New Orleans: The Story of New Orleans Rhythm & Blues* (1974): 1. Blues (Songs, etc.)—Louisiana—New Orleans—History and criticism.

Sources: Blume letter; Ammer, p. 298; Stambler's 1974 *Encyclopedia,* p. 3; *Barnhart Dictionary,* p. 405; 1968–72 LC music/phonorecord catalog, v. 2, p. 531; January-June 1975 LC catalog, *Music: Books on Music and Sound Recordings,* P. 51.

"Originating in the islands of the Caribbean, especially Trinidad, steel bands provide the rhythmic accompaniment for calypso and other popular music."

STEELBAND MUSIC

LC subject tracings for *1962* Spoken Arts LP, *The Silver Swords Steel Band:* 1. Percussion music. 2. Folk music—Virgin Islands of the United States. No title added-entry made for "Steel Band."

STEEL BANDS employed as a primary *Music Index* head as early as 1954.

Sources: Blume letter; Ammer, p. 343; 1963–67 LC music/phonorecord catalog, v. 2, p. 582; 1954 *Music Index Annual Cumulation* (1956), p. 503.

Coda: Rock flourished 18 years before gaining LC's attention. Country music waited over 47 years. When ragtime became a full-fledged subject head it had already passed its 60th anniversary. And Gospel Music, which only this year entered the LC thesaurus, is more than a century old. On the basis of that pattern, it seems safe to predict that REGGAE, RHYTHM AND BLUES, and STEELBAND MUSIC will respectively win LC's imprimatur in 1989, 1998, and 2015. Give or take a decade.

Hide and Seek through the Catalog: A Talk Delivered at the MLA Annual Conference, 1974

Dearly Beloved,

My message for this afternoon
is that catalogers
should watch TV.

Last week we got a book that LC traced
under title and one subject.
The subject was KARATE.

So far nothing exceptional, right?
But if the cataloger happened to be a TV-freak,
he or she should have been a little suspicious.
Because the title of the book
was *Wisdom of Kung Fu*.

Anyone who's caught "Kung Fu" on the tube
knows damn well that there's more to it
than simply chops & kicks & grunts.
It's not just about combat and fighting.
And it's not exactly the same thing as Karate
in either its origin or content,
even though LC not long ago made it a cross-reference *to* KARATE.

So there are grounds for suspicion
on the basis solely of the book's title
& watching David Carradine cavort on the screen.
However, those grounds become even more serious
if the cataloger does what many catalogers increasingly *don't do*:
look at the book itself.
(Believe-it-or-not,
I've heard Tech Services Directors
from big public library systems boast that they no longer check
books or cards.)

Reprinted from *HCL Cataloging Bulletin*, nos. 18—19 (December 1, 1975): 51–5.

Anyway, looking at the book
you'd find that it includes chapters on
Kung Fu customs, training, & medicine—
plus a large selection of Chinese proverbs & sayings
on topics that range from Mysticism to Government.
In fact,
these quotations from Chinese masters & philosophers
account for half or more of the volume.

What's wrong with what LC did?

Two fundamental things:
First, they confused Kung Fu with Karate,
with the result that this particular item would be found,
subject-wise,
only under KARATE,
which is *not* the same thing as Kung Fu.
And, practically speaking,
most libraries probably
haven't even got around yet to putting that cross-reference
into the catalog,
the net result being that there's absolutely no "Kung Fu" access
at all.

Second point is that the book's actual contents have been
seriously mis- or under-represented.
LC furnished no way whatever to get to the quotations, proverbs,
    & maxims.
And there's no connection, through cross-references or anything
    else,
between China and this work.
None.

I'd like this example to serve as the springboard
for a postulate or generalization:
Namely, that if our catalogs are to honestly & usefully represent our
    collections,
and if the cataloging process is to be more than merely a clerical or
    bookkeeping operation,
we've got to practice what I'm going to call "critical revision."
That is, we must critically compare the material in hand
with the cataloging data supplied by external sources like LC,
    Josten, or Baker & Taylor.
If the data are wrong or insufficient,
they should be corrected or expanded.
And that may involve a further area of critical revision:
our "authorities," our basic tools like Sears, Dewey, and the LC
    subject-heading list.

To do justice to the Kung Fu title requires both kinds of critical
    revision:
LC's treatment would have to be amplified through more tracings

& perhaps a contents note.
And "Kung Fu" would have to be transformed
from an x-reference
to a primary head.

To put the postulate another way:
If you're not prepared spiritually & intellectually to QUESTION the
      authorities
and, if necessary, change them—
in other words,
if you think that every LC-card, MARC record, or CIP-entry
is like a tablet inscribed on Mt. Sinai,
you're going to let a helluva lot of material go down the drain
by killing or reducing access to it through the catalog.

A corollary, for the economy-minded,
is that a lot of money spent on selection, acquisition, and processing
is just plain wasted
if the goods are relatively hidden
and consequently under-used.
Lousy cataloging
may also lower the library's credibility
and even turn-off potential users.
E.g., the library might have a number of Gay novels & plays,
but the Gay or interested non-Gay reader
who finds no GAYS—FICTION
or GAYS—DRAMA entries in the catalog
probably won't be able to reach those novels & plays.
And won't think too highly of the library itself,
possibly concluding that the place either hadn't bought any
Gay stuff or was deliberately concealing it.

As another example:
The first subject tracing on Baker & Taylor's
cards for Bill Hosokawa's *Nisei: The Quiet Americans*
is
JAPANESE IN THE U.S.
If that were an accurate descriptor,
one would expect that persons of Japanese descent born in
      America
would have formed a
"Japanese in the U.S. Citizens League."
But they didn't.
Instead, they formed a
Japanese-American Citizens League.
Because that's what they are.
And that's presumably where they'd look in the catalog
for Hosokawa's book & others like it.
But they won't find it there
if you uncritically accepted Baker & Taylor cards.

A third example:
There's much talk lately
about children's "right to read."
But our catalogs don't much reflect nor enhance that right.
They're typically ageist: biased against kids.
For instance,
There *are* books and other media that deal with
mud pies
&
scribbling
&
the first day in school
&
teddy bears
&
temper tantrums
&
the Afro-American holiday, Kwanza,
&
mischief
&
peaceableness
(remember Ferdinand-the-bull?).
But I'll bet that few in this room have ever seen a Josten or LC tracing
for any of those topics.
And so they're not in many catalogs.
Sure, PUTTING them in means more work for us.
But if we don't,
the kids are the losers.

And what about ordinary 1974 *adults*
who look for RHYME
& are stupidly referred to RIME?
or who check for something on AIRPLANES
only to be trundled off to AEROPLANES?
That doesn't do much for the library's credibility
or its "modern image," either.

Another large area where our authorities can't be trusted
—indeed, LC has nearly admitted its own incompetence there—
is in handling material on women & women's issues.
LC hasn't yet recognized that there's something called Sexism.
And LC catalogers apparently don't know how to distinguish
  between
"Feminism"
and the
"Women's Liberation Movement."

To accent the positive & return to TV for a moment:
A lot of people—kids and grown-ups alike—
would be happy to find entries for
"Steve Austin" and "Cyborgs" in the catalog.
And at least a cross-reference from "Six Million Dollar Man."
Such entries could not only lead Austin-fans to the
three Martin Caidin novels on him,
but also capitalize on a TV-connected interest
& show that the library is right there,
up-to-date,
& with it.

I've got to underscore, though, that this is the kind of thing
that LC & most other Big Brothers won't do for you.
You've got to do it for yourself.

Let me quit with this observation:
The name of the game is service,
not "hide and seek."
It's *no* service to our patrons
if
their books,
their records,
&
their films
get magnificently
and
irretrievably
buried.
In
the
catalog.

Cataloging
Cross-Fertilization

Too bad there isn't more cross-fertilization between the LCers who catalog adult and children's materials. If there were, Giacomo Patri's lately reissued, semiautobiographical *White-Collar* (Celestial Arts, 1975) might have enjoyed much better treatment.

It's a "novel in linocuts," a "story told in pictures." Any juvenalia cataloger would instantly recognize the genre, rightly assign the subject descriptor, STORIES WITHOUT WORDS, and instinctively class it as "Easy" *fiction*. However, since Patri's graphic tale solely traveled the "adult" route at LC and Juvie/grown-up "spillover" appears to be minimal there, it not only missed an ideal subject head but also got absurdly tagged as an art book (769.924), thereby locating it so far from "novels" that few—if any—of the very persons for whom it's intended could possibly find it by browsing. Too bad.

Oh, yes. Another thing. Patri's tome—introduced by Rockwell Kent and with an afterword by John L. Lewis—makes powerful statements about the Great Depression, capitalism, and labor solidarity. The author himself regarded *White Collar* as his "contribution to . . . an indispensable understanding of the necessity of unity among all American workers. . . ." But you'd never know it from LC's sorry subject tracings: 1. Patri. Giacomo, 1898- 2. United States—History—1933–1945—Pictorial works. 3. United States in art. Again, too bad. For all of us.

Letter reprinted from *Library Journal* (May 15, 1976): 1158. Published by R.R. Bowker Co. (a Xerox company). Copyright © 1976 by Xerox Corporation.

Nitty-Gritty Subject Heads: A Selection of People-Helping Descriptors LC Hasn't Got Around to Yet

AFFIRMATIVE ACTION ORGANIZATIONS, CENTERS, ETC.
AID TO FAMILIES WITH DEPENDENT CHILDREN
ALTERNATIVE ENERGY SOURCES
ALTERNATIVE LIFESTYLES
APPROPRIATE TECHNOLOGY
BARBERS [DENTISTS, LAWYERS, SURGEONS, etc.], CHOICE OF
BARGAIN-HUNTING
CHARTER FLIGHTS
CHILD ADVOCACY
CIVIL RIGHTS ORGANIZATIONS
COMMUNITY DEVELOPMENT—FUNDING SOURCES
CONSUMER ACTION
CONSUMER ADVOCACY
CONSUMER PROTECTION GROUPS AND AGENCIES
COOKING, MONEY-SAVING
CORPORATE ACCOUNTABILITY
CREDIT UNIONS
DISABLED PERSONS' ADVOCACY
DISABLED PERSONS—PROJECTS AND SERVICES
DROP-IN CENTERS
DRUG ABUSE COUNSELING
DRUG ABUSE PROJECTS AND SERVICES
ENCYCLOPEDIAS AND DICTIONARIES, CHOICE OF
ENERGY-EFFICIENT BUILDINGS
ENVIRONMENTAL PROTECTION GROUPS AND AGENCIES
FEMINIST COUNSELING
FOOD CO-OPS
FRAUD IN ADVERTISING
FRAUD IN AUTOMOBILE MAINTENANCE AND REPAIR
FRAUD IN DOOR-TO-DOOR SELLING
FREE CLINICS
FREE UNIVERSITIES
GOVERNMENT GRANTS

GROUP HOMES
HOME ENERGY CONSERVATION
HUMAN SERVICES
INCEST VICTIMS' SERVICES
INSURANCE, CHOICE OF
JOB HUNTING
LEGAL ASSISTANCE TO SENIORS
LEGAL ASSISTANCE TO THE POOR
MEDICAL ACCOUNTABILITY
MIGRANT WORKERS—RIGHTS
MINORITIES—PROJECTS AND SERVICES
NURSING HOMES, CHOICE OF
PATIENTS' RIGHTS
POOR—RIGHTS
PRISONERS—RIGHTS
PROPOSAL WRITING FOR GRANTS
RAPE CRISIS CENTERS
RUNAWAY YOUTH—PROJECTS AND SERVICES
SENIOR ADVOCACY
SENIOR PROJECTS AND SERVICES
SEX COUNSELNG AND THERAPY
SHOES, CHOICE OF
SOCIAL ADVOCACY
SUING (LAW)
SUPPLEMENTAL SECURITY INCOME PROGRAM
SURVIVAL (ECONOMICS)
SUSPECTS' RIGHTS
TENANTS' RIGHTS
TENANTS' UNIONS
TOYS, CHOICE OF
TRANSSEXUALS—RIGHTS
TRAVEL, LOW-COST
WOMEN'S PROJECTS AND SERVICES
WOMEN'S SHELTERS
YOUTH PROJECTS AND SERVICES
YOUTH SHELTERS

The above rubrics are all used at Hennepin County Library. And here are examples of how the catalog might easily perform a local information-and-referral function by making contact notes under relevant subject headings:

AFFIRMATIVE ACTION—WASHBURN COUNTY, IDAHO

For more information on Washburn County's Affirmative Action program, phone 348-4096.

BUS LINES—TWIN CITIES METROPOLITAN AREA

For MTC bus schedule information, phone 827-7733.

CHILD ABUSE—JASPER, TENNESSEE

For more information on Jasper child protection services, phone 653-1212.

INCOME TAX

To contact the local IRS office for further tax information and forms, phone 930-8833.

SOCIAL SECURITY

To contact the local Social Security office for further information on the basic program, as well as Medicare and Supplemental Security Income, phone 322-5543.

UNITED STATES. PEACE CORPS.

For more information on both the Peace Corps and VISTA, phone ACTION at 725-9526.

UNITED STATES. VOLUNTEERS IN SERVICE TO AMERICA

For more information on both VISTA and the Peace Corps, phone ACTION at 725-9526.

Reprinted with permission from *The U*N*A*B*A*S*H*E*D Librarian: the "how i run my library good" letter*, no. 22 (1977): 8. G.P.O. Box 2631, New York, NY 10001

Guidelines for A/V Materials

The RTSD/CCS/SAC Subcommittee on the Subject Analysis of Audiovisual Materials, chaired by Liz Bishoff, developed these draft guidelines in 1976:

- Supply subject headings to all audiovisual materials in a manner similar to the current alternative subject headings assigned to children's literature by the Library of Congress. The committee suggests that these be form headings such as SHORT FILMS as well as subjects, such as DEATH.

- Multi-item sets and multisubject items should be analyzed to whatever degree the individual item warrants. For example, a filmstrip set titled *Africa, The Dark Continent,* having eight filmstrips, each on a different country, should have eight or nine subject headings, one for each country and one for Africa.

- Change book-oriented form subdivisions to make them applicable to both audiovisual materials and books. For example, GUIDEBOOKS, TEXTBOOKS FOR FOREIGNERS, etc. A study of this problem is strongly suggested to SAC.

- Make the general material designators form subdivisions on an optional basis. A possible authority for these subdivisions would be the list appearing in *AACR,* Chapter 12, revised. A need for this option is dependent on the size of the collection and the physical organization of the collection.

- Provide an explanation of audiovisual subject analysis in the introduction of *Sears* and *LCSH,* including a discussion of the matters discussed in these guidelines.

- Encourage the extension of Cataloging-in-Publication to include audiovisual materials, even if limited to subject headings and classification numbers.

Reprinted from *HCL Cataloging Bulletin,* no. 26 (February 1, 1977): 4–6.

- Assign a Dewey or LC classification number to audiovisual materials. Although the individual library may not physically integrate its materials, the assignment of call numbers provides unification for bibliographies, facilitates automated retrieval, allows for greater flexibility in physical arrangement, and encourages consistency in commercial processing.

- Provide guidance for the creation of subject headigs where none exist. Audiovisual materials need greater currency and frequently deal with very current subjects; therefore frequently no subject heading is available in *Sears* or LCSH.

- The authors of Dewey, LCSH, LC Classification schedules, and Sears request input from the library community regarding questions in application of specific subject headings, suggested changes, etc.

In response to Ms. Bishoff's call for "reactions," the head cataloger sent the following letter on October 21:

> Heartily agree that subject headings should be assigned "to all audiovisual materials," but *not* "in a manner similar to the current alternative . . . headings assigned to children's literature by the Library of Congress." The point here is that they should be applied to A/V items in essentially the *same* fashion as to print, *not* as bracketed "alternatives" or options. In other words, print and A/V material should be subject-cataloged on a basis of parity, recognizing that both categories deserve equal treatment.
>
> Yes, parity requires that "book-oriented form subdivisions" be replaced by terms or constructions applicable to either print or A/V materials. TEXTBOOKS might become TEXTS or simply STUDY MATERIALS. However, the cited example, TEXTBOOKS FOR FOREIGNERS, is doubly unacceptable, not only for its print bias but because it's palpably ethnocentric. E.g., ENGLISH LANGUAGE—TEXTBOOKS FOR FOREIGNERS—SPANISH clearly implies that the hypothetical spanish-speaker is "foreign," an alien. Yet the likelihood is that such a person—perhaps a Chicano in California or Puerto Rican-American in New York City—is U.S.-born. The "solution" is to change the primary heading to ENGLISH AS A SECOND LANGUAGE—a totally neutral, objective descriptor—and then add subheads like —TEXTS—SPANISH,—AUDIO-VISUAL INSTRUCTION—SPANISH,—SELF-INSTRUCTION—SPANISH, —STUDY MATERIALS—SPANISH, etc.)
>
> Concur that the CIP program should encompass A/V materials, but (again) *not* on a second-class basis, i.e., CIP treatment for A/V items should parallel that for print titles (main entry, notes, tracings, classification, etc.).
>
> The next-to-last point is probably unnecessary because (a) few institutions seem predisposed to unilaterally "create" headings, and (b) apart from recommending a solid familiarity with the relevant major scheme (*LCSH, Sears,* etc.), it could only be suggested that heading innovators variously consult reasonable "authorities" (e.g., dictionaries, periodical indexes, current literature, live experts/practitioners) and canvass public service staff re the actual terminology employed by patrons making subject requests.

LC to Seniors: Sorry, Folks

On September 9, 1975, the "officers and members" of Southern California Council R.C.I.A. Unions Retirees' Clubs sent this letter to the chief of LC's Subject Cataloging Division:

Many senior citizens use libraries and realize that the card catalog is an important key to what is in the library! But we find that much of the material we want, or that relates directly to our interests and needs, is either cataloged under subject headings that we'd never think to look for, or under "Aged," a term that frankly upsets us or turns us off completely.

We would like to suggest three things:

1. Substitution of SENIORS for AGED. (We are not antiques yet.)
2. Creation of more meaningful, relevant terms to fit topics—like AGEISM and SENIOR POWER—that we know have been dealt with in books and other media.
3. Greater use of these new (and old) headings—e.g., RETIREMENT—to make library materials more accessible to us.

Frankly, we don't think this is asking too much and hope you will agree with us.

On November 28, the SCD chief replied:

I am most regretful that it took me so long to get around to answering your letter . . . . During that time I have been out of the office visiting various parts of the country, including a trip to your own state two weeks ago (Palo Alto); who could ever make too many trips to California?

All this is not by way of brushing aside your concern for the terminology used in assigning subject headings to material on the older age group of citizens. I and a number of catalogers are not so far removed from that category as to lack understanding and identification.

In a situation like this we try to keep in touch with usage in the literature and in other indexing systems. And for this reason we have never abandoned the term "aged" since it still seems to be favored in general usage, even though any one of us may not identify him- or herself as "aged" in terms of self-perception. We have made references from "Senior citizens" to "Aged" to guide the reader to the material. We have not used "Seniors" alone since in a universal catalog such as that in the

Reprinted from *HCL Cataloging Bulletin,* no. 20 (March 1, 1976): 46–8.

Library of Congress that word could mean, in addition to older citizens, high school students of the last year and, in terms of employment, those with the greatest seniority.

We never consider a question closed. As soon as the move in general literature toward a preference for "senior" becomes evident, we will change. In the meantime, for a vocabulary meant to serve academic and research as well as public libraries we feel it unjustified to produce such a major change in numerous catalogs for a situation where the decision can be somewhat arbitrary.

We also agree that such headings as "Ageism" and "Senior power" are valid concepts and we would certainly establish them as needed for material being acquired by the Library of Congress. However, a reexamination of our current files does not reveal titles that would justify their assignment. You have to remember that in the LC system we have only headings that have been used to designate the contents of entire books, not headings that may be suitable for periodical articles, brochures, or other material which we do not catalog.

We are making an attempt to give wider use to such terms as "Retirement" for material of interest to persons in that situation, even when the book is not about retirement per se. I hope this will result in greater availability of pertinent material.

I hope you do not find our position on retaining the heading "Aged" an insensitive one. However, this is the only heading we can justify as long as we adhere to the basic principle of frequency of use (literary warrant) in American English.

I do wish to thank you sincerely for writing to me. Even when we cannot have total agreement it is good for us here at the Library to know that we have a concerned readership that is willing to make known its preferences in terminology and to offer suggestions for better service to the reading public.

If not "insensitive," the response is surely an unconvincing clutter of non sequiturs, contradictions, and unproven claims. Consider "general usage." *Who* is it that continues to "use" the term "aged"? Academics, clinicians, and LC subject catalogers. *Not* the elderly. Older people in America now almost invariably refer to themselves as "seniors" or "senior citizens." Offered in evidence: *Action for Seniors*, the 1975 "directory of leisure time resources in Greater Minneapolis" published by Community Information and Referral Service, a department of the Community Health and Welfare Council. The roster cites some 199 groups. Of that number, 106 include "senior" or "seniors" in their names. *None* include "aged." This is a purely random sample, from pages 14-15:

Golden Age Club	XYZ Group
Hope's Young At Hearts	Senior Citizens of Our
Senior Citizen Club	Redeemer Lutheran Church
Kewaydin Senior Citizens	Senior Friends
Senior Citizens	Senior Citizen Group
Matthews Center Seniors	Resurrection Leisure Club
Boulevard Club	St. Albert's Seniors
Morris Park Senior Citizens	St. Helena Seniors
Nokomis Lanes Senior Bowling	Parkway Leisure Club
Club	60 Plus Club

"Senior" forms obviously predominate, "Golden Age," "Evergreen," "Forever Fifty," "Sixty Plus," "Leisure," and "Retired" being distant runners-up. Last summer both SAC and LC endorsed Joan Marshall's "Principles for Establishing Subject Headings relating to People and Peoples." The first of those principles declares:

> The authentic name of ethnic, national, religious, social, or sexual groups' should be established if such a name is determinable. If a group does not have an authentic name, the name preferred by the group should be established. The determination of authentic or preferred names should be based upon the literature of the people themselves (not upon outside sources or experts), upon organizational self-identification, and/or upon group members experts.

"Aged" is undeniably the language of outsiders, not the name preferred nor employed by the group itself.

Next, consider the objection that "seniors" could be too easily confused "in a universal catalog" with "high school students of the last year and, in terms of employment, those with the greatest seniority." A *very* red herring, for—as noted long ago in *HCL Cataloging Bulletin*, nos. 8-10, p. 95—"it should be abundantly and instantly clear from the nature of the entries actually displayed under SENIORS in the catalog that it refers to the elderly, *not* to last-year students" nor ranking workers. "Moreover, school-related SENIOR heads would never appear unmodified or unglossed because of the necessity to distinguish between levels: high school, college, etc." Hence, HIGH SCHOOL SENIORS (1966–1971 *LCSH* cumulative supplement, p. 321), COLLEGE SENIORS (1966–1971 *LCSH* cumulative supplement, p. 148). And LC already provides for the employment aspect with SENIORITY, EMPLOYEE (*LCSH*, 7th ed., p. 1159), which can hardly be mistaken for the general age group. Further, the plural noun, "Seniors," almost never refers in either speech or print to laborers *with seniority*. So it's not likely to be misunderstood on that count. The "multiple meanings" case is simply contrived and specious. Worse, even if there *were* a reasonable concern over possible confusions, there's a handy remedy: the scope note (e.g., "Here are entered materials on persons over 60 years of age").

Given that most Seniors use public rather than academic or research libraries, SENIORS *should* certainly appear in public library catalogs. The reasons: to eliminate ageist, demeaning terminology and simultaneously improve access. But, if good for public libraries, then why not for their academic and research counterparts as well? Or is it somehow okay for those "learned" institutions to persist in objectifying and debasing a whole, large category of humanity?

If that reexamination of "current files" failed to yield titles that would justify the assignment of new rubrics like AGEISM and SENIOR POWER, it either wasn't done with much enthusiasm or the examiner didn't know what-in-hell to look for.

It's welcome news that LC is "making an attempt to give wider use to such terms as RETIREMENT . . . even when the book is not about retirement per se." Bravo! But one paragraph earlier came the announcement that "in the LC system we have only headings that have been used to designate the contents of *entire* books. . . ." The two statements not only don't harmonize, but inevitably raise the not-so-innocent question: If an established heading like RETIREMENT can be legitimately assigned to a work that's "not about retirement per se," why can't descriptors like AGEISM and SENIOR POWER be innovated and applied to works that aren't about Ageism and Senior Power per se?

Finally, it's all quite proper to close such missives with sincerity-reeking phrases like "it is good for us . . . to know that we have a concerned readership . . . willing to make known its preferences in terminology and . . . offer suggestions for better service," but it doesn't add up to one small damn if those concerns, preferences, and suggestion are ultimately dismissed with lame excuses and transparent cliches.

Senior Access

Harriet L. Eisman ["Public Library Programs for the Elderly," *Wilson Library Bulletin* (April 1979)] neglected the problem of catalog access to library resources for over-60 users. Such resources, in fact, are typically undercataloged and frequently assigned subject rubrics— like AGED—that not only hinder access, but also reflect an "ageist," essentially disrespectful approach toward the topic and the "elderly" themselves. (E.g., would Ruth Gordon or Maggie Kuhn expect to find entries on senior centers under AGED—SOCIETIES AND CLUBS? And how might they feel about being compelled to make a second look-up under the "Aged" descriptor?)

As a few undercataloging examples:

- *The New Old,* a 1978 Anchor Press title, included substantive material on ageism, death, Senior Power, hospices, mandatory retirement, and self-reliance, as well as resource directories. LC assigned these subject tracings: 1. Aged—United States—Social conditions—Addresses, essays, lectures. 2. Aged—United States—Economic conditions—Addresses, essays, lectures. 3. Aged—United States—Political activity—Addresses, essays, lectures. 4. Age and employment—United States—Addresses, essays, lectures. At Hennepin County Library, we subject-traced the same work this way: 1. Seniors—United States. 2. Seniors— Economic conditions. 3. Seniors—Political activity. 4. Seniors' organizations, centers, etc.—Directories. 5. Ageism in employment. 6. Seniors and death. 7. Ageism—United States. 8. Hospices. 9. Senior power. 10. Mandatory retirement.

- *Maggie Kuhn on Aging,* a 1977 Westminster Press volume, featured sections on "Playpens and Warehouses: Retirement Communities and Homes," "Health," "Mandatory Retirement," and "Changing Life-styles," together with "A Living Will." LC's tracings: 1. Old age. 2. Retirement—United States. 3. Aged— United States. I. Title. HCL's tracings: 1. Ageism. 2. Gray Panthers. 3. Aging. 4. Retirement communities. 5. Euthanasia. 6. Alternative funerals. 7. Seniors—United States. 8. Mandatory retirement. I. Title. II. Title: A living will.

Letter submitted on May 30, 1979, to the *Wilson Library Bulletin,* but never printed.

● Garson Kanin's *It Takes a Long Time to Become Young* (Double-day, 1978) got this LC treatment: 1. Retirement—United States. And this HCL handling: 1. Mandatory retirement. 2. Ageism in employment.

● These are the contents of Leonard Biegel's *Best Years Catalogue: A Source Book for Older Americans* (Putnam, 1978): About aging. Food. Shelter. Health. Safety. Creative leisure. Transportation and travel. Money. Joining and sharing. Communicating. Rights and legacies. LC's subject tracings: 1. Aged—United States—Handbooks, manuals, etc. 2. Aged—Societies and clubs—Directories. HCL's subject tracings: 1. Transportation for seniors. 2. Seniors—health and welfare. 3. Seniors—Housing. 4. Seniors' organizations, centers, etc.—Directories. 5. Seniors—Personal finance.

For more on how to fairly and fully catalog seniors' materials, see:

"CHILDREN AND SENIORS," *HCL Cataloging Bulletin,* no. 20 (March 1, 1976): 16.
"LC to Seniors: Sorry, Folks," *HCL Cataloging Bulletin,* no. 20 (March 1, 1976): 46–8.
"LEGAL ASSISTANCE TO SENIORS," *HCL Cataloging Bulletin,* nos. 18–19 (December 1, 1975): 26
"SENIOR POWER/SENIORS," *HCL Cataloging Bulletin,* nos. 11–13 (March 15, 1975): 26.
"SENIOR PROJECTS AND SERVICES," *HCL Cataloging Bulletin,* no. 21 (May 1, 1976): 26.
"SENIORS," *HCL Cataloging Bulletin,* no. 20 (March 1, 1976): 51
"Seniors by Any Other Name," *HCL Cataloging Bulletin,* nos. 8–10 (September 1, 1974): 94–5.
" 'We Are Not Antiques Yet': L.A. Retirees Enlighten LC," *HCL Cataloging Bulletin,* no. 17 (October 1, 1975): 43.

Ethnic Access

I take for granted that:

- Ethnicity is something positive and valuable, something worth recognizing and encouraging.
- Libraries should stock a wide variety of ethnic materials, including foreign language and bilingual media.
- Apart from special bookmarks, displays, and shelving arrangements, ethnic materials should be easily and fully identified and located through the catalog, primarily by means of subject headings.
- Catalog users, including those whose mother language may not be English, should be able to readily understand the data in catalog records; should (ideally) be able to reach desired subjects on their first try; and should not be offended, prejudiced, confused, misled, or "turned off" by the very terminology used to denote specific topics.

Now, do most catalogs provide full, fair, and intelligible access to ethnic materials?

No.

And the responsibility or "blame" lies in two places:

- At the national level, where (1) the Library of Congress—the principal source of cataloging copy for most libraries—has simply proven insensitive, inept, and inadequate in its treatment of ethnic items; and (2) ALA technical services and special-interest committees—ostensibly the profession's watchdogs and consumer advocates—have stupendously failed to exert any real independence, rarely (if ever) lobbying aggressively on behalf of library consumers and their clienteles.
- At the local level, in our individual libraries, where both technical and public services staff have copped out in two ways: (1) by not pressuring ALA and LC to improve their cataloging practices and codes, and (2) by not initiating at least *some* in-house action to reform and expand catalog access to ethnic materials.

Reprinted from *HCL Cataloging Bulletin*, no. 35 (July/August 1978): 1–7.

I want no one to accept these charges simply on faith. So here's a litle evidence in the form of "loaded" questions:

- How are the earth's darker peoples ordinarily described in the LC subject scheme? Aren't they usually "underdeveloped," "primitive," and exotically "native" or "tribal," in essence represented as species of tropical wildlife?
- Why is it that all religions but Christianity worship qualified or glossed Gods, very definitely *not* the Genuine Article?
- Why do such absurd, inaccurate, and derogatory headings as MAMMIES, YELLOW PERIL, MEDITERRANEAN RACE, TEUTONIC RACE, MONGOLOID RACE, and KAFIR WARS still appear as valid, "legitimate," okay-to-use descriptors?
- Why, on the other hand, have dozens of obvious and important "ethnic" topics *never* been acknowledged nor legitimized? Why are there still no rubrics for the following topics?

INTERETHNIC [or ETHNIC] RELATIONS	COOKING, ETHNIC
JOB HUNTING FOR MINORITIES	ETHNIC ARCHIVES
MESTIZOS	ETHNIC ART
MINORITY LITERATURE	ETHNIC LIBRARIES
MINORITY ORGANIZATIONS	ETHNIC MUSEUMS
MINORITY WOMEN	ETHNIC MUSIC
MINORITY WORKERS	ETHNIC NAMES
OPEN HOUSING	ETHNIC PUBLISHERS AND PUBLISHING
THIRD WORLD LITERATURE	ETHNOCIDE
	INNER CITY CHILDREN
	INNER CITY SCHOOLS

- Why are there no descriptors for subjects of clear, unmistakable interest to specific groups? For instance, why can't Black people directly locate material under these topics?

AFRICAN DIASPORA	BLACK THEOLOGY
AFRO-BEAT MUSIC	HARLEM RENAISSANCE
AFRO-CUBAN MUSIC	HIGHLIFE
ANANSI [the folkloric character]	KWANZA
ANTI-APARTHEID MOVEMENT	RHYTHM AND BLUES MUSIC
BLACK LIBERATION	SOLEDAD BROTHERS
	UJAAMA VILLAGES

- Why can't anyone make subject "hits" for foods like French CREPES and Italian PASTA, Scandinavian crafts like KUBBESTOLS (log chairs) and ROSEMALING, Canadiana like METIS, VOYAGEURS, and VOYAGEUR SONGS, Filipino TINIKLING DANCE, or Southern U.S ZYDECO MUSIC?
- Why the ubiquitous "Oriental" headings that reinforce Kipling-esque stereotypes of Asia as a kind of exotic, inscrutable adjunct to Europe, a pagoda-shaped, dragon-decorated, curry-and-soy-sauce-smelling doll house populated by Charlie Chans and operated largely for the amusement of wonder-craving Westerners?

- Why are the Inuit, Saame, Mbuti, and Oromo not called by their own, their genuine names? Why, instead, are they still termed "Eskimos," "Lapps," "Pygmies," and "Galas"? In other words, why do we persist in laying alien and frequently demeaning labels on these people?

- Why are minority-group victims so often made to seem responsible for their own victimization? And why is their oppression minimized? For example, are Jewish-Gentile relations invariably *JEWISH* "QUESTIONS"? And why, in nearly all our catalogs, does it appear that Japanese-Americans during World War II were merely-if not even helpfully—"evacuated" and "relocated" from the West Coast, instead of *forcibly interned in concentration camps?* Similarly, why is it that the many works on the forced removals suffered by Native Americans are regularly subject-cataloged under INDIANS OF NORTH AMERICAN—LAND TRANSFERS?

- And why do catalogs largely ignore the fact of minority-group rebellion, of fighting back? Where, for instance, are headings for AFRICAN, JEWISH, MESITIZO, PUERTO RICAN, and NATIVE AMERICAN RESISTANCE AND REVOLTS? Or for RED POWER? Or TRAIL OF BROKEN TREATIES? or NATIONAL LIBERATION MOVEMENTS?

- Why are novels in Arnost Lustig's "Children of the Holocaust" series often inaccessible by means of series' or subject tracings? And why is no mention made of the movie versions, even though some of the books include still photos from the films?

- Why does the descriptive cataloging of Helen Cyr's *Filmography of the Third World,* a 1976 Scarecrow Press volume, provide no hint that over 70 pages of annotated entries deal with *North American* minorities—Native Americans, Asian-Americans, Afro-Americans, and Latinos? And why is there absolutely no subject access to that large block of material (the only tracings being, naturally, for UNDERDEVELOPED AREAS)?

- Why does the subject cataloging for John Shearer's "Billy Jo Jive" books overlook the obvious fact that the boy detective himself and most of his companions are Black?

- Why did Florence King's 1977 title, *Wasp, Where Is Thy Sting?,* get no subject tracing for either ANGLO- or BRITISH-AMERICANS?

- Why does *LCSH* mandate no cross-reference from "La Causa" to both UNITED FARM WORKERS UNION and CHICANO MOVEMENT?

- Why, for Barron's *How to Prepare for the TOEFL—Test of English as a Foreign Language,* was there no added entry made for "TOEFL" nor "Test of English as a Foreign Language"?

- Why is there no "Jewish" approach to Charles Reznikoff's *Poems, 1918–1936,* the first in a series of his "Complete Poems" to be issued by Black Sparrow Press?

- Since there's a growing emphasis on bilingual education, why isn't there a direct catalog approach to bilingual materials?

- Despite all the public attention to ethnic identity, ethnic pride, and the value of role models, why can't Black kids find biographies of Hank Aaron, Rod Carew, and Wilma Rudolph listed under AFRO-AMERICAN ATHLETES and Pelé under AFRO-BRAZILIAN ATHLETES? And why, in most catalogs, will no one find anything at all under

"Pelé" except—if they're lucky—a cross-reference to "Nascimento, Edson Arantos do"?

- Although Charles Garry's recent autobiography, *Streetfighter in the Courtroom,* contains whole chapters on Huey Newton, Bobby Seale, Inez Garcia, and George Jackson—people and cases of unquestionably ethnic as well as political interest—why does no contents' note indicate this? And why are there no subject analytics for Newton, Seale, Garcia, and Jackson, not to mention AFRO-AMERICAN DEFENDANTS, LATINO DEFENDANTS, etc.?

The litany could easily continue. But perhaps it's long enough to make the simple point that something's wrong with ethnic cataloging. The "something" nicely breaks down into four components or elements.

1. Biased, inaccurate, and inauthentic subject headings: e.g., UNDERDEVELOPED AREAS; NATIVE RACES; YELLOW PERIL; IBO TRIBE; SOCIETY, PRIMITIVE; and ART, ORIENTAL.

2. Wholesale omissions in the major subject vocabularies or schemes: i.e., the absence of descriptors for topics that are well represented in library materials and likely to be sought by users, but which LC hasn't yet sanctified.

3. "Undercataloging": i.e., the assignment of too few (if any) ethnic-related subject tracings, added entries, and notes, even though the materials warrant them.

4. Descriptive cataloging practices—like indecipherable abbreviations and punctuation marks, as well as ridiculous main-entry forms—that may seriously frustrate catalog use for many patrons, especially the so-called "disadvantaged," who already find libraries forbidding, and those whose primary language is not English.

To state the problem is also to state the major solutions or remedies. So there's no need to recite a catechism of cataloging "shoulds." (That is, we certainly *should* replace UNDERDEVELOPED AREAS with THIRD WORLD. We *should* reduce or eliminate abbreviations. We *should* create and assign subject headings for AFRO-BEAT MUSIC and HIGHLIFE. And we *should* enter "Pelé" under *P* instead of *N*.) What might be more profitable is to suggest a few approaches outside the established boundaries that may further enhance access to ethnic materials:

- Innovate headings for particular characters, places, and themes in literature and lore. And then assign them to the appropriate novels, plays, poetry, and folktales, whether juvenile or adult. For instance, the catalog can afford quick access to the ethnic sleuths in mystery and crime novels by means of headings like:

AFRICAN DETECTIVES	QUARSHIE, DOCTOR
IRISH DETECTIVES	MCGARR, PETER
NAVAHO DETECTIVES	LEAPHORN, JOE
ISRAELI DETECTIVES	SHOMAR, SHOMRI
MEXICAN-AMERICAN DETECTIVES	MENDOZA, LUIS
SWEDISH DETECTIVES	BECK, MARTIN
AFRO-AMERICAN DETECTIVES	TIBBS, VIRGIL
JAPANESE-AMERICAN DETECTIVES	MASUTO, MASAO

- Innovate headings for ethnic-related literary and media awards. And then apply them to winning titles in your own collection. As examples:

CARTER G. WOODSON BOOK AWARDS
CORETTA SCOTT KING AWARD BOOKS
COUNCIL ON INTERRACIAL BOOKS FOR CHILDREN AWARDS
EDWARD LEWIS WALLANT BOOK AWARDS
EPSTEIN AWARDS
MILDRED L. BATCHELDER AWARD BOOKS
SCHWARTZ JUVENILE BOOK AWARDS

- "Trace"—i.e., make added entries for—ethnic presses and organizations connected with individual works in the collection. As a result, the catalog would show under "Julian Richardson Associates," "Third World Press," or "Indian Historian Press" all the material in your library issued by those publishers. And a short explanatory note could be composed for each group or press; e.g.,

---

Council on Interracial Books for Children

Here are entered materials produced by an organization founded in 1966 and dedicated "to promoting antiracist and antisexist literature and instructional materials for children."

Or

Broadside Press

Here are entered materials produced by a Detroit press, founded in 1965 by Dudley Randall, which specializes in "Black poetry broadsides and books."

In sum, libraries may go to much trouble and expense in picking, buying, processing, and publicizing ethnic materials, but if they don't also go to a little trouble and expense in cataloging them, the whole investment may be wasted. Put in positive terms: If the stuff is worth getting, it's surely worth being handled with respect—and in such a way that people can find it.

Gay Access

I assume that (1) libraries should stock plentiful and diverse materials on the Gay experience, for both private and course-connected reading/listening/viewing; (2) apart from special lists and exhibits, Gay materials should be easily and fully identified through the library catalog, primarily by means of subject headings; (3) catalog users should (ideally) be able to reach desired subjects on their first try and should not be offended, prejudiced, confused, misled, or repelled by the very terminology used to denote specific topics; (4) Gay nonfiction should be sensibly and helpfully classified, as well.

Those are my basic assumptions. Now, how does today's cataloging rate in terms of fully and fairly providing access to Gay materials? Badly. For this reason: the homophobia (at worst) or insensitivity (at best) endemic to librarianship has not—until lately—been seriously challenged at either the national level (where subject and classification schemes like *Sears*, *Dewey*, and *Library of Congress* are produced and applied) or locally, in individual school, public, and college libraries (where librarians and media specialists *could* pressure the American Library Association and LC to improve their cataloging codes and practices, and *could* themselves initiate at least some in-house action to reform and expand access to Gay materials). Specifically:

In most catalogs there's no longer a *see also* reference *to* HOMOSEXUALITY *from* SEXUAL PERVERSION. And that's good. There always *have* been subject headings for LESBIANISM and LESBIANS. That's good, too. And just a few years ago, after intense lobbying, GAY LIBERATION MOVEMENT became a nationally respected, "legitimate" rubric. Which is also good. So what's the trouble? Well, it's four-fold:

1. A failure to replace the misleadingly narrow and often derogatory terms, HOMOSEXUALS and HOMOSEXUALS, MALE, with GAYS and GAY MEN.

Reprinted with permission from *Gay Insurgent* 4–5 (Spring 1979): 14–5.

2. A failure to innovate and employ descriptors for topics abundantly represented in library collections but never "validated" by *Sears* or *LC* and thus "buried" in library catalogs; e.g.,

CHRISTIAN GAYS
GAY ARTISTS
GAY AUTHORS
GAY BOOK AWARDS
GAY CLERGY
GAY COUPLES
GAY DETECTIVES
GAY MARRIAGE
GAY PERIODICALS
GAY PRISONERS
GAY PUBLISHERS AND
    PUBLISHING
GAY RESISTANCE AND REVOLTS
GAY RIGHTS
GAY SOLDIERS
GAY STUDIES
GAY TEACHERS
GAY TEENAGERS
HOMOPHOBIA
HOMOPHOBIA IN CHRISTIANITY
    [EDUCATION, LAW, LIBRARIAN-
    SHIP, PSYCHIATRY, etc.]
JEWISH GAYS
LESBIAN MOTHERS

3. A failure to regularly assign appropriate headings, with genre subdivisions, to Gay literature; e.g.,

GAY MEN—DRAMA [FICTION, POETRY, etc.]
GAYS—DRAMA [FICTION, POETRY, etc.]
LESBIANS—DRAMA [FICTION, POETRY, etc.]

4. A failure to create and use a heading for HETEROSEXUALITY, which—as a matter of simple equity—would "balance" and complement the existing forms, BISEXUALITY and HOMOSEXUALITY.

In the *Dewey Decimal Classification*, "Homosexuality" no longer "enjoys" its own special slot under 616.8583 ("Sexual aberrations, manias, perversion"). And that's good. The principal DDC number currently allotted to "Homosexuality"—301.4157—until very recently appeared under the broader caption, "Abnormal sexual relationships." That, however, has been changed to "Variant relationships," which is good. But there's still only *one* five-digit notation specified for nearly *all* material on Homosexuality, Gay men, and Lesbians! The result is a willy-nilly "dumping" and intermixing of disparate books and other media in that single overcrowded number. The remedy? Clearly, to extend the notation. At Hennepin County Library we did it this way:

301.4157   Gay lifestyles
301.41571   Gay men
301.41572   Lesbianism and Lesbians
301.41573   Gay Liberation Movement

As a consequence, general and comprehensive works on Gays, then material exclusively on Gay men, on Lesbians, and on the Gay Liberation Movement are grouped together and consecutively on the shelves instead of becoming one senseless jumble.

So what does all this mean? In brief: that Gay materials—if they are to be found and used—must be made readily accessible through the catalog and must be intelligently classified. If *Dewey, Sears, LC,* or card vendors won't yet do these things the way they should, individual librarians may have to do it themselves. To avoid or shun that task is to consign Gay media to disuse and to keep Gayness itself tightly and shamefully hidden in the cataloging closet.

Readings/Sources:

Berman, Sanford. "The Gays and the Straights." *Wilson Library Bulletin,* v. 50, no. 9 (May 1, 1976): 699.

———. *Prejudices and Antipathies: A Tract on the LC Subject Heads Concerning People.* Metuchen, NJ: Scarecrow Press, 1971, pp. 182-3.

Elrod, J. McRee. "Sexuality: Suggested Subject Headings." *HCL Cataloging Bulletin,* no. 30 (September/October 1977): 28-30.

"GAY MEN (etc.)." *HCL Cataloging Bulletin,* no. 32 (January/February 1978): 4-6.

"HOMOPHOBIA (etc.)." *HCL Cataloging Bulletin,* no. 20 (March 1, 1976): 26-7.

Marshall, Joan K. *On Equal Terms: A Thesaurus for Nonsexist Indexing and Cataloging.* New York: Neal-Schuman, 1977, pp. 60-4, 74-5.

Morgan, Marjorie. "Feedback." *HCL Cataloging Bulletin,* no. 31 (November/December 1977): 19.

———. "Feedback." *HCL Cataloging Bulletin,* no. 37 (November/December 1978): 11.

———. "MeSH 1975: The Gay Person as a Medical Phenomenon." *HCL Cataloging Bulletin,* no. 27 (April 1, 1977): 41-4.

"SRRT Task Force Launches Offensive against 'Homosexuality.'" *HCL Cataloging Bulletin,* no. 8-10 (September 1, 1975): 33-4.

White, David Allen. "Homosexuality and Gay Liberation: An Expansion of the Library of Congress Classification Schedule." *HCL Cataloging Bulletin,* no. 28 (June 1, 1977): 35-8.

Wolf, Steve. "Sex and the Single Cataloger: New Thoughts on Some Unthinkable Subjects." In *Revolting Librarians.* San Francisco, CA: Booklegger Press, 1972, pp. 39-44.

The "Jewish Question" in Subject Cataloging

It's reasonable, I think, to expect that the subject treatment of Jewish materials should do two things:

- Provide full and swift access to those materials by both Jews themselves and interested Gentiles.

- Use headings that:
  Specifically and accurately represent or denote Jewish subjects.
  Don't bias the library patron against either the materials or the topics.
  Reflect the language, experience, and viewpoint of Jews, not Gentiles, of victims, not victimizers.

The two fundamental goals or functions, then, are: access and equity. But, unfortunately, they are not the reality of Judaica subject cataloging, at least not as performed by the Library of Congress and its lockstep followers. And, by extension, they are not the reality of MARC and OCLC records, which rarely betray any serious deviation from LC-established norms.

While it can safely—and sadly—be argued that *no* ethnic nor religious groups, apart from WASPs, enjoy truly adequate and equitable subject treatment, Jews undoubtedly fare worse than all others. I can only guess about why that's the case, but there's no mystery whatever about *how* it happens. There are two modes: First, through the content and form of the vocabulary. And, second, by the way that vocabulary is actually applied.

1. The vocabulary problem itself divides into several aspects:

- Clearly defamatory, palpably *Goyish* terminology like JEWISH QUESTION and—until very recently—that whole sequence of as-

Paper presented at the Association of Jewish Libraries Convention, Cincinnati, June 18, 1979.

sinine and demeaning headings: JEWS AS FARMERS, JEWS AS SOL-DIERS, JEWS AS SCIENTISTS, etc. (which incidentally coexisted for decades with JEWISH CRIMINALS, no "as" considered necessary to express doubt about a Jew's fitness for being a crook).

- A special or peculiar approach to Jews and Judaica, exemplified by the almost exclusive use of —JEWS as an ethnic subdivision under topics like BANKING AND BANKERS, CAPITALISTS AND FINANCIERS, COMMUNISM, and RADICALISM as well as the refusal—absolutely unique in the handling of American minority groups—to recognize Jews as genuine, legitimate citizens of the United States. The sole relevant heading remains JEWS *IN* THE UNITED STATES, even though similar rubrics for other peoples—headings like POLES IN THE UNITED STATES, ITALIANS IN THE UNITED STATES, and ASIANS IN THE UNITED STATES— have been rightly complemented over the past several years with the compound, nonalien forms, POLISH-AMERICANS, ITALIAN-AMERICANS, and ASIAN-AMERICANS. A second- or third-generation Dimaggio or Scarpelli is an "Italian-American," but a second- or third-generation Epstein or Berman is only a "Jew *in* the United States." The LC heading—in stark contrast to CSLA's JEWISH-AMERICANS—bespeaks something of impermanence, and perhaps undesirability, in effect saying: "These people don't really belong here. We don't want them here. And they're sure-as-hell not going to stay here."

- A failure to create and assign headings for Jewish-related subjects amply represented in both print and audiovisual media; e.g.,

KIBBUTZ [which now appears merely as a *see* reference to COLLEC-TIVE SETTLEMENTS—ISRAEL, meaning that typical catalog users searching in the *K*s won't "hit" the subject on their first try and may well be turned-off altogether. Two precedents for the direct and familiar form: the *Index to Jewish Periodicals* uses KIBBUTZIM as a primary descriptor, while Hennepin County Library long ago installed KIBBUTZ (ISRAELI COLLECTIVE SETTLEMENT).]

SHTETL [at Hennepin, emphatically not a "Jewish" library, we've already assigned SHTETL to more than two dozen works, and the *Index to Jewish Periodicals* acknowledges the topic with a heading for JEWS IN EUROPE—SHTETL.]

JEWISH RESISTANCE AND REVOLTS [which at HCL parallels rubrics for AFRICAN RESISTANCE AND REVOLTS, WOMEN'S RESISTANCE AND RE-VOLTS, INDIAN RESISTANCE AND REVOLTS, etc.]

BAS or BAT MITZVAH [the counterpart to BAR MITZVAH.]

BAGELS

GEFILTE FISH

GHETTOES

NAZI FUGITIVES [applicable, e.g., to M. Bar-Zohar's *Avengers* (1967), S. Wiesenthal's *Murders among Us* (1967), and H. Blum's *Wanted! The Search for Nazis in America* (1977).]

ALIYAH BETH

CONCENTRATION CAMP SURVIVORS

ANTISEMITISM IN THE NEW TESTAMENT [lately assigned at HCL, with a
    —FICTION subhead, to Ben Freidman's 1977 novel, *The Anguish of
    Father Rafti.*]

ANTISEMITISM IN THE ARMED FORCES [applied at HCL to Harold W.
    Felton's 1978 biography of Uriah Phillips Levy.]

SEXISM IN JUDAISM

HOMOPHOBIA IN JUDAISM

BILINGUAL MATERIALS—ENGLISH/HEBREW and the corollary BILINGUAL
    MATERIALS—ENGLISH/YIDDISH

JEWISH-AMERICAN POLITICIANS

JEWISH-AMERICAN DETECTIVES

JEWISH GAYS

folkloric persons and places like CHELM, SCHLEMIEHL, and LILITH.

fictional characters like DAVID SMALL, the protagonist of Harry
Kemelman's "Rabbi" stories, and SADIE SHAPIRO, who stars in a
series of novels by Robert Kimmel Smith.

and literary prizes—like the SCHWARTZ JUVENILE BOOK AWARDS, EP-
STEIN AWARDS, and EDWARD LEWIS WALLANT BOOK AWARDS— that
could be applied as labels or tags to the laureate works themselves,
making it easy to identify those award winners that are actually in the
collection.

- A failure to introduce helpful cross-references to existing terms,
  links that would benefit Jewish and non-Jewish catalog users
  alike; e.g.,

COOKING, JEWISH
  x Cooking, Kosher
    Kosher cooking

HOLOCAUST, JEWISH (1933-1945)
  x Shoah

SYNAGOGUES
  x Jewish synagogues
    Shuls
    Temples, Jewish

PASSOVER
  x Pesach

BIBLE. O. T.
  x Bible, Jewish
    Jewish Bible

JEWS—PERSECUTIONS
  x Pogroms
    Programs

ROSH HA-SHANAH
  x Jewish New Year
    New Year, Jewish

MYSTICISM—JUDAISM
  x Jewish mysticism

JEWS—DIASPORA
  x Diaspora, Jewish
    Galut
    Jewish Diaspora
    Jews—Galut

YOM KIPPUR
  x Day of Repentance (Judaism)

ENTEBBE AIRPORT RAID, 1976
  x Israeli Raid, Entebbe Airport, 1976
    Uganda Airport Raid, 1976

- Awkwardly or oddly formulated terms that impair quick access or, in catalogs with few cross-references, totally prevent finding the sought-after topic; e.g.,

AMERICAN LITERATURE —JEWISH AUTHORS	*instead of*	JEWISH-AMERICAN LITERATURE
WARSAW—HISTORY— UPRISING OF 1943	*instead of*	WARSAW GHETTO UP- RISING, 1943
TEREZIN (CONCENTRA- TION CAMP)	*instead of*	THERESIENSTADT (CON- CENTRATION CAMP)
OSWIECIM (CONCENTRA- TION CAMP)	*instead of*	AUSCHWITZ (CONCEN- TRATION CAMP)
AMAUROTIC FAMILY IDIOCY	*instead of*	TAY-SACHS' DISEASE (used by the *Index to Jewish Periodicals*)
NATIONAL SOCIALISM	*instead of*	NAZISM
SLAUGHTERING AND SLAUGHTERHOUSES— JEWS	*instead of*	the more accurate and far less insensitive KOSHER MEAT INDUSTRY AND TRADE (or something similar)

- A failure to recognize the Jewish dimension of certain notable events through *see also* connections; e.g.,

AUSCHWITZ TRIAL, FRANKFURT AM MAIN, 1963-1965

   xx Holocaust, Jewish (1933-1945)
       Jews—Persecutions [or Jews in Europe—Persecutions]

BABIY YAR MASSACRE, 1941

   xx Antisemitism—Ukraine
       Holocaust, Jewish (1933-1945)
       Jews—Persecutions [or Jews in the Ukraine—Persecutions]

- A pervasive and overwhelming "Christian primacy" among the multitude of headings that deal with religion. In nearly every string of descriptors concerning a special facet of spirtuality, worship, or faith, Christianity comes first. There are forms for GOD (AFRICAN RELIGION), GOD (HINDUISM), GOD (ISLAM), and GOD (JUDAISM), but not for GOD (CHRISTIANITY). Why? Because the unglossed, the unmodified GOD, the primary divinity, the God-Before-All-Other-Gods, is unabashedly and undeniably *Christian*. And the same pattern obtains for countless other topics, including ANGELS, SERMONS, CHILDREN'S SERMONS, HERESIES AND HERETICS, PRAYER, ESCHATOL- OGY, CONFIRMATION, PROVIDENCE AND GOVERNMENT OF GOD, DEVO- TIONAL LITERATURE, and THEOLOGY (indeed, the lately added see references to the *un*modified term, THEOLOGY, are from "*Christian* theology" and "Theology, *Christian*"!). Aside from considerations of ethics and fairness, this Christocentrism unquestionably vio- lates the "Establishment Clause" of the First Amendment.

2. The assignment problem is best illustrated with real cases; e.g.,

- In 1978, Pantheon Books reissued Izzy Stone's *Underground to Palestine,* including a new introduction and epilogue by the author. LC assigned three subject tracings: WORLD WAR, 1939–1945—REFUGEES; WORLD WAR, 1939–1945—JEWS; and STONE, ISIDOR F. The last head, for the author, would be redundant in a dictionary. catalog; the first two are appropriate, but not nearly specific nor accurate enough. At HCL, we added: ISRAEL—IMMIGRATION AND EMIGRATION—HISTORY; ZIONISM; PALESTINIAN ARABS; PALESTINE—IMMIGRATION AND EMIGRATION—HISTORY; ALIYAH BETH—PERSONAL NARRATIVES; and ISRAELI-ARAB RELATIONS. (Just for the record, the current LC "equivalent" to ISRAELI-ARAB RELATIONS is *JEWISH*-ARAB RELATIONS, which crazily implies that *all* Jews—everywhere—have had, or are now having, "relations" with Arabs. Both *Sears* and *CSLA* wisely employ the unambiguous "Israeli" form).

- To Marilyn Hirsh's 1978 "easy book," *Potato Pancakes All Around: A Hanukkah Tale,* LC's juvenalia catalogers applied one heading: HANUKKAH—FICTION. And composed this summary:

> A wandering peddler teaches the villagers how to make potato pancakes from a crust of bread.

Okay, as far as it goes. But, again, it doesn't go far enough. At HCL, we inserted this extra note:

> Includes "Grandma Yetta's and Grandma Sophie's recipe for potato pancakes," as well as "a brief explanation of Hanukkah and its history."

And we assigned four more headings, all subdivided by —FICTION: PEDDLERS AND PEDDLING; PANCAKES, WAFFLES, ETC.; COOKING, JEWISH; and SHTETL (EAST EUROPEAN JEWISH COMMUNITY).

- LC subject-cataloged Joe W. Haldeman's *Infinite Dreams,* a 1978 St. Martin's Press volume, under SCIENCE FICTION, AMERICAN. We added a note ("Thirteen short stories, including 'The Mazel tov revolution' and 'Tricentennial' "), another subject tracing (JEWISH-AMERICAN FICTION), and two title added-entries (for "Mazel tov revolution" and "Tricentennial").

- Crowell, in 1977, published Lulla Rosenfeld's *Bright Star of Exile,* subtitled *Jacob Adler and the Yiddish Theater.* LC's trio of subject headings: ADLER, JACOB, 1855–1926; THEATER—JEWS; and ACTORS, JEWISH—BIOGRAPHY. The first tracing, for Adler himself, is unexceptional. However, the next two nicely manage to both bury the "Yiddish" element and mask the biographee's true identity. At HCL we replaced them with YIDDISH THEATER and ACTORS AND ACTRESSES, JEWISH-*AMERICAN*. Also, to further enhance access by readers who might recall only a portion of the title, we made title added-entries for "Star of exile" and "Exile star."

- Maggie Rennert's *Shelanu, an Israel Journal,* appeared in 1979. It got three LC subject tracings: ISRAEL—DESCRIPTION AND TRAVEL; AUTHORS, AMERICAN—20TH CENTURY—BIOGRAPHY; and the wonderfully Byzantine RENNERT, MAGGIE—HOMES AND HAUNTS—ISRAEL—BEERSHEBA. We left the first heading alone, changed the second to AUTHORS, JEWISH-AMERICAN—DIARIES, and replaced the convoluted Beersheba Monster with ISRAEL AND JEWISH-AMERICANS, a homemade descriptor. Also, we made an entry for the permuted title, "An Israel journal," on the premise that some title searchers might forget the first word, "Shelanu."

- Stein and Day, in 1979, issued M. Hirsh Goldberg's *Just Because They're Jewish.* LC assigned a total of four added entries: one for the title plus three for subjects (JEWS—HISTORY, JEWS—ANECDOTES, FACETIAE, SATIRE, ETC., and JEWS—PUBLIC OPINION). That cataloging conveys the unmistakable impression that Goldberg's tome is basically a lighthearted review of the Jewish experience and of popular ideas about Jews. Well, Goldberg's style is surely informal, but the substance of his book is definitely not "funny," nor does it qualify as a "balanced," good-and-bad rundown of "popular opinion" through the ages. At HCL, we made two notes to clarify the author's intent and what's really inside the work:

> On title page: If anything can be misconstrued about the Jews, it will be . . . and has been.
> PARTIAL CONTENTS: The Jews in stereotype.—About that religion that brought you the Ten Commandments.—Praise the Lord and pass the ammunition.—Sticks and stones may break your bones, but names can kill you.—To Hell with Hitler: a journey inside the Holocaust.

Of the three original subject headings, we kept only the first, JEWS—HISTORY, and expanded the treatment with: ANTISEMITISM; JEWISH SOLDIERS; MISCONCEPTIONS (an HCL innovation); JUDAISM; HOLOCAUST, JEWISH (1933–1945): JEWISH RESISTANCE AND REVOLTS; and JEWS—MISCELLANEA.

- Yael Dayan's 1979 novel, *Three Weeks in October,* published by Delacorte & Friede, got one LC subject tracing, for ISRAEL-ARAB WAR, 1973—FICTION. Which is perfectly valid. It might also, however, have been assigned SOLDIERS—ISRAEL—FICTION and the genre heading, ISRAELI FICTION, which can be valuable—particularly in smaller collections—for collocating or listing together all such works. (LC applies genre tracings solely to anthologies by various authors, not to novels, plays, or poetry by a single writer.)

- A collective of radical Jews in Chicago has been producing the tabloid, *Chutzpah,* for about six years. In 1977, New Glide Publications, a small, alternative press in San Francisco, issued

Chutzpah: a Jewish Liberation Anthology. The table of contents includes captions like "Singing in a strange land: Jewish life in America," "Anti-Semitism," "The joy of socialism, the heartbreak of capitalism," and "Two peoples, two states: self-determination in the Middle East." Among the individual essays are "Role models for Jewish women," "The Jewish sorority: sisterhood perverted," "Why we write about Gay Liberation," "Dilemma of a Jewish Lesbian," "Anti-Semites are surfacing like roaches from the woodwork," "That's funny, you don't look Anti-Semitic: perspective on the American left," "Feminist frustration with the forefathers," "Magnus Hirschfeld: Gay Liberation's Zeyde," and "In forests and ghettos: Jewish resistance to the Nazis." All of this any cataloger could have determined purely from the "front matter," without reading a word of text or knowing anything in advance about the collective and its scruffy-looking newspaper. How was it subject-cataloged? With one heading: JEWS—HISTORY—20TH CENTURY—ADDRESSES, ESSAYS, LECTURES. Instead of that feeble, imprecise, and misleading treatment, which also happens to mask or submerge several key, controversial topics that are otherwise very hard to find much about, it should have been assigned at least these seven tracings: JEWISH RESISTANCE AND REVOLTS; ANTISEMITISM; JEWISH WOMEN; ISRAELI-ARAB RELATIONS; SEXISM IN JUDAISM; and JEWISH-AMERICANS. Further, there could have been—but wasn't—a title added-entry for "Jewish liberation anthology."

- LC assigned no subject tracings to Lester Goldberg's 1977 story collection, *One More River.* At HCL, it's findable under SHORT STORIES, JEWISH-AMERICAN and JEWISH-AMERICANS—FICTION.

- Belva Plain's 1978 Delacorte novel, *Evergreen,* received no subject headings at LC. It should, though, be accessible under JEWISH-AMERICANS—FICTION and JEWISH-AMERICAN WOMEN —FICTION.

- LC applied three subject descriptors to Hans Askenasy's 1978 study, *Are We All Nazis?:* VIOLENCE; SOCIAL PSYCHIATRY; and HOMICIDE—PSYCHOLOGICAL ASPECTS. It deserved more, for AUSCHWITZ (CONCENTRATION CAMP); NAZIS—PSYCHOLOGY; HOLOCAUST, JEWISH (1933–1945)—PSYCHOLOGICAL ASPECTS; OBEDIENCE; and ATROCITIES—PSYCHOLOGICAL ASPECTS.

- LC's handling of *The Maimie Papers,* issued in 1977 by the Feminist Press, and Lee Seldes' *Legacy of Mark Rothko,* a 1978 Holt title, neglects in both cases to recognize the Jewishness of the principal figures, one a prostitute, the other a painter.

- Beverly Brodsky McDermott's 1976 *Golem: A Jewish Legend,* got two subject tracings from LC, one for JUDAH LOW BEN BEZALEEL and the other for GOLEM, both subdivided by —JUVENILE LITERATURE. Except for the ageist subhead, those are fine—but insufficient. Even though explicitly subtitled "a *Jewish* legend," and of obvious relevance *to* Jews, where's the explicitly "Jewish" entry point? Missing. Nor did LC's cataloging express other major aspects of this powerful rendering, elements that might prove of special interest and worth to Jewish readers, adults as well as children. These are the further tracings applied at Hennepin: GHETTOES, JEWISH—PRAGUE—LEGENDS; JEWS IN CZECHOSLOVAKIA—PERSECUTIONS—LEGENDS; LEGENDS, JEWISH; and RABBIS—LEGENDS.

If this, then, is the state—the sorry and even shameful state—of Judaica subject cataloging, what can be done about it? Well, there are two things: one is to lobby the Library of Congress, the source of most of our "outside copy," whether in the form of cards, MARC records, or CIP and also the agency responsible for the world's principal English-language subject heading scheme, the "authority" for subject cataloging in most libraries. But don't expect instant results. And don't expect that LC, even if it were miraculously sensitized and reformed overnight, would be *able* to do certain things for your particular library. Which raises the second point: That the best way to improve subject access and equity in your own library is to locally undertake as many reforms as your resources allow. For instance, in no event can LC—no matter how enlightened—make necessary cross-references in *your* catalog. Or assign retrospective award or prize headings. *You* have to do it. Regardless of when LC abandons or alters JEWISH QUESTION, if *you* find the heading inaccurate and indefensible, *you* should eliminate it from your active subject thesaurus and recatalog the titles it has already been assigned to. If you get a new filmstrip on bagel making and there's no "bagel" heading in the LC subject list, it's up to *you* to devise and apply a suitable descriptor. If you want your catalog to show *all* of the Israeli drama, fiction, or poetry you've got—not just anthologies—you'll have to assign the relevant headings yourself to incoming or existing material because LC will probably never do so for novels, plays, and verse by single authors. This "do-it-yourself" approach may strike some as awfully tedious and even sinful, since it indisputably violates the holy canons of standardization and "follow-the-leader." However, my litany of neglect, if not abuse, should have demonstrated that the "leader" can't be wholly trusted.

To reinforce that conclusion, here's the history of what's probably the only serious lobbying effort in the past decade: On August 26, 1975, the newly formed ALA Jewish Caucus sent the following letter to the chief of LC's Subject Cataloging Division:

> ALA's Jewish Caucus applauds LC's increasing sensitivity to the needs and views of American ethnic groups—manifest, for instance, in Mr. Mumford's reply to the October 1974 Nashville Seminar resolution (cf. *HCL Cataloging Bulletin,* nos. 11–13, pp. 80–2) and such recent subject-heading innovations as ITALIAN-AMERICANS, JAPANESE-AMERICANS, and SCANDINAVIAN-AMERICANS (1974 LCSH supplement). Given this new and welcome responsiveness, we herewith request immediate attention to three areas of special concern to us:

1. *Offensive/archaic nomenclature*

JEWISH QUESTION, for reasons already well stated in the literature, must be dismantled. Since, in fact, this form has been applied to works dealing with the relationship between Jews and non-Jews, we suggest its replacement with the completely accurate and altogether neutral JEWS—RELATIONS WITH GENTILES, which would allow permutations like JEWS IN EUROPE—RELATIONS WITH GENTILES, etc. On no account should "Jewish Question" again defile library catalogs, even as a cross-reference.

We trust that all extant JEWS AS . . . constructions will be speedily supplanted by nondefamatory, contracted forms; e.g., JEWISH FARMERS and JEWISH SOLDIERS instead of the present JEWS AS FARMERS and JEWS AS SOLDIERS.

2. *Omissions/inadequacies*

JEWS IN THE UNITED STATES should be promptly complemented by JEWISH-AMERICANS, applicable to material on Jewish citizens and permanent residents in America. This form would totally harmonize with ITALIAN-AMERICANS, JAPANESE-AMERICANS, etc. Also required are such spin-off forms as JEWISH-AMERICAN FICTION; JEWISH-AMERICAN LITERATURE; JEWISH-AMERICAN WOMEN; etc.

We further recommend the deliberate creation and conscientious assignment of Jewish-related rubrics for which literary warrant has long existed and whose employment should measurably enhance access to the relevant materials for Jews and Gentiles alike. Examples: KIBBUTZ (ISRAELI COLLECTIVE SETTLEMENT), SHTETL (EAST EUROPEAN JEWISH COMMUNITY), JEWISH RESISTANCE AND REVOLTS [Directly subdivided], BOYS, JEWISH and BAS MITZVAH. Additionally, several cross-references can be usefully introduced to existing primary heads; e.g.,

---

COOKERY, JEWISH

x Cookery, Kosher
Kosher cookery

Unless subdivided by place, JEWISH-ARAB RELATIONS is seriously inaccurate and misleading. We believe ISRAELI-ARAB RELATIONS would prove an appropriate substitute.

3. *Christian primacy*

The manifold religious headings—like GOD and ANGELS—which automatically endow Christianity with preeminence are altogether unacceptable and must be transformed so that *all* religions enjoy absolute equity. In the two above-cited cases, this can be painlessly accomplished by appending the gloss, (CHRISTIANITY), and reserving application of the *un*glossed form to genuinely comparative or multifaith materials.

We look forward to quick action on these matters. And wish to express our thanks in advance for your cooperation.

The SCD chief replied on December 4, 1975:

I had hoped to be able to answer your letter of late September with an answer that all the questions raised had been considered and solved as requested but I cannot. The fact is that I have been away so much in the past months and we have come to a grinding halt in major changes until we have decided on implementation in our own catalogs.

As a pledge of good faith, however, I did want to let you know that the points are valid ones, I see nothing insurmountable in a resolution along the lines you ask. But I don't think I can give you a final answer until after the first of the year.

Thank you for your considered and specific recommendations. That gives us a point of departure so we can make the best use of our time which we have to subtract from that meant for current cataloging.

Now, the answer was a bit tardy, but certainly sympathetic, inspiring hope for fairly fast reforms. Yet, to this day none of the Caucus requests—save the truncation of "as" forms—has actually been implemented. "Kibbutz" stays a cross-reference; "God" is still unreservedly Christian; New York- and Chicago-born Jews continue to be *temporary* Americans; and as recently as June 6, 1979 the present chief of LC's Subject Cataloging Division wrote Herb Zafren of Hebrew Union College that "elimination of [JEWISH QUESTION] has been considered in the past but has not been achieved because of the difficulty of determining what heading(s) would replace it"— that "explanation" notwithstanding at least three known and weighty precedents: the use of JEWS AND GENTILES by *Sears,* of JEWS AND NON-JEWS by the *Index to Jewish Periodicals,* and Hennepin's six-year-old JEWS—RELATIONS WITH GENTILES. Beyond these precedents, there are two more in LC practice: the recent replacement of RACE QUESTION by RACE RELATIONS and the use of —GOVERNMENT RELATIONS as a subhead under various INDIAN headings, which, in the form of JEWS—GOVERNMENT RELATIONS, might easily be applied to some of the works presently saddled with JEWISH QUESTION. And if, for research purposes, it's desirable to trace the history of the concept itself, however odious, a little imagination could produce an acceptable form like "JEWISH QUESTION" (ANTISEMITIC DOCTRINE).

In sum, there's no realistic basis for expecting much from LC—not soon, anyway—although it would surely be worthwhile for prestigious organizations like AJL and the Church and Synagogue Library Association to firmly demand improvements. It may not seem very professional nor high-minded, but the fact is that LC tends to be most "responsive" when it's most threatened, when it's publicly ridiculed or chastised. That's how Black and women's groups not long ago secured a number of overdue subject-cataloging changes.

If there's any one message with respect to "The 'Jewish Question' in subject cataloging," it's probably that—just as with other varieties or manifestations of either Goyish unconcern or outright anti-Semitism—Jews must take care of themselves, ultimately relying on each other. LC won't do a damn thing unless we force them. And even then, what they produce may not be 100 percent kosher. So it needs to be checked. And corrected. And otherwise made to work. By us. By the people it most affects. By people who are resolved never again to be humiliated nor oppressed. By people who understand that the weapons of oppression include not only whips and guns, but also words.

Sources   Baker, Zachary M. "Problems in Judaica Cataloging." *HCL Cataloging Bulletin*, nos. 23–24 (September 1, 1976): 54-6.

Berman, Sanford. "Counter-cataloging." *Library Journal* (May 1, 1972): 1640.

———"Ethnic Access: New Approaches in Cataloging." *HCL Cataloging Bulletin*, no. 35 (July/August 1978), 1-7.

———"Golems and Goddesses." *HCL Cataloging Bulletin*, no. 22 (July 1, 1976): 29-31.

———*Prejudices and Antipathies*. Metuchen, NJ: Scarecrow Press, 1971, pp. 22-5, 35-8, 55-6, 61-3, 84, 86-8.

"Jewish Caucus Asks for 'Quick Action' on *LCSH* Bias, Omissions." *HCL Cataloging Bulletin*, no. 17 (October 1, 1975): 43-4. Discussion: *HCL Cataloging Bulletin*, no. 20 (March 1, 1976): 3-4.

Kersten, Dorothy B. *Subject Headings for Church or Synagogue Libraries*. Bryn Mawr, PA: Church and Synagogue Library Association, 1978, p. 13.

Westby, Barbara M., ed. *Sears List of Subject Headings*. 11th ed. New York: H.W. Wilson, 1977, pp. 256, 308, 310-1.

Access to Alternatives

It's not enough to simply *acquire* alternative and small press materials. They must also be made easily accessible to library users by means of intelligible, accurate, and generous cataloging.

Most libraries depend heavily, if not totally, on MARC, OCLC, and similar sources for their bibliographic data (i.e., complete records for specific works). And even when such data aren't immediately available through the "tube," on cards, or in the form of Cataloging-in-Publication, libraries tend to rely upon standard Library of Congress practices and tools (like the LC subject heading scheme) to perform in-house, "original" cataloging. This reliance on uniform rules and "authorities" seems eminently sensible and economic. In fact, however, it isn't. For when LC and its imitators catalog an "alternative" or small press item, the results are ordinarily pathetic, characterized by a failure to:

- Assign sufficient subject headings and other added entries (i.e., access points).
- Adequately and helpfully indicate special features or content elements not discernible from the title alone.
- Employ subject terms that faithfully and precisely express what the material is about—in familiar, unbiased language.

If alternative media are, indeed, regularly under- or miscataloged, then much of the money and effort expended on securing and processing them is wasted. The remedy for this malaise is either to catalog them independently of LC or to deliberately correct, expand, and improve the usual "outside copy," as well as employing basic tools—like *LCSH*—in a critical fashion.

Reprinted with the permission of Neal-Schuman, Inc. from *Collection Building*, Special issue, v. 2, no. 2. © 1980 Neal-Schuman Publishers, Inc.

To aid in fairly and effectively cataloging small press, radical, ethnic, women's, and "New Age" works, here are a few guidelines, followed by graphic, comparative examples:

1. Make added entries for sponsoring, producing, or otherwise closely associated presses, groups, and agencies; and, for informational purposes, provide *public notes* in the catalog that briefly identify such producers and organizations.

Guidelines

● Sample added entries

Blofeld, John.
   Taoism; the road to immortality. Shambhala, 1978.
     I. Shambhala Publications.

Entrance: 4 Chicano poets...
   Greenfield Review Press, copyright 1975.
     I. Greenfield Review Press.

Kleyman, Paul, 1945–
   Senior power: growing old rebelliously. Glide Publications, copyright 1974.
     I. Glide Publications

Bruchac, Joseph, 1942–
   compiler.
   Words from the house of the dead; prison writings from Soledad . . . Crossing Press, copyright 1974.
     I. Crossing Press.

Krivananda.
   Eastern thoughts, Western thoughts. Ananda Publications, copyright 1973.
     I. Ananda Publications.

Lesbian lives; biographies of women from The ladder . . .
   Diana Press, copyright 1976.
     I. Diana Press

● Sample notes

Shambhala Publications.
   Here are entered materials produced by a San Francisco house "dedicated to exploring and mapping man's inner world, and to expressing creatively the potential of man's inner evolution through the medium of books of quality."

Diana Press.
   Here are entered materials produced by an Oakland, California, press that publishes "feminst books by women, for women."

New Glide Publications.
   Here are entered materials produced by a nonprofit, community-based press in San Francisco which emphasizes women's issues and new lifestyles. Founded in 1968 as Glide Publications, a program of the Glide Foundation, the press in early 1977 became completely independent.

Kids Can Press.
   Here are entered materials issued by a press "formed to provide Canadian urban children with an alternative literature reflecting their own environment, and to counter damaging sexual stereotypes found in most children's books."

Feminist Press.
Here are entered works issued by a non-profit press that specializes in "reprints of neglected women's writings, biographies, & materials for non-sexist curriculum at every educational level."

Crossing Press.
Here are entered materials issued by a Trumansburg, New York, press that specializes in "books that people need, i.e., food for spirit, body, and soul: poetry books, cookbooks, and children's stories."

Liberation Support Movement.
Here are entered materials produced by an organization, founded in 1968, "whose purpose is to raise North American consciousness of and solidarity with national liberation movements."

West End Press.
Here are entered materials produced by a Cambridge, Massachusetts, house dedicated to "recapturing the common experience of . . . writers of the 30s—a collective experience of expression, a sharing of social and personal understanding, a common solidarity against poverty and the threat of war and fascism."

Booklegger Press.
Here are entered works issued by a "feminist collective of information freaks" in San Francisco.

Urban Information Interpreters, Inc.
Here are entered materials produced by a Washington-based organization that seeks to "attack . . . poverty, racism and repression in the social system . . . through information access."

2. Make added entries for subtitles and catch-titles that catalog users may remember and seek.

• Sample title added-entries

Bruchac, Joseph, 1942- compiler.
Words from the house of the dead; prison writings from Soledad.

I. Title. II. Title: Prison writings from Soledad. III. Title: The house of the dead. IV. Title: Soledad prison writings.

Kleyman, Paul, 1945-
Senior power; growing old rebelliously.

I. Title. II. Title: Growing old rebelliously.

Entrance: 4 Chicano poets...

I. Title: 4 Chicano poets. II. Title: Chicano poets.

Krivananda.
Eastern thoughts, Western thoughts . . .

I. Title. II. Title: Western thoughts, Eastern thoughts.

3. Impose no upper limit on subject tracings, applying as many as necessary to substantially and accurately reflect the content of each work.

4. Assign subject tracings to novels, short stories, poetry, and other literary genres on the same basis as subject tracings are assigned to nonfiction.

5. Reform biased, imprecise, clumsy, or antique subject descriptors that misrepresent, defame, or obscure the topics they ostensibly denote; e.g.,

Use	Instead of
COLONIZED PEOPLES	NATIVE RACES
FILMS	MOVING–PICTURES
FREEDOM OF SPEECH [THE PRESS, etc.]	LIBERTY OF SPEECH [THE PRESS, etc.]
GUN CONTROL	FIREARMS—LAWS AND REGULATIONS
MIDDLE EAST	NEAR EAST
MULTINATIONAL CORPORA-TIONS	CORPORATIONS, INTER-NATIONAL
NEW RELIGIOUS MOVEMENTS	RELIGIONS, MODERN
RECORDS	PHONORECORDS or SOUND RECORDINGS
TAPES	PHONOTAPES
THIRD WORLD	UNDERDEVELOPED AREAS
TRADITIONAL RELIGION	RELIGION, PRIMITIVE
UNITED STATES—COLONIES	UNITED STATES—TERRITORIES AND POSSESSIONS and UNITED STATES—INSULAR POSSESSIONS
WORKING CLASSES	LABOR AND LABORING CLASSES
WORLD WAR, 1914–1918	EUROPEAN WAR, 1914–1918

6. Establish new descriptors to represent subjects not currently "legitimized" nor recognized in the LC thesaurus. For instance, as of early 1980, *none* of these terms—each the unquestionable theme or genre of already cataloged works—appears in *LCSH*:

ACID RAIN	ANIMAL LIBERATION
AFRICAN [GAY, INDIAN, JEWISH, SLAVE, WOMEN'S, etc.] RESISTANCE AND REVOLTS	ANTI-NUCLEAR MOVEMENT
	APARTHEID
	APPROPRIATE TECHNOLOGY
AGEISM	BAKKE CASE
AGRIBUSINESS	"BEAT" FICTION [POETRY, etc.]
ALTERNATIVE ENERGY SOURCES	CATHOLIC RADICALISM
	CLASS STRUGGLE
ALTERNATIVE LIFESTYLES	CLASSISM
ALTERNATIVE MEDICINE	COLLECTIVES
ANARCHA–FEMINISM	CONSUMER ADVOCACY

DECENTRALIZATION
DECRIMINALIZATION OF
  MARIJUANA
DECRIMINALIZATION OF
  PROSTITUTION
DEPROGRAMING
DISABILITY RIGHTS
  MOVEMENT
ECO-FICTION
EDELIN CASE
EUROCOMMUNISM
EX-CONVICTS—RIGHTS
FAMILY PLANNING
FARM ORGANIZING
FEMINIST ESSAYS [FICTION,
  FILMS, POETRY, etc.]
FOOD AS A WEAPON
FOOD CO-OPS
FORT WORTH FIVE
FREE CLINICS
FREE UNIVERSITIES
GASOHOL
GAY RIGHTS
GHETTOES
HANDICAPISM
HOLISTIC HEALTH
HOMESTEADING
HOSPICES
INNER CITY
KOREAN LOBBYING
  SCANDAL
LABOR EDUCATION
LABOR ORGANIZING
LABOR PERIODICALS
  [SONGS, etc.]
LABOR SOLIDARITY
LIBERTARIANISM
MANDATORY DEPOSIT
  LEGISLATION
MEDICAID AND ABORTION
MENTAL PATIENTS' LIBERA-
  TION MOVEMENT
MILITARY EXPENDITURES
MILITARY-INDUSTRIAL
  COMPLEX

MIND CONTROL
MINORITY WOMEN
NAZIS
NEOCOLONIALISM
NEOPAGANISM
"NEW AGE"
NEW LEFT
NEW RIGHT
NUCLEAR POWER AND
  CANCER
NUCLEAR POWER AND CIVIL
  RIGHTS
PATIENTS' RIGHTS
POLICE RIOTS
POLICE SHOOTINGS
PROLETARIAN FICTION
PUNK ROCK MUSIC
RADICAL THEATER
RED POWER
ROSENBERG CASE
SELF-CARE
SELF-HELP LAW
SELF-HELP PSYCHOLOGY
SELF-MANAGEMENT [or
  WORKERS' CONTROL]
SILKWOOD CASE
SIMPLE LIFE
SKILL-SHARING
SKOKIE CASE
SUSPECTS' RIGHTS
TENANTS' RIGHTS
TENANTS' UNIONS
TRAIL OF BROKEN TREATIES,
  1972
UJAMAA VILLAGES
UNDERGROUND COMIC
  BOOKS, STRIPS, ETC.
UNEMPLOYED
  ORGANIZING
WAGES FOR HOUSEWORK
  MOVEMENT
WOMEN'S MOVEMENT
WOMEN'S SHELTERS
YOUTH LIBERATION

(The Hennepin County Library *Authority File*, semiannual *New Periodicals Index*, Alternative Press Centre subject heading list, and Joan Marshall's *On Equal Terms* may prove helpful in establishing new forms; but daily newspapers, TV, radio, and the alternative product itself—whether a magazine, book, film, pamphlet, tape, record, or poster—constitute the best, most contemporary and authentic guides or "authorities.")

7. Compose notes to clarify contents, indicate special features, and show relationships to other works, persons, or groups.

LC/OCLC	**Alternative**

Seldman, Neil N.
  Common'sense radicalism. Mutualist Books, c1977.

  1. Environmental policy—United States. 2. Decentralization in government—United States. I. Title.

Seldman, Neil N.
  Common sense radicalism. Mutualist Books, copyright 1977.

  1. Radicalism—United States. 2. Appropriate technology. 3. Decentalization. 4. Community organization. 5. Alternative economics. I. Mutualist books. II. Title.

Madness network news reader.
  Edited by Sherry Hirsch [and others]. Glide Publications [1974].

  Essays, poems, letters, and graphics from the Madness network news.
  Bibliography: p. 187–92.

  1. Psychiatry—Addresses, essays, lectures. I. Hirsch, Sherry, 1947-comp. II. Madness network news.

Madness network news reader;
  edited by Sherry Hirsch and others. Glide Publications, 1974.

  Essays, poems, letters, graphics, and reading lists from the Madness network news.
  PARTIAL CONTENTS: The madhouse.-The cure. Old treatments. Current treatment: shock therapy, psychosurgery and drugs. The politics of hospitalization. The final "solution."-The resistance.

  1. Antipsychiatry. 2. Mental Patients' Liberation Movement. 3. Psychiatric malpractice. 4. Shock therapy. 5. Psychiatric hospitals. I. Hirsch, Sherry, 1947-compiler. II. Madness network news. III. Glide Publications.

Resources for Community Change.
  Gonna rise again! Economic organizing for hard times . . . R.C.C., 1976.

  1. Labor and laboring classes—United States—Political activity—Addresses, essays, lectures. 2. Unemployed—United States—Addresses, essays, lectures. I. Title.

Resources for Community Change.
  Gonna rise again! Economic organizing for hard times . . . R.C.C., 1976

  1. Unemployment—United States. 2. Working classes—United States. 3. Strikes and lockouts—Handbooks, manuals, etc. 4. Labor oganizing. 5. Labor education. I. Title. II. Title: Economic organizing for hard times. III. Title: Organizing for hard times.

Epica Task Force.
  Puerto Rico: a people challenging colonialism; a people's primer . . . Epica, 1976.

  1. Puerto Rico—Economic conditions—1918-2. Puerto Rico—Polictics and government—1952-3. Puerto Rico—History—1952- I. Title.

Epica Task Force.
  Puerto Rico: a people challenging colonialism; a people's primer . . . Epica, 1976.

  1. Puerto Rican resistance and revolts. 2. Colonized peoples—Puerto Rico. 3. United States—colonies.

San Francisco Women's History Group.
  What have women done? . . . United Front Press, 1975.

  "A photo essay on the history of working women in the United States."

  1. Women—United States—History. 2. Women—United States—Employment. 3. Feminist—United States—History. I. Title.

San Francisco Women's History Group.
  What have women done? . . . United Front Press, 1975.

  "A photo essay on the history of working women in the United States."

  1. Women workers—United States—History—Pictoral works. 2. Women labor unionists—United States—History—Pictorial works. 3. Working class women—United States—History—Pictorial works. I. United Front Press. II. Title.

LC/OCLC

Franke, Richard W.
   East Timor: the hidden war . . . East Timor Defense Committee, 1976.

   1. Timor, Portuguese—History.
   1. Fretilin. 2. National liberation movements—East Timor. 3. Colonized peoples—East Timor. 4. East Timor. I. East Timor Defense Committee. II. Title. III. Title: The hidden war.

Ehrenreich, Barbara.
   Complaints and disorders; the sexual politics of sickness. By Barbara Ehrenreich and Deirdre English . . . Feminist Press, 1973.

   (Glass Mountain pamphlet, no. 2.)

   1. Women—Health and hygiene—Sociological aspects. 2. Gynecology—History. I. English, Deirdre, joint author. II. Title

Edwards, Alison.
   Rape, racism, and the white women's movement; an answer to Susan Brownmiller . . . Sojourner Truth Organization, 1975?

   1. Rape. 2. Race problems. 3. Brownmiller, Susan. Against our will: men, women and rape. I. Title.

Mass, Bonnie.
   Population target: the political economy of population control in Latin American . . . Latin American Working Group, 1976.

   1. Birth control—Latin America. 2. Birth control—Economic aspects—Latin America. 3. Latin America—Population. I. Latin American Working Group. II. Title.

Nguyen Khiac Vien.
   Tradition and revolution in Vietnam . . . Indochina Resource Center, 1974.
   CONTENTS: Some reflections on ending the war.-The judo lesson-Confucianism and Marxism in Vietnam.-Water, rice, and men.-The Vietnamese experience and the Third World.-The American war: an interview with Jeune Afrique.-The old banyan tree.

   1. Vietnam (Democratic Republic, 1946-)—Addresses, essays, lectures. I. Title.

Alternative

Franke, Richard W.
   East Timor: the hidden war . . . East Timor Defense Committee, 1976
PARTIAL CONTENTS: Fretilin: East Timor's genuine liberation movement.-Indonesia goes to war.-Washington's hand in the invasion. 1. Fretilin. 2. National liberation movements—East Timor. 3. Colonized peoples—East Timor. 4. East Timor. I. East Timor Defense Committee. II. Title. III. Title: The hidden war.

Ehrenreich, Barbara.
   Complaints and disorders; the sexual politics of sickness. By Barbara Ehrenreich and Deirdre English . . . Feminist Press, 1973.

   (Glass Mountain pamphlets no. 2)

   1. Sexism in medicine. 2. Sexism in gynecology. I. English, Deirdre, joint author. II Feminist Press. III. Title: The sexual politics of sickness. IV. Title: Disorders and complaints. V. Title. VI. Series.

Edwards, Alison.
   Rape, racism, and the white women's movement; an answer to Susan Brownmiller . . . Sojourner Truth Organization, 1975?

   1. Rape. 2. Racism. 3. Brownmiller, Susan. Against our will: men, women, and rape. 4. Women's movement. I. Sojourner Truth Organization. II. Title. III. Title: The white women's movement.

Mass, Bonnie.
   Population target; the political economy of population control in Latin America . . . Latin American Working Group, 1976.

   1. Birth control—Latin America. 2. Population control—Latin America. 3. Latin America—Population. 4. Imperialism, American—Latin America. I. Latin American Working Group. II. Title: III. Title: Population control in Latin America.

Nguyen Khiac Vien.
   Tradition and revolution in Vietnam . . . Indochina Resource Center, 1974.
   PARTIAL CONTENTS: Some reflections on ending the war.-Confucianism and Marxism in Vietnam.-The Vietnamese experience and the Third World.-The American war: an interview with Jeune Afrique.

   1. Vietnam—History. 2. Revolutions—Vietnam. 3. Communism—Vietnam. 4. National liberation movements—Vietnam. I. Indochina Resource Center. II. Title.

LC/OCLC

Ehrenreich, Barbara
    Witches, midwives, and nurses; a history of women healers. Barbara Ehrenreich and Deirdre English . . . Feminist Press, 1978.

    (Glass Mountain pamphlet, no. 1)

    1. Midwifery. 2. Women. I. English, Deirdre. II. Title.

International Telephone and Telegraph
    Corporation.
    Subversion in Chile: a case study in U.S. corporate intrigue in the Third World . . . Bertrand Russell Peace Foundation, 1972.

    (Spokesman books)

    "The documents reproduced in this book are the internal memoranda of the ITT-International Telephone and Telegraph Corporation . . ."
    On spine: ITT-CIA: subversion in Chile.

    1. International Telephone and Telegraph Corporation. 2. Chile—Politics and government—1970. 3. United States—Foreign relations—Chile. 4. Chile—Foreign relations—United States. I. Bertrand Russell Peace Foundation. II. Title. III. Title: ITT-CIA: subversion in Chile.

Klare, Michael T., 1942-
    Supplying repression . . . Field Foundation, 1977.

    1. Military assistance, American. 2. Civil rights. 3. Political rights. I. Field Foundation. II. Title.

Bergman, Arlene Eisen.
    Women of Viet Nam . . . Peoples Press, 1975.

    1. Women—Vietnam. 2. Feminism—Vietnam. I. Title.

Alternative

Ehrenreich, Barbara.
    Witches, midwives, and nurses; a history of women healers. By Barbara Ehrenreich and Deirdre English . . . Feminist Press, 1978.

    (Glass Mountain pamphlets, no. 1)

    1. Midwifery. 2. Women physicians. 3. Sexism in medicine. 4. Women medical personnel. I. English, Deirdre, joint author. II. Feminist Press. III. Title. IV. Title: Women healers: a history. V. Title: Nurses, witches, and midwives. VI. Title: Midwives, witches, and nurses. VII. Series: Glass Mountain pamphlets, no. 1.

Subversion in Chile; a case study in
    U.S. corporate intrigue in the Third World . . . Bertrand Russell Peace Foundation, 1972.

    (Spokesman books)

    "The documents reproduced . . . are the internal memoranda of the ITT . . ."
    On spine: ITT-CIA: subversion in Chile.

    1. International Telephone and Telegraph Corporation. 2. Chile—Politics and government—1970-. 3. United States—Foreign relations—Chile. 4. Chile—Foreign relations—United States. 5. Imperialism, American—Chile. 6. Corporate accountability. 7. Multinational corporations—Case studies. I. Bertrand Russell Peace Foundation. II. International Telephone and Telegraph Corporation. III. Title: ITT-CIA: subversion in Chile. IV. Title: CIA-ITT: subversion in Chile. V. Title: U.S. corporate intrigue in the Third World. VI. Series.

Klare, Michael T., 1942-
    Supplying repression . . . Field Foundation, 1977.

    1. Military assistance, American—Third World. 2. Repression, Political—Third World. 3. Police—Third World. 4. Military-industrial complex—United States I. Institute for Policy Studies. II. Title.

Bergman, Arlene Eisen.
    Women of Viet Nam . . . Peoples Press, 1975.

    1. Women—Vietnam. 2. Feminism—Vietnam. 3. Sexism—Vietnam. 4. Women's resistance and revolts—Vietnam. I. Peoples Press. II. Title.

LC/OCLC

Alternative

The History book . . . Peace Press, 1977, c1974.

1. World history—Pictorial works. 2. Europe—History. 3. Africa—History. I. Rydberg, Phal. II. Schmorleitz, Carol Baum.

The History book . . . Peace Press, 1977, copyright 1974.

1. World history—Pictorial works. 2. Europe—History. 3. Africa—History. 4. Imperialism—History. 5. Third World—History. 6. Capitalism—History. 7. Colonized peoples—History. 8. Working classes—History. I. Rydberg, Phal, joint author. II. Schmorleitz, Carol Baum, translator. III. Peace Press.

West, Celeste.
The passionate perils of publishing. By Celeste West and Valerie Wheat . . . Booklegger Press, 1978.

1. Publishers and publishing. 2. Authorship—Handbooks, manuals, etc. 3. Publishing as a profession. I. Wheat, Valerie. II. Title. III. Title: Booklegger's guide to: The passionate perils of publishing.

West, Celeste.
The passionate perils of publishing. By Celeste West and Valerie Wheat . . . Booklegger Press, 1978.

Cover title: Booklegger's guide to the passionate perils of publishing.
PARTIAL CONTENTS: The literary-industrial complex. Publishers owned by conglomerates. Publishers' merger mania.-Roll yr own: a guide for new publishers, self-publishers, and authors.-Discovering the wild & free press. Guides, directories, indexes. Alternative review & news media. Selected distributors.-Feminists in print.-Kids' liberated literature.-The library free press.

1. Self-publishing 2. Publishers and publishing. 3. Alternative press—Directories. 4. Small press publication—bibliography. 5. Small press distributors—Directories. 6. Alternative press—Bibliography. 7. Women's publishers and publishing—Directories. 8. Women's publishers and publishing—Bibliography. 9. Children's literature, Nonsexist—Publishing—Directories. 10. Libraries—Periodicals—Bibliography. 11. Big business and publishing. I. Wheat, Valerie, joint author. II. Booklegger Press. III. Title. IV. Title: The perils of publishing.

Kleps, Art.
Millbrook: the true story of the early years of the psychedelic revolution . . . Bench Press, c1977.

1.Hallucinations and illusions. 2. Leary, Timothy Francis, 1920- 3. Millbrook, N.Y. I. Title.

Kelps, Art.
Millbrook: the true story of the early years of the psychedelic revolution . . . Bench Press, copyright 1977.

1. Leary, Timothy Francis, 1920- 2. Millbrook, New York. 3. Psychedelic experience. I. Bench Press. II. Title. III. Title: The psychedelic revolution.

LC/OCLC

Butler, Sandra, 1938-
  Conspiracy of silence; the trauma of incest . . .
New Glide Publications, c1978.

  1. Incest. 2. Sex crimes—United States. I. Title.

The Briarpatch book . . . New Glide Publications;
  Reed Book, 1978.

  A collection of 1st 8 issues of the Briarpatch
review.

  1. Small business—Management—Addresses,
essays, lectures.

The history of shock treatment . . .

  Bibliography. . . .
  Includes indexes.

  1. Shock therapy—History—Addresses, essays,
lectures. I. Frank, Leonard Roy, 1932-

Chutzpah Collective.
  Chutzpah. . . .

  Bibliography. . . .

  1. Jews—History—20th century—Addresses, essays, lectures. I. Title.

Alternative

Butler, Sandra, 1938-
  Conspiracy of silence; the trauma of incest . . .
New Glide Publications, copyright 1978.

  PARTIAL CONTENTS: The children.-the
agressors.-The mothers.-The family.-History of a
survivor.

  1. Incestuous assault. 2. Incest victim services.
I. New Glide Publications. II. Title. III. Title: The
trauma of incest.

The Briarpatch book . . . New Glide Publications;
  Reed Books, 1978.

  Reprint of Briarpatch review: a journal of right
livelihood & simple living, issues 1–8, Spring
1975– Autumn 1977.

  1. Briarpatch Network. 2. Small business. 3.
Skill-sharing. 4. Alternative economics. 5. Alternative lifestyles. 6. Appropriate technology. 7. Simple life. I. New Glide Publications. II. Reed Books.
III. Title: Briarpatch review book. IV. Title: Right
livelihood book. V. Title: Simple living book.

Frank, Leonard Roy, 1932- editor.
  The history of shock treatment. Edited and published by Leonard Roy Frank. Copyright 1978.

  Includes "chronologically arranged selections"
and "four original articles," as well as "ECT death
chronology," "Shock doctor roster," glossary, and
bibliographies.

  1. Insulin shock therapy—History. 2. Electric
shock therapy—History. 3. Metrazol shock therapy—History. 4. Shock therapy—History. 5. Shock
therapy—Bibliography. 6. Anti-psychiatry. 7. Psychiatric malpractice. 8. Patients' rights. 9. Mental Patients' Liberation Movement. I. Title. II. Title: ECT
death chronology. III. Title: Shock doctor roster.

Chutzpah Collective.
  Chutzpah: a Jewish liberation anthology. Edited
by Steven Lubet and others. New Glide Publications,
copyright 1977.

  PARTIAL CONTENTS: Singing in a strange land:
Jewish life in America. Role models for Jewish women. The Jewish sorority: sisterhood perverted. Why
we write about Gay Liberation.-Anti Semitism.-The
joy of socialism, the heartbreak of capitalism.-Two
peoples, two states: Self-determination in the Middle
East.-In forests and ghettos: Jewish resistance to the
Nazis.-The Rosenberg case: we are all your children.

LC/OCLC

Chutzpah Collective (cont'd)

Brown, Rita Mae.
   Rubyfruit jungle . . . Daughters, inc. [973]

   I. Title.

Callenbach, Ernest.
   Ecotopia: the notebooks and reports of William
Weston . . . Banyan Tree Books . . . [1975]

   I. Title.

Maury, Inez, 1909-
   My mother the mail carrier-Mi mama la cartera . . .
illustrated by Lady McCrady; translated by Norah E.
Alemany . . . Feminist Press, c1976.

   English and Spanish.
   SUMMARY: A five-year-old describes the loving
and close relationship she has with her mother, a
mail carrier, and also relates some aspects of her
mother's job.

   1. Spanish language—Readers. [1. Mothers and
daughters—Fiction. 2. Mothers—Employment—
Fiction. 3. Postal service—Letter carriers—Fiction.
4. Spanish language—Readers.] I. McCrady, Lady.
II. Title. III. Title: Mi mama la cartera.

I.F. Stone's weekly (Motion picture).
   I.F. Stone Project, 1973.
   Made by Jerry Bruck, Jr.

   SUMMARY: Presents a portrait of Izzy Stone, who
created a newspaper to bring the truth to the common man.

   1. Stone, Isidor F., 1907– I. Stone (I.F.) Project
(Firm).

Alternative

(cont'd)
   1. Jewish radicalism. 2. Jewish gays. 3. Jewish
resistance and revolts. 4. Anti-Semitism. 5. Jewish
women. 6. Jewish-Americans. 7. Israeli-Arab relations. 8. Sexism in Judaism. 9. Rosenberg Case. I.
Libet, Steven, editor. II. New Glide Publications. III.
Title. IV. Title: Jewish liberation anthology.

Brown, Rita Mae.
   Rubyfruit jungle. Daughters, 1973.

   1. Lesbians—Fiction. 2. Women radicals—Fiction.
3. Feminist fiction. I. Daughters, inc. II. Title. III. Title:
Ruby fruit jungle.

Calenbach, Ernest.
   Ecotopia: the notebooks and reports of William
Weston . . . Banyan Tree Books . . . 1975.

   1. Ecology—Northwestern States—Fiction. 2.
Eco-fiction. 3. Utopias—Fiction. 4. Alternative
economics—Fiction. 5. Appropriate technology—
Fiction. I. Banyan Tree Books. II. Title.

Maury, Inez, 1909-
   My mother the mail carrier: Mi mama la cartera.
Illustrated by Lady McCrady. Translated by Norah E.
Alemany. Feminist Press, copyright 1976.

   In English and Spanish.

   1. Mother and daughter—Fiction. 2. Working
mothers—Fiction. 3. Five-year-olds—Fiction. 4. Mail
carriers—Fiction. 5. Children's literature, Nonsexist.
6. Bilingual materials—English/Spanish. 7. Single-
parent family—Fiction. 8. Latino families—Fiction. 9.
Children's literature, Spanish. I. McCrady, Lady, illustrator. II. Title: Mama la cartera. III. Title. IV. Title:
Mi mama la cartera.

I.F. Stone's weekly (Motion picture).
   I.F. Stone Project, 1973.   Made by Jerry Bruck,
Jr. Distributed by Open Circle Cinema.

   SUMMARY: A profile of reporter, social critic, and
antiwar activist "Izzy" Stone, whose Weekly made
journalistic history because of its candor, independence, and exposés.
   1. Journalists, Jewish-American. 2. Stone, Isidor F.,
1907- 3. Radical journalists. 4. Investigative journalism. 5. Journalism, Political. I. Bruck, Jerry. II. Open
Circle Cinema. III. Title: Stone's weekly.

LC/OCLC

Alternative

Joyce at 34 (Motion picture).   Joyce Chopra and
Claudia Weill. Released by New Day Films,
1973.

SUMMARY: Tells how an independent filmmaker
and her husband face new challenges when they
become parents. Shows how both wife and husband
struggle to adapt to the sudden stress caused by a
conflict of career, love, and male privilege.

1. Family. 2. Parent and child. 3. Role playing. I.
Chopra, Joyce. II. Weill, Claudia. III. New day Films.

Joyce at 34 (Motion picture).   Joyce Chopra and
Claudia Weill. Released by New Day Films,
1973.

SUMMARY: Examines the life of a filmmaker/
mother and her family, including segments dealing
with the husband's role and with the grandmother
and her friends who earlier had to decide between
career and family.

1. Women filmmakers. 2. Working mothers. 3.
Father and child. 4. Sex role. 5. Feminist films. 6.
Women's films. I. Chopra, Joyce. II. Weill, Claudia.
III. New Day Films.

Shange, Ntozake.
Sassafrass . . . Shameless Hussy Press, c1976.

I. Title

Shange, Ntozake.
Sassafrass . . . Shameless Hussy Press, copyright
1976.

1. Afro-American women—Fiction. 2. Feminist fiction. I. Shameless Hussy Press. II. Title.

Men's lives (Motion picture).   Josh Hanig and Will
Roberts. Released by New Day Films,   1974.

SUMMARY: Uses a series of candid interviews in
order to show what American boys and men believe
about the American concept of masculinity.

1. Men. 2. Boys. 3. Masculinity (Psychology)—
Public opinion. 4. National characteristics,
American—Public opinion. I. Hanig, Josh. II.
Roberts, Will. III. New Day Films.

Men's lives (Motion picture). Josh Hanig & Will
Roberts. Released by New Day Films, 1975.

SUMMARY: Documentary about masculinity in
America, examining society's influence on men and
how men view both themselves and women.

1. Academy Award films. 2. Men—Lifestyles. 3.
Manhood (Psychology). 4. Sex role. 5. Men's libera-
tion. 6. Men—Interviews. 7. Boys—Interviews. I.
Hanig, Josh. II. Roberts, Will. III. New Day Films.

Angola: Victory is certain   (Phonodisc). Paredon
Records . . . [1970]

Title on slipcase: A vitoria e certa.
"Songs of the liberation army of MPLA. Recorded
in the liberated zones by members of the Liberation
Support Movement."

Angola: Victory is certain   (Phonograph record).
Songs of the Liberation Army of MPLA (Movimento
Popular de Libertacao de Angola) Paredon. . .1970.

Title on slipcase: a vitoria e certa.
"Recorded in the liberated zones by members of
the Liberation Support Movement."

LC/OCLC

Angola: Victory is certain (cont'd)

Sung in Portuguese and Mbunda.
Words of the songs, with English translations and notes . . . inserted in slipcase

1. Movimento Popular de Libertacao de Angola—Songs and music. 2. Songs, Angolan. I. Title: Victory is certain. II. Title: A vitoria e certa.

[No entry found]

[No entry found]

[No entry found]

[No entry found]

Alternative

(cont'd)

Sung in Portuguese and Mbunda.
Includes text with English translations and notes .

1. Songs, Angolan. 2. Movimento Popular de Libertacao de Angola—Songs and music. 3. Revolutionary ballads and songs, Angolan. 4. National liberation movements—Angola—Songs and music. I. Paredon Records. II. Liberation Support Movement. III. Title: Victory is certain. IV. Title: A vitoria e certa. V. Title: Songs of the Liberation Army of MPLA.

The politics of prostitution: resources for legal change. Written Jennifer James and others. 2d ed. Social Research Associates, 1977.

1. Prostitution, Female—Law and legislation. 2. Decriminalization of prostitution. I. James, Jennifer, joint author. II. Social Research Associates.

Spiritual community guide #4. Spirtual Community Publications/NAM, copyright 1978.

PARTIAL CONTENTS: Resources for a new age. Whole mind/whole body. Education. Community. Mother earth. Science & technology. Arts.-Guide to spiritual growth centers.-Community directory.

1. "New Age" centers, oranizations, etc.—Directories. 2. Therapeutic centers, groups, etc.—Directories. 3. Occult centers, organizations, etc.—Directories, 4. Cults—United States—Directories. 5. Counter-culture—United States—Directories. I. Spiritual Community Publications. II. Title: Spiritual growth centers guide.

Lyons, Gracie.
Constructive criticism: a handbook. Issues in Radical Therapy, copyright 1976.

1. Self-help psychology. 2. Criticizing. 3. Defensiveness (Psychology). 4. Self-criticism. I. Issues in Radical Therapy. II. Title.

MacNeil, Rita.
Born a woman (Phonograph record). Boot Records . . . 1975.

1. Feminist songs. 2. Women—Songs and music. I. Boot Records. II. Title.

LC/OCLC

Alternative

[No entry found]

Virgo rising (Phonograph record).
   The once and future woman.
Thunderbird . . . 1973.

   "Songs of sisterhood," written and performed by
Malvina Reynolds, Janet Smith, Charley's Aunts,
Nancy Raven, Kit Miller, Mollie Gregory, and Joan
Lowe.

   1. Feminist songs. I. Reynolds, Malvina. II. Raven,
Nancy. III. Charley's Aunts (Musical group). IV.
Smith, Janet. V. Gregory, Mollie. VI. Title: The once
and future woman.

[No entry found]

Continuous woman (Motion picture). Twin Cities Women's Film Collective, copyright 1974

   SUMMARY: Studies the strengths and alternatives
of women through the eyes of five women who recognize their own strengths.

   1. Alternative lifestyles. 2. Women—Interviews. 3.
Women—Social conditions. 4. Sex role. 5. Lesbian-
ism. 6. Women—Minneapolis. 7. Women's films. I.
Twin Cities Women's Film Collective.

[No entry found]

My people are my home (Motion picture). Twin Cities
   Women's Film Collective. Released by Femme
   Films, copyright 1976.

   SUMMARY: Examines Midwestern women's history through the writing and life of Meridel LeSueur,
Minnesota poet and novelist. Uses historical photographs and film footage.

   1. Women's films. 2. Women—Middle West
(United States)—History. 3. Authors, Women. 4.
LeSueur, Meridel. I. Twin Cities Women's Film Col-
lective. II. Femme Films.

[No entry found]

Mountaingrove, Ruth.
   Turned on woman songbook. New Woman Press,
1975.

   Includes 29 songs.
   PARTIAL CONTENTS: Be a woman for yourself.-
Invisible woman.-Love song.-Turned on woman.-
Vision.-Witches song.

   1. Feminist songs. 2. Women—Songs and music.
I. New Woman Press. II. Title. III. Title: Invisible women. IV. Title: Witches song.

LC/OCLC

Alternative

[No entry found]

All our Lives: a women's songbook.
Edited by Joyce Cheney, Marcia Deihl, and Deborah Silverstein. Diana Press, copyright 1976.

"Theory, words and music ('The bloods,' 'I'm tired of fuckers fucking over,' 'Bread and roses,' and dozens more), a reference list, other resources such as tapes, songbooks, records, and photos."

1. Women—Songs and music. 2. Music, Popular (Songs, etc.)—United States. 3. Feminist songs. 4. women's music. I. Deihl, Marcia, 1949-editor. II. Cheney, Joyce, 1950-editor. III. Silverstein, Deborah, 1949-editor. IV. Diana Press. V. Title: A women's songbook. VI. Title: The bloods. VII. Title: Bread and roses.

Alloy, Evelyn.
Working women's music: the songs and struggles of women in the mills, textile plants and needle trades; complete with music for playing . . . [Musical notation by Martha Rogers] . . . New England Free Press, c 1976.

1. Work-songs. 2. Textile workers—Songs and music. I. Rogers, Martha. II. Title.

Alloy, Evelyn.
Working women's music: the songs and struggles of women in the mills, textile plants and needle trades. Complete with music for playing . . . Musical notation by Martha Rogers . . . New England Free Press, copyright 1976.
PARTIAL CONTENTS: The rebel girl.-Bread and roses.-Solidarity forever.-The union is our leader.-Which side are you on?

1. Work-songs. 2. Textile workers—Songs and music. 3. Women workers—Songs and music. 4. Labor songs. 5. Radical songs. 6. Women's music. I. Rogers, Martha, joint author. II. New England Free Press. III. Title: The rebel girl. IV. Title: Bread and roses. V. Title: Solidarity forever. VI. Title: The union is our leader. VII. Title: Which side are you on? VIII. Title.

LeSueur, Meridel.
Song for my time: stories of the period of repression . . . West End Press, 1977.

I. Title.

LeSueur, Meridel.
Song for my time: stories of the period of repression . . . West End Press, 1977.

1. Proletarian fiction. 2. Short stories, American. 3. Repression, Political—United States—Fiction. 4. Radicalism—United States—Fiction. 5. Working classes—United States—Fiction. I. West End Press. II. Title.

Organize! A working women's handbook [Jean Maddox . . . et al.] . . . Union W.A.G.E. Educational Committee, 1975

1. Trade-unions—United States. 2. Women in trade-unions—United States. I. Maddox, Jean.

Organize! A working women's handbook. By Jean Maddox and others . . . Union W.A.G.E. Educational Committee, 1975.

1. Women workers. 2. Women labor unionists. 3. Labor organizing. I. Maddox, Jean, joint author. II. Union W.A.G.E. Educational Committee. III. Title: A working women's handbook.

LC/OCLC

Babson, Steve.
   Why do we spend so much money? [By Steve Babson, designed, edited and illustrated] by Nancy Brigham . . . Popular Economics Press, 1977.

   1. Economics. I. Brigham, Nancy, editor. II. Title.

Warrior, Betsy.
   Working on wife abuse . . . 1978.
"Publications and films" p. 64–72.

   1. Wife beating—Directories. I. Title.

Berkeley Holistic Health Center.
   The holistic health handbook: a tool for attaining wholeness of body, mind, and spirt . . . Compiled by . . . Edward Bauman . . . [et al.] . . . And/Or Press, 1978

   1. Health. 2. Therapeutics, Physiological. I. Bauman, Edward. II. Title.

Vocations for Social Change.
   No bosses here: a manual on working collectively . . . Vocations for Social Change, 1976.

   1. Cooperative societies—United States. I. Title.

Trail of broken treaties: B.I.A., I'm not your Indian anymore . . . Akwesasne Notes, 1974.

   "This book contains information published in various issues of Akwesasne notes, as well as additional information not published before."

Alternative

Babson, Steve.
   Why do we spend so much money? By Steve Babson; designed, edited, and illustrated by Nancy Brigham . . . Popular Economics Press, 1977.

   1. United States—Economic conditions. 2. Consumer education. 3. Big business—United States. 4. Capitalism. 5. Prices. 6. Finance, Personal. 7. Corporate accountability. I. Brigham, Nancy, editor. II. Popular Economics Press. III. Title.

Warrior, Betsy.
   Working on wife abuse . . . 1978.

   Directory of women's shelters, feminist counseling centers, and "women working on all aspects of wife abuse," together with an annotated list of "publications and films."
   Scope: United States and Canada.

   1. Women's shelters—Directories. 2. Feminist counseling and therapy—Directories. 3. Battered women— Bibliography. 4. Battered women—Filmography. 5. Women's projects and services—Directories. 6. Battered women—Research—Directories. 7. Wife beating—Bibliography. 8. Wife beating—Research—Directories. 9. Wife beating—Filmography. I. Title. II. Title: Wife abuse directory.

Berkeley Holistic Health Center.
   The holistic health handbook; a tool for attaining wholeness of body, mind, and spirit. Compiled by . . . Edward Bauman and others . . . And/Or Press, 1978.

   1. Holistic health. 2. Alternative medicine. I. Bauman, Edward, joint author. II. And/Or Press. III. Title.

Vocations for Social Change.
   No bosses here: a manual on working collectively. Cover and graphics by Randy Elliott; photographs by Shelley Rother. Vocations for Social Change, 1976.

   1. Collectives. I. Title. II. Title: A manual on woking collectively. III. Title: Working collectively: a manual.

Trail of broken treaties: B.I.A., I'm not your Indian anymore . . . Akwesasne Notes, 1974.

   Includes the "Twenty points of the Trail of Broken Treaties," data on the BIA Papers Case, and additional material either reprinted from Akwesasne notes and other sources or previously unpublished.

LC/OCLC

Trail of Broken Treaties (cont'd)
   1. United States, Bureau of Indian Affairs. 2. Indians of North America—Government relations. I. Akwesasne notes.

Dorfman, Ariel.
   How to read Donald Duck: imperialist ideology in the Disney comic. Ariel Dorfman, Armand Mattelart; translation and introd. by David Kunzle . . . International General, 1975.

   Translation of Para leer al Pato Donald.

   1. Comic books and children. 2. Disney (Walt) Productions. I. Mattelart, Armand, 1936– joint author. II. Title.

Morgan, Richard, 1950-
   How to challenge your local electric utility: a citizen's guide to the power industry . . . by Richard Morgan and Sandra Jerabek . . . Environmental Action Foundation, [1974].

   1. Electric utilities—United States. 2. Consumer education. 3. Political participation. I. Jerabek, Sandra, joint author. II. Title.

Alternative

(cont'd)
   1. United States. Bureau of Indian Affairs. 2. Indians of North America—Government relations. 3. Trail of Broken Treaties, 1972. 4. American Indian Movement. 5. B.I.A. Papers Case. 6. Indians of North America—Treaties. I. Akwesasne notes. II. Title: B.I.A., I'm not your Indian anymore. III. Title: I'm not your Indian anymore.

Dorfman, Ariel, 1942-
   How to read Donald Duck; imperialist ideology in the Disney comic. By Ariel Dorfman and Armand Mattelart; translation and introduction by David Kunzle . . . International General, 1975.

   "First published as Para leer al Pato Donald in Chile 1971, and since the . . . 1973 coup . . . has been banned and burned there."
   PARTIAL CONTENTS: From the child to the Noble Savage.-From the Noble Savage to the Third World.-Ideas machine.-Conclusion: power to Donald Duck?-Selected bibliography of Marxist writings on cultural imperialism and comics.

   1. Censorship—Chile—Case studies. 2. Disney characters—History and criticism. 3. Comic books, strips, etc.—History and criticism. 4. Comic books, strips, etc.—Political aspects. 5. Social values in comic books, strips, etc. 6. Third World in comic books, strips, etc. 7. Propaganda, American—Case studies. 8. Donald Duck (Comic book series). 9. Cultural imperialism, American. I. Mattelart, Armand, 1936- joint author. II. Kunzle, David, editor. III. International General. IV. Title. V. Title: Imperialist ideology in the Disney comic.

Morgan, Richard, 1950-
   How to challenge your local electric utility: a citizen's guide to the power industry. By Richard Morgan and Sandra Jerabek. Environmental Action Foundation, 1974.

   1. Electric utilities. 2. Electric utilities—Rates. 3. Consumer action. 4. Corporate accountability. I. Environmental Action Foundation. II. Jerabek, Sandra, joint author. III. Title. IV. Title: A citizen's guide to the power industry.

LC/OCLC

Alternative

Gay sunshine interviews . . . edited by Winston Leyland . . . Gay Sunshine Press, 1978.

1.Artists—Interviews. 2.Homosexuals—Interviews.
I. Leyland, Winston, 1940-

Gay sunshine interviews, volume 1. Edited by Winston Leyland . . . Gay Sunshine Press, 1978.

PARTIAL CONTENTS: William Burroughs.-
Charles Henri Ford.-Jean Genet.-Allen Ginsberg.-
John Giorno.-Lou Harrison.-Christopher Isher-
wood.-Harold Norse.-Peter Orlovsky.-John Rech.-
Gore Vidal.-Tennessee Williams.

1. Gay authors—Interviews. 2. Gay musicians—
Interviews. I. Leyland, Winston. 1940- editor.
II. Gay Sunshine Press. III. Burroughs, William S.,
1914- IV. Ford, Charles Henri. V. Genet. Jean.
1910- VI. Ginsberg, Allen, 1926- VII. Giorno. John.
VIII. Harrison, Lou. 1917- IX. Isherwood. Christopher, 1904- X. Norse, Harold. XI. Orlovsky. Peter.
XII. Rechy, John. XIII. Vidal. Gore. 1925- XIV. Williams. Tennessee. 1911-

Schiffman, Muriel.
    Self-therapy techniques for personal growth . . .
Self Therapy Press [1972, c1967]

1. Success. 2. Psychotherapy. . Title.

Schiffman, Muriel.
    Self-therapy techniques for personal growth . . .
Self Therapy Press, 1972, copyright 1967.

PARTIAL CONTENTS: How to feel a hidden
emotion.-Communication in marriage.-The meaning
of self-acceptance.

1. Self-help psychology. 2. Emotions. 3. Marriage.
4. Self-acceptance. I. Self Therapy Press. II. Title. III.
Title: Personal growth self-therapy techniques.

Edmond, Wendy.
    All work and no pay: women, housework, and the
wages due . . . edited by Wendy Edmond and Suzie
Fleming . . . Power of Women Collective and Falling
Wall Press, [1975]

1. Women—Social conditions. I. Fleming, Suzie,
joint author.

Edmond, Wendy, editor.
    All work and no pay: women, housework, and the
wages due. Edited by Wendy Edmond and Suzie
Fleming . . . Power of Women Collective and Falling
Wall Press, 1975.

PARTIAL CONTENTS: The housewife.-No end to
the working day.-This is nursing. Introduction to a
struggle.-Mother-led union.-Organizing on the second job.-A general strike.

1. Women workers. 2. Women labor unionists. 3.
Women and homemaking. 4. Sexism in nursing. 5.
Sexism in emloyment. 6. Labor organizing. 7. Wages
for Housework Movement. I. Fleming, Suzie, editor.
II. Power of Women Collective. III. Falling Wall Press.
IV. Title. V. Title: Women, housework, and the wages
due. VI. Title: Housework, women, and the wages
due.

LC/OCLC

Ordinary women: an anthology of poetry by New York City women . . . edited by Sara Miles . . . [et al.]; introd. by Adrienne Rich . . . Ordinary Women Books, c1978.

1. American poetry—Women authors. 2. American poetry—New York (City). 3. American poetry—20th century. I. Miles, Sara, 1952.

The beat journey . . . ed. by Arthur and Kit Knight . . . c1978.

(The Unspeakable visions of the individual: v. 8)

1. Authors, American—20th century—Interviews. 2. Authors, American—20th century—Correspondence. I. Knight, Arthur Winfield, 1937- ed. II. Knight, Kit, ed.

[No entry found]

[No entry found]

Alternative

Ordinary women: an anthology of poetry by New York City women. Edited by Sara Miles and others; introduction by Adrienne Rich . . . Ordinary Women books, copyright 1978.

1. American poetry—20th century. 2. Women's writings, American. 3. Women—New York (City)—Poetry. 4. Working class women—New York (City)—Poetry. I. Miles, Sara, 1952—editor. II. Ordinary Women Books. III. Title: Poetry by New York City women. IV. Title: New York City women's poetry.

The beat journey; edited by Arthur and Kit Knight . . . Unspeakable Visions of the Individual, copyright 1978.

Includes interviews with Allen Ginsberg, Michael Mcclure, and John Clellon Holmes, poetry by Joanna McClure, Philip Whalen, and Gregory Corso, letters by Jack Kerouac, Holmes, and William Burroughs, and photos by Fred W. McDarrah.

1. Authors, American—20th century—Interviews. 2. Authors, American—20th century—Correspondence. 3. "Beat" literature. I. Knight, Arthur Winfield, 1937- editor. II. Knight, Kit, editor. III. Unspeakable Visions of the Individual. IV. Ginsberg, Allen, 1926. V. McClure, Michael. VI. Holmes, John Clellon.

Brisby, Stewart, editor.
Born into a felony; access to the society within. Edited by Stewart Brisby & Walt Shepperd. Pulpartforms Unltd., copyright 1978.

Anthology of photos, poetry, discussions, graphics, and short essays that provide "a window of experience on that part of society which is prison."

1. Prisoners' writings, American. 2. Prisoners, Afro-American. 3. Prisoners—United States. 4. Prisons—United States—Poetry. 5. Prisons—United States—Pictorial works. 6. Prisons—United States. 7. Prisons—Poetry. 8. Prisons—Pictorial works. I. Shepperd, Walt, editor. II. Pulpartforms Unltd. III. Title. IV. Title: Access to the society within.

Communities, journal of cooperative living.
A guide to cooperative alternatives; edited by Communities, journal of cooperative living. Editors: Paul Freundlich, Chris Collins, and Mikki Wenig. Community Publications Cooperative, copyright 1979.

LC/OCLC

Alternative

[No entry found]

(cont'd)

PARTIAL CONTENTS: Community organizing.-Health & well-being.-Economics & work.-Food.-Housing.-Communications & networking. Akwesasne notes.-Family life & relationships.-Energy & environment. New Alchemy.-Politics.-Education.-Decision making. Clamshell Alliance.-Culture.-Self & spirit.-Intentional communities. Twin Oaks.-Directory of intentional communities.

1.Cooperatives—Information services. 2. Community organization—Information services. 3. Communes—United States—Directories. 4. Health—Information services. 5. Self-management—Information services. 6. Alternative economics—Information services. 7. Food co-ops—Information services. 8 Nutrition centers, groups, etc.—Directories. 9. Housing co-ops—Information services. 10. Alternative housing—Information services. 11. Akwesasne notes. 12. Alternative press—Information services. 13. New Alchemy Institute. 14. Appropriate technology—Information services. 16. Clamshell Alliance. 17. "New Age" centers, groups, etc.—Directories. I. Freundlich, Paul, editor. II. Community Publications Cooperative. III. Title. I.V. Title: Cooperative alternatives: a guide.

The Power of women and the subversion of the community /[by] Mariarosa Dalla Costa and Selma James. 3rd ed. . . . Falling Wall Press Ltd. 1975.

Women and the subversion of the community first published as an article, Donne e sovversione sociale, in Potere femminile e sovversione sociale, Padova, 1972; A woman's place originally published in 1952.
CONTENTS: Dalla Costa, M. Women and the subversion of the community.—James, S. A woman's place.

1. Feminism—Italy—Addresses, essays, lectures. 2. Women and socialism—Addresses, essays, lectures. I. Dalla Costa, Mariarosa. Potere femminile e sovversione sociale. Donne e sovversione sociale. English. 1975. II. James, Selma. A woman's place. 1975. III. Title.

Dalla Costa, Mariarosa.
The power of women and the subversion of the community; by Mariarosa Dalla Costa and Selma James. 3rd ed. . . . Falling Wall Press. 1975. copyright 1972.

CONTENTS: Women and the subversion of the community, by M. Dalla Costa.-A woman's place, by S. James.
"Women and the subversion of the community" first appeared as an article, Donne e sovversione sociale, in Potere femminile e sovversione sociale . . . 1972; "A woman's place" originally published in 1952.

1. Women's movement—Italy. 2. Women and homemaking. 3. Wages For Housework Movement. 4. Women and socialism. 5. Capitalism and the family. 6. Class struggle. 7. Sexism in employment. 8. Women workers. I. James, Selma, joint author. II. Falling Wall Press. III. Title. IV. Title: Women and the subversion of the community. V. Title: A woman's place. VI. Title: The subversion of the community.

LC/OCLC

Alternative

The Lesbian reader: an Amazon quarterly
anthology/edited by Gina Covina and Laurel
Galana . . . Amazon Press, 1975.

   1. Lesbianism—United States. 2. Lesbianism in
literature. 3. Women's writings, American. I. Covina,
Gina, ed. II. Galana, Laurel, ed. III. Amazon
quarterly.

The Lesbian reader; an Amazon quarterly anthology. Edited by Gina Covina and Laurel Galana . . .
Amazon Press, 1975.

   Includes short stories, poetry, essays, and
bibliography.

   1. Lesbianism. 2. Women's writings, American. 3.
Lesbians. 4. Love poetry. 5. Lesbians—Fiction. 6.
Lesbians—Poetry. I. Covina, Gina, editor. II. Galana,
Laurel, editor. III. Amazon quarterly. IV. Amazon
Press.

Friends, Society of. Program on Government
Surveillance and Citizens' Rights.
   The police threat to political liberty: discoveries
and actions of the American Friends Service Com-
mittee Program on Government Surveillance and
Citizens' Rights, 1979 . . . AFSC, 1979.

   1. Police—United States. 2. Privacy, Right of—
United States. 3. Intelligence service—United
States. 4. Civil rights—United States. I. Title.

American Friends Service Committee. Program on
Government Surveillance and Citizens' Rights.
   The police threat to political liberty; discoveries
and actions of the American Friends Service Com-
mittee Program on Government Surveillance and
Citizens; rights, 1979 . . . AFSC, 1979.

   PARTIAL CONTENTS: Rebellions and repres-
sions of the Sixties.-Some revelations of the
Seventies.-Digging into the cities. Seattle. Los
Angeles. Philadelphia. Baltimore. Jackson,
Mississippi.-Economic and political intimidation.-
Physical intimidation.-The LEIU.-Collusion among
government and private organizations.

   1. Police misconduct—United States. 2. Repression, Political—United States. 3. Police surveillance—United States. 4. Law Enforcement Intelligence Unit. 5. FBI. 6. Political surveillance—United
States. I. Title.

[No entry found]

Grossman, Richard.
   Energy, jobs and the economy. By Richard Grossman and Gail Daneker; introduction by Harvey Was-
serman. Alyson Publications; distributed by Carrier
Pigeon, copyright 1979.

   'Much of this book originally appeared under the
title Jobs and energy, published by Environmentalists for Full Employment."
   PARTIAL CONTENTS: The myth about energy
expansion.-Jobs from conservation.-Jobs from the
sun.-Inaction at the Departments of Energy and
Labor.

   1. Energy conservation and employment. 2. Energy policy—United States. 3. Environmental protection loyment. 4. Solar energy and employment. 5.
Environmental Movement. 6. United States. Dept. of
Energy. 7. United States. Dept. of Labor.

LC/OCLC

Alternative

[No entry found]

(cont'd)

8. Labor policy—United States. I. Daneker, Gail, joint author. II. Environmentalists for Full Employment. III. Alyson Publications. IV. Carrier Pigeon (firm). V. Title. VI. Title: Jobs and energy. VII. Title: Jobs, energy, and the economy.

Baird, Peter, 1950-
   Beyond the border: Mexico & the U.S. today/Peter Baird & Ed McCaughan; with investment profile by Marc Herold; designed by Rini Templeton . . . North American Congress on Latin America [1979].

   1. United States—Foreign economic relations—Mexico. 2. Mexico—Foreign economic relations—United States. 3. Migrant agricultural laborers—United States. 5. Investments, American—Mexico. I. McCaughan, Ed, 1950- joint author. II. North American Congress on Latin America. III. Title.

Baird, Peter, 1950-
   Beyond the border; Mexico & the U.S. today. By Peter Baird & Ed McCaughan; with foreign investment profile by Marc Herold. Index by Zoia Horn; designed by Rini Templeton, assisted by Tessa Martinez and Elizabeth Patelke . . . North American Congress on Latin America, copyright 1979.

   1. United States—Foreign economic relations—Mexico. 2. Mexico—Foreign economic relations—United States. 3. Migrant workers—Mexico. 4. Migrant workers—United States. 5. Investments, American—Mexico. 6. Working classes—Mexico. 7. Agribusiness—Mexico. 8. Agribusiness—United States. 9. Labor unions—Mexico. 10. Multinational corporations—Mexico. 11. Immigrant workers, Mexican. I. McCaughan, Ed, 1950–joint author. II. North American Congress on Latin America. III. Title. I. Title: Mexico & the U.S. today.

[No entry found]

People, pride & politics: building the North Star country (Audio cassette). Pandora Productions; distributed by Educational Exploration Center, 1978.

   CREDITS: Songs by Pete Seeger, Jean Bluestein, Susan Reed, Martha Schlamme, and others; narration by Rachel Kranz..
   SUMMARY: An oral history of Midwest farmers and workers in the early 20th Century, based on Meridel LeSueur's 1945 book, North Star country.
   CONTENTS: Early farm organizing.-Farm organizing in the Depression.-Labor.-Unemployed organizing in the Depression.-Three Midwestern grassroots organizers (Roz Lindesmith, Clarence Sharp, and Madge Hawkins).-Immigration to the North Star country.

   1. Farm life—Middle West—Personal narratives. 2. Farmers—Middle West—Interviews. 3. Oral history—Middle West. 4. Protest songs. 5. Radicalism—Middle West—History. 6. Depression— 1929—Middle West. 7. Labor organizing—Middle West—Personal narrtives. 8. Unemployed organizing—Middle West—Personal

LC/OCLC

Alternative

[No entry found]

(cont'd)

narratives. 9. Farm organizing—Middle West—Personal narratives. 10. Immigrant workers—Middle West—History. 11. Labor unions—Middle West—History. 12. Labor songs. I. LeSueur, Meridel, 1900– III. Pandora Productions. IV. Kranz, Rachel, V. Education Exploration Center. VI. Lindesmith, Roz. VII. Sharp, Clarence. VIII. Hawkins, Madge. IX. Title: Building the North Star country. X. Title: The North Star country.

Iran erupts/edited by Ali-Reza Nobari . . . Iran-American Documentation Group, Stanford University, c1978.

   1. Iran—Politics and government— 1945- 2. Iran—Social conditions. 3. Iran—History— 1945- I. Nobari, Ali-Reza, ed. II. Iran-American Documentation Group.

Nobari, Ali-Reza, editor.
   Iran erupts. Iran-American Documentation Group, Stanford University, copyright 1978.

   Includes material by Abol-Hassan Banisadr.
   PARTIAL CONTENTS: Instead of the Shah, an Islamic Republic.-Two interviews with . . . Ayatollah Khomeini.-Iran and the multinationals.-Repression in Iran.-The Shah's dreams of glory.-Torture in Iran.-The Iranian Black Friday.

   1. Iran—Politics and government— 1945– 2. Iran—History— 1945– 3. Torture—Iran. 4. Repression, Political—Iran. 6. Mohammed Reza Pahlavi, Shah of Iran, 1919– 7. Revolutions—Iran. 8. "Black Friday" Massacre, Teheran, September 8, 1978. I. Iran-American Documentation Group. II. Khomeini, Ruholla. III. Banisadr, Abol-Hassan. IV. Title.

Mitchell, Larry.
   The faggots and their friends between revolutions/text by Larry Mitchell; drawings by Ned Asta . . . Calamus Books, c1977.

   1. Homosexuality, Male. I. Title.

Mitchell, Larry.
   The faggots & their friends between revolutions. Text by Larry Mitchell; drawings by Ned Asta . . . Calamus Books, copyright 1977.

   1. Gay fables. 2. Gay men—Fiction. 3. Homophobia—Fiction. 4. Gay Liberation Movement—Fiction. I. Asta, Ned, Illus. II. Calamus Books. III. Title.

[No entry found]

Hefner, Keith, editor.
   Children's rights handbook for teachers, youth workers and student organizers. Editor: Keith Hefner . . . Youth Liberation Press, copyright 1979.

   "Published as a special double issue of FPS: a magazine of young people's liberation (#63/64)."
   PARTIAL CONTENTS: Children's rights and social work.-The invention of childhood [comic strip].-A look at children's oppression, and some suggestions for change.-Changing childhood [comic strip].-The case for child advocacy.

   1. Children's rights. 2. Child advocacy. 3. Ageism. 4. Children—Comic books, strips, etc. I. Youth Liberation Press. II. Title.

LC/OCLC

Alternative

Lichty, Ron.
 The do-it-yourself guide to alternative publishing/ edited by Ron Lichty . . . Alternative Press Syndicate. c1976.

 1. Newspaper publishing. 2. Journalism—United States. I. Title.

Lichty, Ron, editor.
 The do-it-yourself guide to alternative publishing; edited by Ron Lichty . . . Alternative Press Syndicate. copyright 1976.

 PARTIAL CONTENTS: How to do it.-How it's been done. Publishing a multiple-edition newspaper, by J. Kois. Investigative reporting; an interview, by D. Porter. Photojournalism, by J. Fries. Special problems of the Underground Press, by J.M. Gora.

 1. Newspaper publishing. 2. Alternative press. 3. Self-publishing. 4. Photojournalism. 5. Investigative journalism. I. Alternative Press Syndicate. II. Title. III. Title: Alternative publishing guide.

Dodson, Betty.
 Liberating masturbation: a meditation on self-love . . . 1976, c1974.

 1. Women—Sexual behavior. 2. Masturbation. I. Title.

Dodson, Betty.
 Liberating masturbation; a meditation on self-love. Copyright 1974.

 Includes both paged and unpaged drawings by the author, as well as material on consciousness-raising, "Bodysex workshops," and vibrators.

 1. Masturbation. 2. Orgasm, Female. 3. Women—Sexuality. 4. Sex manuals. 5. Erotic art. 6. Vibrators. 7. Consciousness-raising. I. Title.

[No entry found]

Blank, Joani.
 Good vibrations: the complete woman's guide to vibrators; being a treatise on the use of machines in the indolent indulgence of erotic pleasureseeking, together with important hints on the acquisition, care, and utilization of said machines, and much more about the art and science of buzzing off. Invented and handlettered by Joani Blank; illustrated by Tee Corinne. Down There Press, copyright 1976.

 1. Vibrators. 2. Masturbation. 3. Sex manuals. 4. Women—Sexuality. I. Down There Press. II. Title. III. Title: The complete woman's guide to vibrators. IV. Title: Buzzing off. V. Title: Woman's guide to vibrators.

Nomadic Sisters.
 Loving women . . . illustrated by Ann Miya. 3d ed. rev . . . Nomadic Sisters, c1976.

The Nomadic Sisters.
 Loving women; illustrated by Ann Miya. 2d ed., revised. copyright 1976.

LC/OCLC

Alternative

Nomadic Sisters (cont'd)

1. Lesbians. 2. Women—Sexual behavior. I. Miya. Ann. II. Title.

(cont'd)

Includes material on dildos and vibrators.

PARTIAL CONTENTS: Ninety-nine out of a hundred do.-I know a place.-Going down, down, down.-Give the lady a hand or gimme five.

1. Women—Sexuality. 2. Lesbians—Sexuality. 3. Homosexuality. 4. Masturbation. 5. Vibrators. 6. Dildos. 7. Sex manuals. I. Miya, Ann, illus. II. Title. III. Title: Women loving.

Proposed: A Subject Cataloging Code for Public, School, and Community College Libraries

1. Use English-language terms whenever possible; e.g.,

Vocabulary

FREE ENTERPRISE	*not*	LAISSEZ-FAIRE

2. Prefer American words and phrases to Anglicisms; e.g.,

LABOR UNIONS	*not*	TRADE UNIONS

3. Use direct, contemporary language; e.g.,

AIR FREIGHT	*not*	AERONAUTICS, COMMER-CIAL—FREIGHT
BAY OF PIGS INVASION, 1961	*not*	CUBA—HISTORY—INVA-SION, 1961
BUSES	*not*	MOTOR-BUSES
BUSINESS ENGLISH	*not*	ENGLISH LANGUAGE—BUSINESS ENGLISH
CIA	*not*	UNITED STATES. CENTRAL INTELLIGENCE AGENCY.
DOWSING	*not*	DIVINING-ROD
DRIVER EDUCATION	*not*	AUTOMOBILE DRIVER EDUCATION
EDUCATIONAL GUIDANCE	*not*	PERSONNEL SERVICE IN EDUCATION
ENERGY TECHNOLOGY	*not*	POWER (MECHANICS)
EXCISE TAX	*not*	TAXATION OF ARTICLES OF CONSUMPTION
FLASH PHOTOGRAPHY	*not*	PHOTOGRAPHY, FLASHLIGHT
FORENSIC MEDICINE	*not*	MEDICAL JURISPRUDENCE
FOUNDATIONS	*not*	ENDOWMENTS
GRAVESTONES	*not*	SEPULCHRAL MONUMENTS
KGB	*not*	RUSSIA. COMMITTEE FOR STATE SECURITY.
MODEL RAILROADS	*not*	RAILROADS—MODELS
MOONSHINING	*not*	DISTILLING, ILLICIT
NUCLEAR WEAPONS	*not*	ATOMIC WEAPONS
OFFSHORE OIL	*not*	PETROLEUM IN SUBMERGED LANDS
PSYCHIC HEALING	*not*	MENTAL HEALING
ROBOTS	*not*	AUTOMATA
TRUCKING	*not*	TRANSPORTATION, AUTO-MOTIVE—FREIGHT
UNDERWATER PHOTOG-RAPHY	*not*	PHOTOGRAPHY, SUB-MARINE

Reprinted from *HCL Cataloging Bulletin*, no. 39 (March/April 1979): 1–5.

4. Follow natural word order, avoiding inversions; e.g.,

ADOPTED CHILDREN	*not*	CHILDREN, ADOPTED
AMERICAN MUSIC	*not*	MUSIC, AMERICAN
BLACK HOLE OF CALCUTTA	*not*	CALCUTTA, BLACK HOLE OF
MILITARY PRISONS	*not*	PRISONS, MILITARY
NATURAL GAS	*not*	GAS, NATURAL
SPONTANEOUS HUMAN COMBUSTION	*not*	COMBUSTION, SPON-TANEOUS HUMAN

5. Create headings for popular literary and media genres; e.g.,

CAPTIONED FILMS	OCCULT FICTION
CAUTIONARY TALES AND VERSE	"REGENCY" NOVELS
	SUSPENSE FILMS
FANTASTIC ART	TALL TALES
FEMINIST ART [ESSAYS, FIC-TION, etc.]	TEENAGERS' FILMS [LITERA-TURE, etc.]
"GOTHIC" FICTION	TRIVIA

6. Create headings for popular fictional or folkloric characters, groups, and places; e.g.,

BABE THE BLUE OX	MARPLE, MISS JANE
BACH, P.D.Q.	MIGHTY MOUSE
BROWN, FATHER	THE NORTHS
CHEWBACCA	PADDINGTON-THE-BEAR
CLAUDINE	PELLUCIDAR
COYOTE THE TRICKSTER	ROGERS, BUCK
GRAND FENWICK	SPOCK, MR.
GREEN KNOWE	THRUSH GREEN, ENGLAND
HOLMES, SHERLOCK	WHITEOAK FAMILY
THE HULK	WOOSTER, BERTRAM
MAGOO, MR.	

7. Create headings for major literary and media awards, to be applied to the laureate works themselves; e.g.,

ACADEMY AWARD FILMS	GOLDEN KITE AWARD BOOKS
CALDECOTT MEDAL BOOKS	GOLDEN SPUR AWARD BOOKS
CORETTA SCOTT KING AWARD BOOKS	HUGO AWARD WINNERS
	NEWBERY MEDAL BOOKS
EDGAR AWARD BOOKS	SCHWARTZ JUVENILE BOOK AWARDS
GAY BOOK AWARDS	

8. Whenever possible, use familiar rather than scientific or taxonomic terms for plants, animals, diseases, drugs, etc.; e.g.,

ASIATIC WILD HORSE	*not*	EQUUS PRZEWALSKII
DIOXIN	*not*	TETRACHLORODIBENZO-DIOXIN
DNA	*not*	DEOXYRIBONUCLEIC ACID
GRAY REEF SHARK	*not*	CARCHARINUS MENISORRAH
MINNOWS	*not*	FUNDULUS HETEROCLITUS

8. (cont'd), Plants, animals, diseases, drugs, etc.

PBB'S	*not*	POLYBROMINATED BIPHENYLS
SLOTHS	*not*	BRADYPUS TRIDACTYLUS
TAY-SACHS' DISEASE	*not*	AMAUROTIC FAMILY IDIOCY
WHITE-FOOTED MOUSE	*not*	PEROMYSCUS LEUCOPUS

9. Establish new terms as soon as materials are received dealing with topics that no existing descriptors adequately represent. (For example, most libraries now have materials on ENVIRONMENTAL EDUCATION, ADOPTEES' RIGHTS, KIRIGAMI, JOB SHARING, MATH ANXIETY, SLEEPING PILLS, POOL PLAYERS, THE FIFTIES, THE SIXTIES, the BATES METHODS, SPACE PROGRAMS, SORORITIES, VANITY PRESSES, NATIONAL HEALTH INSURANCE, the CHARISMATIC MOVEMENT, TWO-CAREER COUPLES, PICK-UP TRUCKS, RADIO COLLECTIBLES, DISCO SKATING, PROPOSITION 13 and NEWS MEDIA, but such materials can't be found under those subject headings in most catalogs.)

10.   Avoid sex, ethnic, age, and other bias in people-related terms; prefer self-declared group names; e.g.,

CHILD REARING	*not*	CHILDREN—MANAGEMENT
CITY COUNCIL MEMBERS	*not*	CITY COUNCILMEN
DISABLED PERSONS	*not*	HANDICAPPED
ENGLISH AS A SECOND LANGUAGE—TEXT-BOOKS—SPANISH	*not*	ENGLISH LANGUAGE—TEXT-BOOKS FOR FOREIGNERS—SPANISH
HUMANS	*not*	MAN
IGBO (AFRICAN PEOPLE)	*not*	IBO TRIBE
INUIT	*not*	ESKIMOS
SENIORS	*not*	AGED

Assignment

1. Assign sufficient subject tracings to every work—whether adult or juvenile, fiction or nonfiction, print or audiovisual—to fully and fairly reflect its content; e.g.,

Aiken, Joan, 1924-
  The smile of the stranger. Doubleday, 1978.
 	
    1. "Regency" novels. 2. Seventeen-year-olds—Fiction. I. Title.
	not	Aiken, Joan, 1924-
		  The smile of the stranger. Doubleday, 1978.
		
		    I. Title.

MacLeod, Charlotte.
  Rest you merry. Published for the Crime Club by Doubleday, 1978.
 	
    1. American detective and mystery stories. 2. Academic libraries—Fiction. 3. Librarians—Fiction. 4. Christmas stories. I. Title.
	not	MacLeod, Charlotte.
		  Rest you merry. Published for the Crime Club by Doubleday, 1978.
		
		    I. Title.

1. Subject tracings, (cont'd)

King, Billie Jean.
  Tennis love; a parents' guide to the sport. By Billie Jean King and Greg Hoffman; illustrations by Charles M. Schulz. Macmillan, copyright 1978.
  1. Tennis for children. 2. Tennis—Psychological aspects. 3. Peanuts characters. I. Hoffman, Greg, 1946- joint author. II. Schulz, Charles Monroe, illus. III. Title. IV. Title: A parents' guide to tennis.
	not	King, Billie Jean.
		  Tennis love; a parents' guide to the sport. By Billie Jean King and Greg Hoffman; illustrations by Charles M. Schulz. Macmillan, c1978.
		  1. Tennis. 2. Tennis—Psychological aspects. I. Hoffman, Greg, 1946- joint author. II. Title.

2. Subdivide directly by place; e.g.,

AGRICULTURE—SICILY	*not*	AGRICULTURE—ITALY—SICILY
EDUCATION—ALSACE	*not*	EDUCATION—FRANCE—ALSACE
EDUCATION—MINNEAPOLIS	*not*	EDUCATION—MINNESOTA—MINNEAPOLIS
PREDATORY ANIMALS—SERENGETI PLAIN, TANZANIA	*not*	PREDATORY ANIMALS—TANZANIA—SERENGETI PLAIN

3. Do not employ such subheadings as:

—ADDRESSES, ESSAYS, LECTURES	—DOCTRINAL AND CONTROVERSIAL WORKS
—AMATEURS' MANUALS	—JUVENILE LITERATURE
—CONGRESSES	—POPULAR WORKS

4. Use subheadings like —HANDBOOKS, MANUALS, ETC. and —UNITED STATES on a selective basis, depending on the library's collection; e.g.,

BRICKLAYING	*not*	BRICKLAYING—HANDBOOKS, MANUALS, ETC.
CARPENTRY	*not*	CARPENTRY—HANDBOOKS, MANUALS, ETC.
FEDERAL AID TO LIBRARIES	*not*	FEDERAL AID TO LIBRARIES—UNITED STATES
INCOME TAX	*not*	INCOME TAX—UNITED STATES
PUBLIC HEALTH LAWS	*not*	PUBLIC HEALTH LAWS—UNITED STATES

Baker Street Blackout

Four new novels lately arrived at HCL in which the ever-popular Sherlock Holmes appears as a protagonist. None of these works bore the "Doyle" by-line, and so would be inaccessible to Sherlockians making a *D* search either in the catalog or on the fiction shelves. Similarly, LC catalogers failed to make added *Schlagwort* entries even for the three books that included the telltale "Sherlock Holmes" or "by John H. Watson" in their titles. Unsurprisingly, the subject tracings acknowledged neither Holmes nor his best-known associates, Dr. Watson and Prof. Moriarty, although these two characters figured in at least three of the works. Indeed, two titles were assigned no subject headings at all, while two others got single descriptors representing "real-life" persons—Teddy Roosevelt and Bertrand Russell—whom the novelists deliberately manipulated into Holmes encounters. The issue here is not whether the fictional materializations of Roosevelt and Russell *should* have merited any subject treatment, but rather why the appearance of a no-less-eminent and well-known personality—namely, Holmes—should not have warranted equal attention. Perhaps such disparate and discriminatory treatment might be termed *fictionism*: i.e., a bias against fictional characters. But whatever it's called, it means—in practice —that the Roosevelt and Russell fans can easily locate *their* heroes' literary reincarnations through the catalog, while the Holmesians can't.

Reprinted from *HCL Cataloging Bulletin*, no. 40 (May/June 1979): 1–2.

Here are the details, which incidentally show that several other characters—"real" and "fictional" alike—also failed to "make it" into the MARC record:

MARC

Collins, Randall, 1941–
    The case of the philosophers' ring, by Dr. John H. Watson, in which Sherlock Holmes and Bertrand Russell encounter the world's most evil genius/ unearthed by Randall Collins. New York: Crown Publishers, c1978.

    p. cm.

    1. Russell, Bertrand Russell, 3d Earl, 1872–1970—Fiction. I. Title.

Estleman, Loren D.
    Sherlock Holmes vs. Dracula; or, The adventure of the sanguinary count/by John H. Watson as edited by Loren D. Estleman. 1st ed. Garden City, N.Y.: Doubleday, 1978.

    214p.: 22 cm.

    I. Title.

Jeffers, Harry Paul, 1934–
    The adventure of the stalwart companions: heretofore unpublished letters and papers concerning a singlular collaboration between Theodore Roosevelt and Sherlock Holmes/edited and annotated by H. Paul Jeffers. 1st ed. New York: Harper & Row, c1978

    190p.: 21 cm.

    1. Roosevelt, Theodore, Pres. U.S., 1858–1919—Fiction. I. Title.

HCL

Collins, Randall, 1941–
    The case of the philosophers' ring; by Dr. John H. Watson. Unearthed by Randall Collins. Crown, copyright 1978.

    152p.

    Includes unpaged photos.

    1. Russell, Bertrand Russell, 3d Earl, 1872–1970—Fiction. 2. Watson, John Hamish, born 1852—Fiction. 3. Holmes, Sherlock, born 1854—Fiction. 4. Wittgenstein, Ludwig, 1889–1951—Fiction. 5. Crowley, Aleister, 1875–1947—Fiction. 6. Detective and mystery stories, American. I. Title. II. Title: The philosophers' ring case.

Estleman, Loren D.
    Sherlock Holmes vs. Dracula; or, The adventure of the sanguinary count. By John H. Watson, as edited by Loren D. Estleman. Doubleday, 1978.

    214p.

    1. Dracula—Fiction. 2. Holmes, Sherlock, born 1854—Fiction. 3. Watson, John Hamish, born 1852—Fiction. 4. Detective and mystery stories, American. I. Title. II. Title: The adventure of the sanguinary count. III. Title: The sanguinary count adventure.

Jeffers, Harry Paul, 1934–
    The adventure of the stalwart companions; heretofore unpublished letters and papers concerning a singular collaboration between Theodore Roosevelt and Sherlock Holmes. Edited and annotated by H. Paul Jeffers. Harper, copyright 1978.

    190p.

    1. Roosevelt, Theodore, 1858–1919—Fiction. 2. Holmes, Sherlock, born 1854—Fiction. 3. Detective and mystery stories, American. I. Title. II. Title: The stalwart companions adventure.

MARC

Kaye, Marvin.
    The incredible umbrella/Marvin Kaye. 1st ed.
Garden City, N.Y.: Doubleday, 1979.

    p. cm.

    I. Title.

HCL

Kaye, Marvin.
    The incredible umbrella. Doubleday copyright
1979.

    217p.

    "Doubleday science fiction."

    1. Fantastic fiction, American. 2. Gilbert and Sulli-
van operettas—Fiction. 3. Holmes,Sherlock, born
1854—Fiction. 4. Dracula—Fiction. 5. Moriarty,
James, born 1846—Fiction. 6. Frankenstein
Monster—Fiction. I. Title.

JUVENALIA

Two categories of library wares suffer particular neglect, frequently being poorly cataloged, if cataloged at all: audiovisual items and children's materials. *AACR2* and the earlier-noted guidelies for A/V subject cataloging constitute, in tandem, an enlightened and useful approach toward nonprint which could ultimately liberate films, tapes, records, kits, slides, etc. from their historic second-class status. But the "follies and deficiencies" that beset children's cataloging in 1976 still await correction, in spite of plentiful precedents and innovations like those recorded in "Kids' Stuff."

"The Natives Are More than Restless" deals primarily with language but also illustrates how librarians can function as active, rather than typically passive, consumers.

The Natives
Are More than Restless

On April 10, 1974, the head cataloger directed this letter to Children's Press, Inc.:

> While cataloging Allan Carpenter's and Michael Maginnis' 1973 title, *Burundi*, in your "Enchantment of Africa" series, I discovered two serious flaws (which I'm frankly surprised the 48 Northwestern University advisors missed):
>
> 1. The caption for the "above left" photograph on page 40 reads "German settlers sit in front of their hut." Having lived in Germany for more than 6 years, I think myself reasonably competent to recognize or identify bona fide "Germans." However, I see *none* in the picture. Nor could several colleagues here.
>
> 2. Even more disturbing is the use of the defamatory word "native." It appears in at least two picture captions, on pages 75 and 78 ("A native marriage" and "Native men are taught . . ."). I directed extensive documentation and arguments against this term on pages 90-4 of my own 1971 study, *Prejudices and Antipathies* (enclosed). Here are further data and reputable opinions on the same issue:
>
> - That *native* is not much distant, connotatively, from *nigger* Isabelle Suhl discloses in her analysis of the popular, highly touted Doctor Dolittle series of children's books. In particular, she reveals that a passage in the original, "official" edition of Hugh Lofting's *Voyages of Doctor Dolittle*, "You know what those *niggers* are—that ignorant!," became—in a later, "revised" paperback version: "You know what those *natives* are—that ignorant!" See "The 'real' Doctor Dolittle," *Interracial Books for Children*, v. 2, nos. 1-2 (Spring/Summer 1968): 6. (Emphasis added.)
>
> - Noting that "certainly as a black youngster the communications media had rendered 'native' as repulsive a word to me as 'black,'" a former New York junior high school teacher reported, in the July-August 1970 *Integrated Education*, on a classroom study she conducted with 17 students. Most equated the word "native" with "Negroes," "Africa," "cannibals," "savagery," or "primitive, uncivilized people." Definitions culled from six standard dictionaries, dating from 1959 to 1963, echoed, if not underpinned, these equations. "Our children," the teacher concluded, "have consulted the authorities. And the authorities have spoken. Natives are black and yellow, Africans and Asians, savage and barbarians!" See Janet Morgan, "Sensitive native or native sensitivity?" pages 35-9.

Reprinted from *HCL Cataloging Bulletin*, nos. 11–13 (March 15, 1975): 78–9.

As a result of these comments and enclosures, I trust that (a) the caption relating to "German settlers" will be corrected in future printings or revisions, and (b) "native" wil be consistently and consciously avoided in all "Enchantment of Africa" volumes, precisely as Dr. Fafunwa, the eminent Nigerian educator, demanded several years ago. (The cited examples, for instance, could be simply and suitably recast as "An African marriage," "A Burundi marriage." "African men are taught," or "Burundi men are taught.")

Joan Downing, Children's Press editor, replied on October 21, 1974:

Thank you for pointing out the errors in *Burundi*, from our "Enchantment of Africa" series. We are checking our film and the proper corrections will be made in the next printing.

Although the editors make every effort to avoid errors, they do occur. We appreciate your contacting us.

So far, so good. However, a later, four-page-long critique of three other series' titles (*Liberia, Tanzania,* and *Zaire*), including extensive comments by Ms. Christine Obbo, an Ugandan doctoral candidate in Anthropology at the University of Wisconsin (Madison), has gone unanswered. Copies of that May 29th document—which, among other things, noted many factual errors, more "native" eruptions, and several instances of both ethnocentric and sexist bias—are available on request.

For the record, Ms. Obbo concluded, after closely examining these three "Enchantment" titles: "Very sketchy work! I would not recommend them for an African audience . . . . The important contemporary issues—like free primary education in Tanzania—are not even touched upon. . . ." Overall, the material seemed inexact, oversimplified, superficial, stereotypic, and bland: mediocre, assembly-line stuff. If Ms. Obbo rightly judged these volumes unsuitable for Africans, they must also be regarded as not-good-enough for Americans. The subjects deserve better treatment. And so do our readers. *Why, then,* do most of these titles so readily and unreservedly win the *Children's Catalog* imprimatur (for example, see the 1974 supplement, pages 41-2)?

Follies & Deficiencies: LC's Cataloging of Children's Materials

Lois Doman Rose and Winifred E. Duncan write glowingly of "LC's National Standard for Cataloging Children's Materials" [*SLJ* (January): 20-23] But if the object is to maximize access to juvenile books and media for kids, teachers, parents, and librarians alike, there's not much to glow about. By uncritically accepting LC cataloging as *the* standard, our "leaders" and "experts" in effect standardized a host of follies and deficiencies. Moreover, in their reflexive endorsement of LC's Annotated Card Program—i.e., age-segregated cataloging—they reinforced a divisive and damaging ageism in professional attitudes and practice.

If anything, cataloging data and formats for *all* libraries—school, public, and academic—should be detoxed, rendered more intelligible and helpful to everyone, regardless of age. Among other things, that would mean rigorous title-page cataloging, an end to abbreviations, and the elimination of utterly useless, often perplexing elements like "1st ed.," centimeter spine lengths, brackets, Roman paging, and Bibliography notes.

Yet LC cataloging means just the reverse. It means frequently ponderous or improbable main entries like "Dodgson, Charles Lutwidge, 1832-1898," "Thompson, George Selden," and "Rabinowitz, Shalom, 1859-1916" for authors whose names most commonly appear (and are most generally known) as Lewis Carroll, George Selden, and Sholom Aleichem. It means not only the customary abbreviations and "descriptive" rubbish, but also (thanks to *ISBD*) a whole new array of occult punctuation and secret Latin codes. Not even the familiar "illus," remains any longer. For some wonderfully mad reason it's now further truncated to merely "ill."

And LC cataloging—despite the terrific hoopla about "liberally applied" and "modernized" subject headings—also means the often miserly, timorous assignment of rubrics from a thesaurus that's itself too limited to adequately reflect the richness, depth, and variety of both children's materials and children's interests. Instead of opening up and promoting the goods, LC cataloging may conceal or mutilate them. Indeed, the usually well-done "Summaries" almost invariably suggest intriguing and eminently traceable themes that

Reprinted with permission from *School Library Journal*, v. 22, no. 8 (April 1976): 50. R.R. Bowker/A Xerox Corp.

the subject headings fail to represent. This, for example, is the annotation for Robin and Jocelyn Wild's *Mouse Who Stole a Zoo* (Coward, 1972): "Hating to see the zoo animals living in cages, a clever mouse devises a scheme to set them free." And here's the "Summary" for Mordecai Richler's *Jacob Two-Two Meets the Hooded Fang* (Knopf, 1975): "Unjustly imprisoned by the Hooded Fang and other big people, Jacob Two-Two awaits the aid of the members of Child Power to free him and two hundred other children." The ACPers assigned *no* subject tracings whatever to either title.

Repeatedly, catch-all descriptors like "animals," "family life," "tales," and "toys" are applied to works that merit much more specific, interesting, and perhaps even exuberant treatment. Repeatedly, key ethnic, racial, or controversial aspects of a work are simply overlooked. Or muted. With the result that in this dawning age of "multicultural education" and frank talk about social issues it's impossible—courtesy of LC cataloging—to determine (from the subject assignments) that Sharon Bell Mathis' *Listen for the Fig Tree* (Viking, 1974) takes place during Kwanza and partly explores the problem of alcoholic parents. Or that Manus Pinkwater's *Wingman* (Dodd, 1975) deals with a Chinese-American boy; Lucille Clifton's *The Times They Used To Be* (Holt, 1974) features an Afro-American girl; Patricia Dizenzo's *Phoebe* (Holt, 1970) concerns a pregnant teenager; and Arnold Adoff's *Black is Brown is Tan* (Harper, 1973) depicts a multiracial family.

And seldom, again due to that highly touted "standard," will anyone find anything subject-cataloged under such obvious and warranted heads as: BACKYARDS; BEDTIME; CLEVERNESS; COUSINS; DIRTINESS; DISOBEDIENCE; FAMILY REUNIONS; FIRST DAY IN SCHOOL; MINIATURE PERSONS; MOVING TO A NEW NEIGHBORHOOD; MUD PIES, PUDDLES, PARTIES, ETC.; NEW BABY IN FAMILY; PLAYING HOUSE; TEASING; TEDDY BEARS; THREE-YEAR-OLDS [FOUR-YEAR-OLDS, ETC.]; WHISPERING; and WORKING PARENTS.

Why catalog kids' stuff separately? Why not totally abandon the apartheid-like subhead, JUVENILE LITERATURE, thus permitting truly age-integrated catalogs? If some ACP descriptors are in fact more modern and less technical than *Library of Congress Subject Headings* forms, they ought to be employed with *all* material, the goal being to develop *one* thesaurus of specific, sensible terms that fit, equally well, both grown up and juvie material. Some children's works, of course, demand special handling since they deal with topics that don't appear in adult-oriented literature. But that only requires the formulation of accurate, appropriate headings to mirror those topics, the new forms then entering the *total* thesaurus.

If annotations have proven useful on juvenile entries, why not do the same for adult titles? And why not, as a demonstration of good faith toward the young, finally dismantle that Victorian relic, DISCIPLINE OF CHILDREN, and replace CHILDREN—MANAGEMENT with something at once unbiased and honest like CHILD-REARING?

Sure, let's have a cost-saving, harmony-making "standard." But let's concoct it to serve everyday, honest-to-God people—however old, however young. The one we've got now doesn't.

Kid's Stuff: A Grabbag of HCL Subject Headings for (Mostly) Children's Media

ABSENT-MINDEDNESS
ADOPTION, INTERNATIONAL
ADOPTION, INTERRACIAL
ADOPTION, SINGLE-PARENT
ALONENESS
ALPHABET SONGS
ANDERSON, EVERETT
ANIMAL BABIES
ANNOYANCE
APACHE CHILDREN
APARTMENT HOUSE LIFE
APPEARANCES
ARROGANCE
ASIAN CHILDREN
AUNTS AND UNCLES
AWAKENING
BACKYARDS
BAD DAYS
BAD LUCK
BAS MITZVAH
BATHTUBS
BEAR HUNT (GAME)
BEDTIME
BEEZUS
BILINGUAL MATERIALS
BITING
BLIND CHILDREN'S MATERIALS
BLUE JEANS
BOASTS AND PRAISES
BOBBSEY TWINS
BOSSINESS
BOY ASTRONAUTS
BOY DETECTIVES
BOY GUERRILLAS
BOY MAGICIANS
BOY/GIRL RELATIONS
BOYS, AFRO-AMERICAN
BOYS, AMERINDIAN
BOYS AND DOLLS

BOYS, CHINESE
BOYS, CHINESE-AMERICAN
BOYS, CHOCTAW
BOYS, DAKOTA
BOYS, ETHIOPIAN
BOYS, HONDURAN
BOYS, INUIT
BOYS, JEWISH
BOYS, LATINO
BOYS, MENDE
BOYS, MEXICAN-AMERICAN
BRACES (DENTISTRY)
BROWN, LEROY
BROWNIES AND ELVES
BUGS BUNNY
BUILDING BLOCKS (TOYS)
BULLYING AND BULLIES
BUNK BEDS
BUSY PARENTS
CALDECOTT MEDAL BOOKS
CANDY STRIPERS
CARDBOARD CRAFTS
CARING (PERSONAL QUALITY)
CARNEGIE MEDAL BOOKS
CARTER G. WOODSON BOOK
  AWARDS
CATNAPPING (ABDUCTION)
CAUTIONARY TALES AND VERSE
CAUTIOUSNESS
CHAOS
CHASES
CHELM (IMAGINARY VILLAGE)
CHEMISTRY SETS
CHILD ARTISTS
CHILD COWHANDS
CHILD DETECTIVES
CHILD REBELS
CHILDREN AND ALCOHOLIC
  PARENTS

CHILDREN AND BIRDS
CHILDREN AND CANDY
CHILDREN AND CHOCOLATE
  PUDDING
CHILDREN AND DOCTORS
CHILDREN AND EYEGLASSES
CHILDREN AND PLANTS
CHILDREN AND RELIGION
CHILDREN AND SENIORS
CHILDREN AND SURGERY
CHILDREN AND TRAVEL
CHILDREN AND WAR
CHILDREN—EATING HABITS
CHILDREN IN TELEVISION
  ADVERTISING
CHILDREN OF CRIMINALS
CHILDREN OF DIVORCED
  PARENTS
CHILDREN OF THE POOR
CHILDREN OF UNMARRIED
  PARENTS
CHILDREN, PRESCHOOL
CHILDREN'S CHANTS
CHILDREN'S DANCES
CHILDREN'S LIBERATION
CHILDREN'S LITERATURE,
  NON-RACIST
CHILDREN'S LITERATURE,
  NON-SEXIST
CHILDREN'S LITERATURE,
  OJIBWE
CHILDREN'S MUSIC
CHILDREN'S SCIENCE BOOK
  AWARDS
CHILDREN'S TELEVISION
  PROGRAMS
CHILDREN'S WIT AND HUMOR
CHINATOWN (NEW YORK)
CHINATOWN (SAN FRANCISCO)

Reprinted with permission from *The U*N*A*B*A*S*H*E*D Librarian; the "how i run my library good" letter*, no. 25 (1977): 7–8, G.P.O. Box 2631, New York, NY 10001.

CHINESE CHILDREN
CHINESE NEW YEAR
CHINESE ZODIAC
CHRISTOPHER ROBIN
CLEVERNESS
COMMUNES AND CHILDREN
CORETTA SCOTT KING AWARD
  BOOKS
COUNCIL ON INTERRACIAL
  BOOKS FOR CHILDREN
  AWARDS
COUNSELING FOR TEENAGE
  GIRLS
COUNTING SONGS
COUSINS
CRITICIZING
DEAF CHILDREN'S MATERIALS
DEFINITIONS, UNUSUAL
DETERMINATION (PERSONAL
  QUALITY)
DIFFERENT AND SIMILAR
  THINGS
DIGGING
DIRTINESS
DISABLED CHILDREN
DISAPPOINTMENT
DISCOURTESY
DISGUISES
DISNEY CHARACTERS
DISOBEDIENCE
DOGNAPPING
DOLL THEFTS
DOUBLE-MEANINGS
  (LANGUAGE)
DOWNHILL CAR RACING AND
  RACERS
DRESSING
DREW, NANCY
DUKES AND DUCHESSES
DUNN, DANNY
EARLY RISERS
EASY AND DIFFICULT THINGS
EASY READERS
EASY READERS, OJIBWE
ECOLOGY—ACTION PROJECTS
EIGHT-YEAR-OLDS
EIGHTEEN-YEAR-OLDS
EIGHTH-GRADERS
ELEVEN-YEAR-OLDS
EMPTY LOTS
ENCHANTMENT
ENGAGEMENT PARTIES
EXAGGERATION
EXCITEMENT
EXPLANATIONS, UNUSUAL
FAIRY GODMOTHERS
FAITHFULNESS
FAMILY, MULTI-ETHNIC
FAMILY, MULTI-RACIAL
FAMILY REUNIONS
FATHER AND DAUGHTER
FATHER-SEPARATED CHILDREN

FERNALD, ALVIN
FERRIS WHEELS
FIFTEEN-YEAR-OLDS
FINGER PUPPETS
FINGERPRINT ART
FINISHING THINGS
FIRST DAY IN SCHOOL
FIRST-GRADERS
FIRST YEAR OF MARRIAGE
FIVE-YEAR-OLDS
FLATNESS
FOLLOWING DIRECTIONS
FOOLISHNESS
FOSTER CHILDREN
FOUNTAINS OF YOUTH
  (LEGENDARY SPRINGS)
FOUR-YEAR-OLDS
FOURTEEN-YEAR-OLDS
FRECKLES
FRIGHTFUL SOUNDS
FRIGHTS
FROG SOUNDS
FRONTIER AND PIONEER
  CHILDREN
FRONTIER AND PIONEER GIRLS
GENIES
GINGERBREAD COOKIES
GIRL ADVENTURERS
GIRL ATHLETES
GIRL DETECTIVES
GIRL JOCKEYS
GIRL REBELS
GIRLS, AFRO-AMERICAN
GIRLS, AMERINDIAN
GIRLS, ATTITUDES TOWARD
GIRLS, GREEK-AMERICAN
GIRLS, INUIT
GIRLS, JEWISH-AMERICAN
GIRLS, LATINO
GIRLS, PUERTO RICAN
GIRLS—RIGHTS
GOALS AND OBJECTIVES
GOBLINS
GOLDEN KITE AWARD BOOKS
GOOD LUCK
GOTHAM (IMAGINARY
  VILLAGE)
GRANDFATHERS
GRANDMOTHERS
GRAYMALKIN, MRS.
GREAT-GRANDMOTHERS
GREED
GREEN
GROUCHES, GRUMPS, AND
  GRINCHES
HAIRCUTTING, CHILDREN'S
HASTINESS
HELPFULNESS (PERSONAL
  QUALITY)
HEYDON, TOBY
HICCUPS
HIDDEN-PICTURE BOOKS

HIDE-AND-SEEK (CHILDREN'S
  GAME)
HIGH SCHOOL JUNIORS
HIGH SCHOOL SOPHOMORES
HOLES
HOLIDAY COSTUMES
HOMESICKNESS
HOUSEGUESTS
HOUSES, IMAGINARY
HUGGINS, HENRY
IMAGINARY PLAYMATES
IN AND OUT (LOCATIONS)
INDEPENDENCE (PERSONAL
  QUALITY)
INDIFFERENCE (PERSONAL
  QUALITY)
INFATUATION
INNER CITY
INNER CITY SCHOOLS
INNOCENCE (PERSONAL
  QUALITY)
INSENSITIVITY
INVECTIVES AND INSULTS
INVISIBILITY
IRMA SIMONTON BLACK
  AWARD BOOKS
JACK-O'-LANTERNS
JANE ADDAMS CHILDREN'S
  BOOK AWARDS
JOKES
JUMP-ROPE RHYMES
JUNKYARDS, GARBAGE
  DUMPS, ETC.
KARLSSON, ELVIS
KATE GREENAWAY MEDAL
  BOOKS
KAZOO
KWANZA
LEMONADE STANDS
LIGHT AND DARKNESS
LIVING AND NON-LIVING THINGS
LOLLIPOPS
LOST CHILDREN
LOST DOGS
LOVE, PATERNAL
McGURK, JACK P.
MAKEPEACE, CHARLOTTE
MAKEPEACE, EMMA
MAKING FACES
MAKING FRIENDS
MALONE, BEANY
"MAN IN THE MOON"
MENTALLY ILL TEENAGERS
MIDDLE CHILD
MILDRED L. BATCHELDER
  AWARD NOMINEES
MINIATURE PERSONS
MISFITS (PERSONS)
MITTENS
MONEY-MAKING SCHEMES FOR
  CHILDREN
MOONLIGHT

MORNING
MOTHER AND DAUGHTER
MOTHER AND SON
MOTHER-SEPARATED
  CHILDREN
MOVING TO A NEW
  NEIGHBORHOOD
MUD PIES, PUDDLES, PARTIES,
  ETC.
NARNIA (IMAGINARY LAND)
NATURE CRAFT
NEATNESS AND MESSINESS
NENE BOOK AWARDS
NEW BABY IN FAMILY
NEW ENGLAND ROUND TABLE
  OF CHILDREN'S LIBRARIANS
  AWARD BOOKS
NEWBERY MEDAL BOOKS
NINE-YEAR-OLDS
NINETEEN-YEAR-OLDS
NONSENSE SONGS
NOSINESS
OBSERVING THINGS
OLD AND NEW THINGS
OLMSTEAD, OX
ONE-CHILD FAMILY
OPPOSITES
ORANGE (COLOR)
OVERDOING THINGS
OVERENTHUSIASM
OVERNIGHT VISITS
OVERWEIGHT BOYS
OVERWEIGHT CHILDREN
OVERWEIGHT GIRLS
PADDINGTON-THE-BEAR
PANDA BEARS (TOYS)
PAPER ROUTES
PARENT-SEPARATED
  CHILDREN
PEACEABLENESS
PEANUTS CHARACTERS
PECOS GANG
PENNINGTON, PATRICK
PERSONAL SPACE
PESTS (PERSONS)
PETS IN APARTMENT HOUSES
PIGGLE-WIGGLE, MRS.
PIGS
PIGTAILS
PLAYING DOCTOR
PLAYING DOLLS
PLAYING HOSPITAL
PLAYING HOUSE
PLAYING SCHOOL
POLICE AND CHILDREN
POP-UP CARDS, BOOKS, ETC.
POPPINS, MARY
POSSIBILITIES
POTATO PRINTING
PRETENDING
QUIMBY, RAMONA
RAG DOLLS

RAINY DAYS
RALPH THE MOUSE
REDHEADS
REFUGEE CHILDREN
RESOURCEFULNESS
  (PERSONAL QUALITY)
RHYMING SLANG
RIGHT AND LEFT (DIRECTIONS)
ROCKING HORSES
ROLLER-SKATING
RUDISILL, SIR ROGER DE
RUNNING ERRANDS
RURAL CHILDREN
SANCHEZ, ESPERANZA
SCARECROWS
SCHLEMIEHL (FOLKLORIC
  CHARACTER)
SCHWARTZ JUVENILE BOOK
  AWARDS
SCHOOL LUNCH PROGRAMS
SCRIBBLES AND SCRIBBLING
SECOND-GRADERS
SECRETS
SECURITY BLANKETS
SELFISHNESS
SELF-PITY
SEPARATED FRIENDS,
  RELATIVES, ETC.
SESAME STREET CHARACTERS
SEVENTEEN-YEAR-OLDS
SEX ROLE AND CHILDREN
SEX ROLE AND TOYS
SHADOWS
SHOW-AND-TELL
  PRESENTATIONS
SHOW-OFFS
SILENCE AND SILENT THINGS
SILLINESS
SILVER, MISS
SIX-YEAR-OLDS
SIXTEEN-YEAR-OLDS
SIXTH-GRADERS
SIZE AND SHAPE
SKILLS
SLEDDING
SLEEPINESS
SMALLNESS AND BIGNESS
SMOKEY THE BEAR
SNIFFLES AND SNEEZES
SOFT TOYS
SPECIES IDENTITY
SPELLING BEES
"SPOILED" CHILDREN
SPOTLIGHT CLUB
SPOTS (MARKS)
STABLE, GEORGE
STANTON, WILL
STEPBROTHERS AND
  STEPSISTERS
STERN, HANNIBAL
STICKBALL
STREET GAMES

STRING-BALLS
SUPERNATURAL SOUNDS
SURPRISE PARTIES
TAG (GAME)
TALENT SHOWS
TALKATIVENESS
TALL TALES
TALLNESS AND SHORTNESS
TEA PARTIES
TEASING
TEDDY BEARS
TEEN AGE
TEENAGE BOYS
TEENAGE FATHERS
TEENAGE GIRLS
TEENAGE GIRLS' PROJECTS
  AND SERVICES
TEENAGE LITERATURE
TEENAGE MARRIAGE
TEENAGE MOTHERS
TEENAGE PREGNANCY
TEENAGE SPIES
TEENAGERS
TEENAGERS AND SENIORS
TEENAGERS' PLAYS
TEENAGERS—RIGHTS
TEMPER TANTRUMS
TEN-YEAR-OLDS
THIRTEEN-YEAR-OLDS
THREE INVESTIGATORS
THREE-YEAR-OLDS
TONGUE-TWISTERS
TRAIL BIKES
TRAIN RIDES
TRANSFORMATIONS (MAGIC)
TREASURE HUNTING
TRUSTFULNESS
TUG OF WAR (GAME)
TWELVE-YEAR-OLDS
UNDERSTANDING (PERSONAL
  QUALITY)
UNHAPPINESS
UNKINDNESS
UP AND DOWN (DIRECTIONS)
USEFULNESS
VACATIONS FOR PARENTS
WAGONS (TOYS)
WASTEFULNESS (PERSONAL
  QUALITY)
WHISPERING
WICKEDNESS
WINNIE-THE-POOH
WISHING AND WISHES
WOODY WOODPECKER
WORKING MOTHERS
WORKING PARENTS
YOUNGER BROTHERS AND
  SISTERS
YOUTH LIBERATION
  MOVEMENT
YOUTH—RIGHTS
YO-YO (TOY)

DEWEY

Let it be stated clearly and candidly: The *Dewey Decimal Classification* is doubtless the best available scheme for nonresearch libraries. Its present faults stem not so much from anything intrinsic to *DDC* itself, but rather from how LC classifiers apply it (e.g., "By Their Call Numbers Ye Shall Know Them," "Deweying the Supernatural," "Cataloging Castaneda") and how the scheme's Forest Press stewards maintain and revise it ("*DDC 19*: An Indictment").

As in most other cataloging areas, there needs to be reform at the top. Nonetheless, each local *DDC*-using library also bears a responsibility to ensure that the LC-assigned notations "fit," that successive revisions and overlays don't generate a senseless mishmash on the shelves, that call numbers keep within manageable limits, and that staff and patron utility governs *DDC* policy (e.g., deciding to employ 92, 921, or *B* for individual biographies—rather than classing them with "specific disciplines or subjects"—if that's where the public prefers them).

It should be noted that although DCD assigns Dewey numbers for the rest of the country, it does *not* do so for the Library of Congress, since LC doesn't *have* a Dewey-classed collection.

By Their Call Numbers
Ye Shall Know Them

The head cataloger on January 14, 1976 sent this letter to the program manager of the Cataloging-In-Publication program at the Library of Congress:

364.172 appears as the CIP Dewey number for Mort Olshan's *Winning Theories of Sports Handicapping: Football, Basketball, Baseball* (Simon and Schuster, 1975). That six-digit combination, according to the latest (18th) edition of the *Dewey Decimal Classification*, denotes "Gambling" as an "offense against public morals." However, the book itself deals with sports betting or handicapping in an unmistakably factual, practical, and even sympathetic way. It is emphatically *not* written from a hostile nor criminological perspective. Thus, the assigned notation not only misrepresents the work, but may also bias a reader who understands the number's significance or the ordinary library browser who finds the volume shelved—because of the 364—in the CRIME section.

Such wanton mislabeling seriously disturbs me as both a librarian and library user. And I suspect it will equally disturb the publisher and author, all the more so since they explicitly state on page 6:

This book is not intended to encourage or promote any type of gambling in any jurisdiction where said gambling may be contrary to local laws.

It is the purpose of this book to give the vast American sporting public a clearer understanding of the science of sports handicapping.

If no appropriate, nonjudgmental DDC number was available to LC's classifiers, they should have created one. That's precisely what we did here last year, innovating 796.04—within the schedule for "Athletic and outdoor sports and games"—to cover "Sports betting." And 796.04 is the number we've just assigned to Olshan's title.

While it's too late to repair the CIP data, perhaps LC could still make some amends by correcting its MARC entry and catalog cards. Otherwise, the treatment will remain grossly inaccurate. Misleading. And unfair.

cc: Chief, Decimal Classification Division,
Processing Dept., Library of Congress

Simon & Schuster

*   *   *

Reprinted from *HCL Cataloging Bulletin*, no. 20 (March 1, 1976): 11–2.

Melvin H. Buxbaum's *Benjamin Franklin and the Zealous Presbyterians* (1975) deals with religion in colonial America and especially Franklin's attitude toward Calvinists, whom he loosely termed "Presbyterians." It has little, if anything, to do with international relations or diplomacy. Yet 973.32, its LC/CIP Dewey number, translates into "Relations of the United States with other nations" during the period of "Revolution and Confederation, 1775-1789." Which underscores again the necessity to closely check out those sometimes wayward digits, for timesaving "shortcuts" may actually result in costly mistakes. (HCL classed Buxbaum's study in 277.302, which we hope signifies "Christian Church in the colonial United States.")

*   *   *

In October 1975, Judith Schaeffer and Susan J. Alessi, cataloger and adult services head at the Merrick (New York) Library, complained in a letter to LC's assistant cataloging director that placing Serge Groussard's *Blood of Israel: The Massacre of the Israeli Athletes, the Olympics, 1972* (1975) "in the Dewey Classification for Olympics [796.48] shows gross insensitivity." They noted that Bro-Dart/McNaughton "managed quite easily to classify this account of political terrorism and massacre in 364.152—murder and suicide." Responding to their criticism, the chief of LC's Decimal Classification Division concurred that the work had been misclassed, explaining that error with the remarkable admission that Groussard's title had been cataloged "from Cataloging-In-Publication data, *which is often insufficient for a complete analysis of the work*"! (Emphasis added.) For the full exchange, see *"Blood of Israel* cataloging," *Unabashed Librarian*, no. 17 (Fall 1975): 8.

*   *   *

As a further gloss on LC praxis, this is how the DCD chief answered the Olshan and Buxbaum points:

> First, the work on gambling by Olshan: We really goofed on that one, didn't we? The correct number is 796. We are introducing into the text of Dewey 19 at 795 the note: "Class here gambling: class gambling on a specific activity with the activity." Since there is so much literature on betting on the ponies, there is a special number at 798.401. However, we do not think the literature on betting on athletic games justifies a separate number. In this connection, I would like to remonstrate mildly your practice of establishing new numbers without knowing whether we are establishing the same number or a different one or none. I recommend that you read section 4.32 on page 51 of volume 1 of the *DDC*.
>
> The same stricture applies to your addition of 02 to the number 277.3 for Christian church in the colonial United States. Here, as a matter of fact, your addition will conflict with the number that Edition 19 will provide, namely 277. 307.
>
> As for the book on Benjamin Franklin, again we goofed but in a more understandable way. First let me explain that we work at a tremendous disadvantage with many CIP publications because all we have is the title page, front matter, and blurb. Lacking sufficient information we classed this work with the biography of Benjamin Franklin, the comprehensive number for which has been established as 973. 320924[B]. Now that we have examined the book, we agree with you that the work should be in 277.3. We are reclassing this work to 277.3 and the work on gambling to 796.

Deweying the Supernatural

If a recently discovered manuscript on painting technique and theory by the French artist, Paul Cézanne, were just published under a title like *The World View of Paul Cézanne* and LC placed it in 759.4, the classification would prompt no special notice nor complaint. But what if a book appeared with the title, *World View of Paul Cézanne: A Psychic Interpretation*, and was composed largely of material *dictated* in late 1975 and early 1976 by Cézanne—who died in 1906—to Jane Roberts, a "sensitive" who since 1963 has been busily transcribing (and selling) whole reams of wisdom and advice communicated by "Seth," a "personality 'no longer focused in physical reality'"? What Dewey number should *that* get? Well, Prentice-Hall issued just such a volume last year. And it *got* 759.4, which violates at least three cardinal principles of classification:

- Material should be classed where browsers would most likely *seek* it.

- Similar materials should be found in the same or nearby Dewey ranges.

- Material should not be classed in such a way that it seems to be something that it really isn't.

The Roberts' tome would have been best classified with other "automatic writings," including the Seth/Roberts canon itself, in 133.93 ("Spiritualism: psychic phenomena"). It emphatically does *not* belong in 759.4 ("French painting") because Cézanne did not *demonstrably* author nor sanction the work, and "stenographer" Roberts has no particular credentials for expounding on nineteenth century French art. Thus, the book is not what serious 759.4 browsers are presumably looking for, and the very classification makes it appear to be what it isn't. Further, to shelve it in the 700s is, in effect, to deny the material to 133 browsers, whom it is far more likely to interest and who should reasonably expect to find precisely such titles in the "Spiritualism" section.

Reprinted from *HCL Cataloging Bulletin*. no. 36 (September/October 1978): 38–40.

In a similar vein, LC has lately cataloged several works on "Reincarnation Therapy"—e.g., Morris Netherton and Nancy Shiffrin's *Past Lives Therapy* (Morrow, 1978)—in 615.851 ("Mental therapies"). But the arguably greater audience or readership for material like the Netherton/Shiffrin opus, in which "a renowned psychologist shows how your present problems and anxieties are the result of what has happened to you in your past incarnations, stretching back centuries," is not those persons who browse in "Medical sciences." Rather, it's the folks who are "into" Reincarnation. And to class *Past Lives Therapy* in the 610s is tantamount to validating or defining as "scientific" a "therapy" that's essentially metaphysical, if not totally occult. Even on the sole basis of like-to-like, these titles should be classed in 129.4 ("Origin and destiny of individual souls: incarnation and reincarnation").

Richard de Mille's review of Carlos Castaneda's *Second Ring of Power* (1977) in the *Skeptical Inquirer*, v. 2, no. 2 (Spring/Summer 1978): 114, begins:

> This book, the *Library Journal* said, "raises the question whether Castaneda's journey should continue to be viewed as nonfiction" (November 1, 1977, p. 2267). About time, I should think. Nevertheless, despite a year's warning from me [in *Castaneda's Journey: The Power and the Allegory* (Capra Press, 1976)], the Library of Congress goes right on classifying Don Juan books as Yaqui history.

And although the Don Juan series has, indeed, been variously and convincingly termed "fictional ethnography," "anthrofantasy," and "hoax," de Mille is not quite right on two counts:

1. The second published of Castaneda's "brilliant frauds," *Journey to Ixtlan: The Lessons of Don Juan* (1972), was classed by LC in 133.4 ("Magic, witchcraft, demonology").

2. All other titles, from *The Teachings of Don Juan* (1968) through *Tales of Power* (1974) and *Second Ring of Power* (1977), have been LC classified 299.7 ("Religions of North American Indian origin"). Further, they have been uniformly subject-traced YAQUI INDIANS—RELIGION AND MYTHOLOGY, not YAQUI INDIANS—HISTORY.

Even with these corrections, however, de Mille's criticism remains basically valid: Don Juan, Castaneda's alleged seer, is only nominally "Yaqui," and the "recorded" events or experiences are mainly paranormal in nature. Consequently, anyone desiring genuine, detailed information on *Yaqui* (or overall Native American) culture and religion would be disserved by finding Castaneda's materials on the shelf at 299.7 or in the catalog under YAQUI INDIANS. Where *do* they belong? Some, of course, would soberly and forcefully recommend *F* (Fiction) or perhaps 398.4 ("The paranatural and legendary as subjects of folklore"). But it would render no disservice to browsers, author, *or* critics if LC's second-time classification— *133.4*—were consistently assigned to *all* the Don Juan titles. The number simply denotes "Witchcraft," and Don Juan is endlessly referred to by Castaneda himself as a "brujo" or "sorcerer." (In fact, Castaneda's *Journey to Ixtlan* was accepted as a doctoral dissertation in Anthropology at UCLA as *Sorcery: A*

Description of the World.) Moreover, a 133 notation doesn't necessarily imply that any so-classed work is "scientific" *or* "fraudulent," but it *does* appropriately signal that the topic (whatever its treatment) lies within the broad category of "Parapsychology and occultism," and *not*—in this particular case—within the sphere of either Religion or Social Science. Finally, as a complement to this classification reform, the subject tracing, YAQUI INDIANS—RELIGION AND MYTHOLOGY, deserves replacement by the exquisitely direct and noncontentious WITCHCRAFT. (Strangely, the very title rightly classed by LC in 133.4—i.e., *Journey to Ixtlan*—bore only these two subject tracings: 1. Juan, Don, 1891- 2. Hallucinogenic drugs. That is, the tracings utterly failed to reflect or to harmonize with the topic represented by the DDC number.)

As a last example of the apparent confusion in handling the current tidal wave of esoterica, there's Arnold Lieber's *Lunar Effect: Biological Tides and Human Emotion* (Anchor Press, 1978). LC classed this in 155.91 ("Psychology of influence, pattern, example: physical influences"). Now, that *might* seem altogether right and proper, except that the psychiatrist author explicitly defines his work as "the first synthesis of an overall perspective of cosmobiology" (page 120): a new "discipline" concerned with planetary, stellar, lunar, and cosmic influences on humans. Lieber maintains he's not an astrologist nor an occultist, but nevertheless hints strongly that this cosmic "science" may well solve such enigmas as the Bermuda Triangle (which *is* no special enigma, as countless investigations and an hour-long "Nova" documentary have conclusively shown). Nor is Lieber, much like generations of astrologers, able to isolate the vector, the medium, the instrument for his claimed "lunar effect" on human psyches. In sum, it can be confidently predicted that the book will prove of greater congeniality, if not delight, to 133 browsers than to persons scanning the 155s. Again, the LC classifier failed to perceive this material—like Castaneda's and Roberts'—in its true "New Age"/psi/parascience context. At HCL, it has been accommodated by a brand-new number: 133.59, representing "Cosmobiology." And two other psi topics have also been assigned specific, unambiguous notations: Psychic archaeology (133.87) and Astral projection (133.89).

Incidentally, the above-mentioned Roberts tome underwent a curious subject treatment: apart from a heading for Cézanne, it received only the much-too-broad and inexact PSYCHICAL RESEARCH. Preferable to that second rubric would have been LC's own SPIRIT WRITINGS or the HCL substitute, AUTOMATIC WRITINGS (PSYCHIC PHENOMENA).

Cataloging Castaneda

On May 18, 1978, Richard de Mille sent the following letter to the director for cataloging at the Library of Congress:

> Some years ago, Curtis D. MacDougall wrote in *Hoaxes* about the Library's policy on correcting catalog cards when a work is discovered to be a hoax . . . . As author of *Castaneda's Journey* and of a sequel in preparation, *The Don Juan Papers: Further Castaneda Controversies*, I should like to have a letter, to be quoted in the *Don Juan Papers*, stating current policies and thinking on discovered hoaxes and present or prospective application of such policies and thinking to the Don Juan hoax. Specifically, I should like to know whether Carlos Castaneda's works (68-17303, 79-139617, 72-83221, 74-10601, 77-22107) will continue to be classified E99.Y3, and, if so, what reasons are given for the continuation.
>
> Some background may be useful. The following anthropological authorities have denied that the Don Juan books should be recognized as ethnography dealing with Yaqui culture:
>
> - Edward H. Spicer. *American Anthropologist*, April 1969, 71:320-322.
> - Keith H. Basso. *Annual Review of Anthropology*, 1973, 2:246. ("Should not be mistaken for ethnography.")
> - William & Claudia Madsen. *Natural History*, June 1971, 80(6):80.
>
> The following authorities have said the books are not anthropology:
>
> - Agehananda Bharati. *The Realm of the Extra Human: Agents and Audiences*, Mouton, 1976:9. ("Quasi-anthropology.")
> - Ralph Beals. *Los Angeles Times Book Review*, 17 July 1977:2. ("Not anthropology.")
>
> The following have seriously questioned the factuality of the Don Juan books as personal memoirs:
>
> - Edmund Leach [anthropologist]. *New York Review of Books*, 5 June 1969: 12-13.
> - David Silverman [sociologist]. *Reading Castaneda*. Routledge & Kegan Paul, 1975: xi.
> - Stan Wilk [anthropologist]. *American Anthropologist*, Dec. 1977, 79:921.
> - *Library Journal*, 1 Nov 1977, 102:2267.
> - *Publishers Weekly*, 6 Sep 1976, 210(10):60; 28 Nov 1977, 212(22):42.

Reprinted from *HCL Cataloging Bulletin*, no. 37 (November/December 1978): 1–3.

The following have confidently judged the Don Juan books to be fiction:

- R. Gordon Wasson. *Economic Botany*, Jul-Sep 1974, 28:245-246.
- Weston La Barre. *The Peyote Cult*. Schocken, 1975: 271-275.
- *Booklist*, 1 Dec 1977, 74:599.
- John Leonard. *New York Times*, 29 Dec 1977:C18.
- Robert Bly. *New York Times Book Review*, 22 Jan 1978:7:22.
- David Farren. *Los Angeles Times Book Review*, 5 March 1978:4.

On August 18, the director replied:

The Library is currently operating under two policies depending upon whether the misrepresentation is in the descriptive elements of a work or in the subject content.

In descriptive cataloging, a misrepresentation is corrected as soon as "the truth" becomes known. In certain situations (e.g., authorship ascription), supporting documentation would need to be fairly strong.

In subject cataloging, the general policy is to follow the statements of the author and publisher as long as the item has been issued as a legitimate work on the subject. Reclassification would not be undertaken without a statement from the author and/or publisher that a misrepresentation had occurred, although others may have determined that the work is one of the imagination. The basic goal in book classification is to bring similar works together on the shelves. Such an arrangement best serves the library user when browsing through the book stacks in search of material of interest. The cataloger fulfills his role by identifying the topics of particular works and placing them with other works on the same topics. While some of these works may be outstanding contributions, others may be poor in quality, based on inaccurate research, or even outright frauds. The cataloger does not and should not place value judgments on these works. For these reasons, Castaneda's works continue to be classified in E99.Y3.

On August 28, Mr. de Mille wrote Hennepin County Library:

In your bulletin [no. 36, page 39], you call *Ixtlan* Castaneda's second book; it was his third. My statement that the Library of Congress continues to classify his books as Yaqui history depended on an *assumption* about the E99 classification, and may itself be unreliable . . . .

If it is true that LC described *Ixtlan* under subject headings only of Don Juan and hallucinogenic drugs, this would conflict not only with the DDC number, as you say, but with the content of the book, which is noted for its departure from the drug theme: it is precisely the book in which the drug theme was abandoned in favor of drugless mystical methods.

De Mille is right about the Castaneda canon being uniformly classed in E99. In fact, the precise LC notation for Don Juan titles, as the director indicates, is E99.Y3. True, that number *appears* to fall within the "American history" schedule, but the E51-99 sequence actually functions as a catchall for material on "Indians of North America," encompasing such varied aspects as ethnography, religion, history, folklore, and, finally, specific "tribes." (The Y3 in Castaneda classmarks specifically denotes "Yaqui.") So it's clear that with the lone exception of *Journey to Ixtlan,* the Don Juan cycle has been consistently assigned both Dewey and LC numbers that in effect declare: "These works primarily deal with Native American, particularly Yaqui, culture and religion." And the subject tracing YAQUI INDIANS—RELIGION AND MYTHOLOGY, applied to every title but *Ixtlan*, is absolutely explicit on that score.

The director for cataloging states that "the basic goal in book classification is to bring similar works together on the shelves," that "the cataloger fulfills his [sic!] role by identifying the topics of particular works and placing them with other works on the same topics," and that "the cataloger . . . should not place value judgments on these works." Now, it's entirely possible to agree on every one of those points and *still* conclude that Castaneda's output has been woefully *mis*classed. Why? Simply because—whether "hoaxes" or not—Mr. C's Donjuaniana does *not* primarily nor essentially nor even ostensibly deal with *Yaqui Indians*. Not even the publisher makes such claims. The jacket notes, as an example, for *Tales of Power* never mention "Yaqui." They do, however, describe that work as "the culmination of [Castaneda's] extraordinary initiation into the mysteries of sorcery." Indeed, terms like "sorcery," "sorcerer," "unknown," "mysterious," "secrets," and "tricks" appear more than ten times in the space of five short paragraphs. The publishers may not have admitted a fraud, but they've transmitted the unmistakable message that *Tales of Power*, e.g., in *their* opinion concerns witchcraft and the occult, *not* Yaqui ethnography or religion. And thus the cataloger—à la the director—would best fulfill his or her role vis-à-vis Castaneda by "identifying the topics" of C's volumes as basically paranormal, with an accent on "witchcraft," and therefore genuinely "place them with other works on the same topics," namely in 133.4 (Dewey) or BF1563-84 (LC).

DDC 19: An Indictment

In open-stack libraries—public, school, or college—classification performs *one* primary function: It allows patrons (and staff) to successfully "retrieve" material in particular genres and subject areas by browsing, without first making a catalog search. It does this through the assignment of notations or call numbers derived from a standard scheme. The scheme, ideally, is organized so that all major disciplines and topics, old and new, are fully represented, with related or congenial fields and forms appearing near one another.[1] The scheme, in short, should be logical, comprehensive, and contemporary.

To permit successful browsing, the notations or call numbers themselves—the shorthand surrogates for topics and genres—must be:

- Reliably constant in meaning or value. (What 301.412 signifies today, it should also signify tomorrow.)[2]

- Moderate in length. (A notation longer than seven or eight digits, that is, four or five digits beyond the decimal point, not only becomes nearly impossible to remember, but also invites labeling, shelving, and keyboarding errors.)[3]

A classification scheme like Dewey should be managed by its stewards, producers, and designers in a way that promptly reflects new scholarship, research, and publishing developments while simultaneously respecting the needs and limitations of its consumers in the "real" library world.

Reprinted from *Library Journal* (March 1, 1980): 585–9. Published by R.R. Bowker Co. (a Xerox company). Copyright © *1980 by Xerox Corporation.*

Forest Press in mid-1979 issued a three-volume 19th edition of the *Dewey Decimal Classification,* which the Decimal Classification Division at the Library of Congress began to implement in January 1980.[4] According to Benjamin A. Custer, *DDC 19* editor and former DCD chief, writing before publication:

> Completely remodeled provisions will appear for the following:
>
> - 301–307 Sociology will be expanded from the former 301, making use in addition of 302–307, numbers that have not been used for nearly 20 years, when they were the standard subdivisions of the social sciences.
>
> - 324 The political process will be revised from the former 324 and 329, and will supply detailed numbers for political parties of the United States and many other countries.

In addition to the relocations in the phoenix schedules [301–307 and 324], there will be about 340 other relocations. . . . Not surprisingly, nearly half of these are in the social sciences and technology classes, 300 and 600.[5]

Forest Press should immediately recall the 19th edition and DCD refuse to further implement it for these reasons:

1. Phoenix schedules, however satisfying to ivory-tower scheme-makers, create absolute havoc on library shelves and effectively undermine both successful browsing and the library's own credibility.[6] The common management nostrums—to either reclassify all the affected materials or insert wooden dummies that refer from old to new numbers and vice versa—are laughably unrealistic, particularly in a time of budgetary retrenchment, staff shortages, and continuing backlogs.[7] If a new phoenix in fact replaced a hopelessly outdated, confused, and constricted schedule with something indisputably more thorough and modern, a substitute also highlighted by consistently shorter basic notations than the original, an understandable—if still tenuous—argument might be made for it. That is not, however, the case with *DDC 19*'s 301–307 substitution for the earlier 301/309 ranges, e.g.,

- "Social control and socialization," 301.15 in *DDC 18,* becomes 303.3 in Edition 19, the chief advantage being a one-digit-shorter notation, but nevertheless a notation completely alien and unknown to regular, live browsers *and* library staff.

- *DDC 18,* in its 301.43–.435 sequence, provided discrete numbers for "Children," "Adolescents," "Mature and middle-aged persons," and "Aged persons." Edition 19, by contrast, retrogressively specifies places for only "Young people" (up to age 20), "Adults," and "Adults aged 65 and over" (305.2–.26). "Teenagers" have thus been eliminated as a separate, shelve-together category, and the new edition entirely fails to introduce a useful notation for "Young adults" (ages 18–25).[8]

- Edition 18 allotted one number *each* to "The sexes and their relations" (301.41), "Men" (301.411), and "Women" (301.412). *DDC 19* allocates *no* number to "The sexes and their relations," instead declaring that "comprehensive works on specific sexes" should be classed in the single slot for "Men" (305.3). A whole, vital category of comparative "sexual relations" materials, which previously enjoyed a distinct location, is now illogically and unreasonably subsumed under the number for *one* of the two sexes. Further, while the "Women" sequence has been rightly expanded (from one number to four), "Men" underwent no comparable refinement. And it may be strongly claimed that *both* topics deserve even *more* than four numbers apiece.[9]

- Although Edition 18 can hardly be credited with a wholly up-to-date and accurate breakdown for "Sexuality" themes, at least it recognized individual subjects or subject clusters like "Courtship," "Dating," "Premarital relations," and "Incest/Bestiality/Sadism/Masochism," investing each with a special number. *DDC 19* lumps *all* those previously separated topics into *one* number, 306.7 ("Institutions pertaining to relations of the sexes"). Further, it continues the unpardonable neglect of Gays by again assigning only *one* five-digit spot to "Homosexuality," making no provision for the independent collocation of materials dealing uniquely with Gay men, Lesbians, and the Gay Liberation Movement.[10] Moreover, "Bisexuality" has been ineptly subsumed under "Homosexuality," while "Transvestism," "Transsexuality," and "Heterosexuality," all ignored in Edition 18, similarly appear nowhere in *DDC 19*—not in the schedules nor the index.[11]

  2. Like the phoenixes, numerous single-number relocations destroy the integrity, the trustworthiness, of old and/or new numbers without compensating benefits, e.g.,

- "Subject cataloging" has been switched from 025.33 to the new 025.47, now following—rather than preceding—"Classification." And "Abstracting" and "Indexing" alike have been transferred from the abolished 029s to the revamped 025.4s. What was the compelling need to move them at all? And if it were agreed that, yes, indexing *should* inhabit the same shelf space as "subject cataloging," why not inflict minimal devastation by simply expanding 025.33 to accommodate the indexing topics (which even in Edition 19 run to six digits, anyway)?

- "Safety" is wantonly transferred from 614.8 to 363.1 and "Product hazards" from 614.3 to 363.19, distances of nearly 300 digits! And "Family planning" is forcibly and illogically moved from the 300s to the 600s.

- The four places traditionally and appropriately specified for North American Indians—970.1, "History and civilization"; 970.3, "Specific peoples"; 970.4, "Specific places"; and 970.5, "Government relations"—have been rendered "optional." This means, from a purely practical standpoint, that DCD won't apply them and consumers therefore won't find them on LC cards and other "outside copy." What *will* DCD apply instead? The newly "preferred" 970.00497 as a catchall for the first three notations, and 323.1197 in place of 970.5. There's an adjective that nicely describes such changes. It's *irresponsible*.

3. Expansions of many fields and subjects that *should* have been effected years ago by means of the semiannual *Dewey Decimal Classification Additions, Notes, and Decisions* have not *yet* been instituted. The overriding example is "Popular music." Edition 18 accorded this genre, which is of tremendous import to public and school collections, a *single* finite number: 780.42. Edition 19 practically repeats that woeful treatment, merely inserting a four-number "Popular song" sequence at 784.5 (encompassing country, blues, rock, and soul *vocal* music), which prompted this comment:

> Public libraries, in particular, have for years been ill served by Dewey music schedules that allocate a single notation for "Popular music." That sole number, presumably, is sufficient to accommodate thousands of records and tapes in genres as diverse as blues, rock, country, and soul. Well, it *doesn't* accommodate them. And while the Dewey directors had long ago promised a 780 phoenix for Edition 19, it won't be there. The explanation: "serious reservations" among members (whoever they are) of the Decimal Classification Editorial Policy Committee. But a whole phoenix isn't necessarily required. What *is* needed—and could have been supplied *already*—is a sensible, useable breakdown for pop music. Forest Press, et al. not only *haven't* met this demonstrated need, but probably won't do so—at least until Edition 20 (i.e., about 1986). Which is inexcusable.[12]

What *could* have been done to bring overdue relief and consistency to "pop music" classifying *without* wrecking the integrity of existing 780 numbers? Perhaps something akin to the sequence developed over several years at Hennepin County Library:

780.4	General special
.42	Popular music
	Class jazz in 785.42, ragtime in 785.422. Further divide .42 schedule like numbers following "78" in 784.1-.3 (Vocals) and 785-789 (Instrumentals); e.g., blues vocal, 780.42643.
.421	General popular
	Examples: Mancini, Welk, Streisand, Sinatra, Martin, Andrews Sisters
.422	Country-Western
.423	Bluegrass
.424	Rock
	Class Rock opera in 782.2
.42499	Disco
.425	Soul
	Including Rhythm and Blues
.426	Blues
.427	Reggae

• Scores of new topics for which ample literary warrant exists—and often *has* existed for years—remain unrepresented in either the schedules or index, with the result that increasing holdings in these areas are likely to be scattered or buried under imprecise or too-broad numbers rather than collocated in specified and expectable places. As examples, indicating how and when HCL validated each subject:

Topic	HCL Number	Established
Alternative medicine[13]	610.42	November 1978
Appropriate technology	604.3	September 1977
Backpacking [*DDC* subsumes under "Walking," 796.51]	796.53	July 1977
Ballooning	797.57	July 1977
Barbershop quartets	784.72	September 1978
Battered women	362.882	July 1977
Belly dancing	793.325	April 1974
Bermuda Triangle	001.946	November 1977
Biorhythm theory	133.34	November 1978
Cinematic poetry	791.4354	September 1974
Computer art	744	September 1978
Copy art	778.1	November 1979
Dance drill teams, chorus lines	793.326	September 1977
Ethnic publishers	070.596	March 1975
Frisbee	796.23	July 1977
GI Movement ("Including coffeehouses, underground press, American Servicemen's Union, antiwar activities")	355.227	August 1975
Genetic engineering ("Including cloning and sex selection")	575.3	July 1977
Governesses/wet nurses/nannies	649.2	January 1974
Government grants	336.395	May 1978
Greenhouses [*DDC* subsumes under "Farm buildings," 728.92]	728.93	May 1978
Hang gliding	797.553	June 1975
High-fiber cooking	641.5637	September 1977
Holistic health	610.42	November 1978
Homesteading	630.43	August 1975
Hospices	362.19604	July 1978
Ice skate dancing	793.336	April 1977
Jury reform	347.0753	October 1975
Kirlian photography	778.38	September 1976
Mainstreaming (Education)	371.9046	September 1978
"New Age"	132	May 1979
Oral history	907.204	March 1978
Orienteering	796.55	April 1977
Packhorse camping	796.546	September 1977
Paddle tennis [*DDC* subsumes under "Racket games," 796.34]	796.344	March 1979
Paddleball	796.348	March 1979
Parent education	649.107	July 1977
Planned unit development	333.382	November 1977
Police misconduct	363.25	January 1974
Popular culture	301.17	January 1978
Protest songs	784.67	May 1976
Psychic archaeology	133.87	September 1978
Pyramid energy	118.2	April 1977
Race walking	796.427	March 1975
Rape victims	362.883	September 1977
Rock opera	782.2	April 1974
Roller skate dancing	793.336	April 1977
Rope skipping	796.45	December 1976
Runaway services [*DDC* subsumes under "Maladjusted young people," 362.74]	362.75	April 1977

Topic	HCL Number	Established
Senior Power	301.43532	October 1975
Singing commercials	784.69	July 1977
Skateboarding [*DDC* subsumes under "Roller skating," 796.21]	796.22	September 1976
Small presses	070.598	June 1975
Space colonies	629.447	September 1977
Sports betting	796.04	October 1975
Style manuals (Journalism/ publishing)	070.0202	July 1978
Volunteer workers/volunteerism	331.53	September 1976
War games [*DDC* subsumes under "Indoor diversions," 793.9]	794.4	April 1974
Women and labor unions	331.882	March 1975
Women's music	780.46	September 1976
Women's publishers	070.596	March 1975
Women's songs	784.65	May 1976
Wood heating	697.041	August 1975

In sum, it is time to reform totally the process of *DDC* revision, perhaps according to these guidelines:

- Concoct no more phoenix schedules.
- Make no more relocations except when approved by two-thirds of an editorial board composed of representatives *elected*—on a proportional basis—by the public, school, and academic libraries that actually *use* Dewey. (This formula would exclude from voting membership all Library of Congress and Forest Press personnel, as well as library school faculty.)[14]
- Integrate new or expanded topics within existing schedules by adding digits to current numbers, reviving latent notations, or redefining the scope of active numbers.

Notes

1. Berman has posited as one of three "cardinal principles of classification" that "similar materials should be found in the same or nearby Dewey ranges." See "Deweying the Supernatural," *HCL Cataloging Bulletin*, no. 36 (September/October 1978): 38 [*Joy of Cataloging*, pp. 171–3].

2. Maurice Freedman observes that "both users and classifiers ... profit from the *non*duplication of numbers with different subject matters. It is a horror in the real world to have totally different categories of materials occupying the same Dewey number. It is bad enough that a given subject is split between two numbers, but when a multiplicity of categories reside at the same address, the user's resultant confusion is the kind of public service problem that libraries can do without." See "Better Latent than Never—A Few Short Comments on the Proposed *DDC19*, and the Custer/ Comaromi Statements in HCLCB no. 35," *HCL Cataloging Bulletin*, no. 37 (November/December 1978): 6.

3. John P. Comaromi, who chaired the Decimal Classification Editorial Policy Committee and has since succeeded Custer as chief

of the Library of Congress Decimal Classification Division, recently suggested that "if your library is large or intends to become so, use the Dewey number to its fullest extent. If that is impossible, set your limit on number length at seven-past-the-decimal point. . . ." See "*DDC 19*: The Reclass Project," *HCL Cataloging Bulletin*, no. 35 (July/August 1978): 14. Freedman ("Better Latent than Never," p. 9) subsequently responded that to:

> extend Dewey numbers at least seven-past-the-decimal-point is one of the most impractical suggestions made and the one I would recommend that all nonresearch libraries ignore. The Branch Libraries of the New York Public Library, possibly the largest public library in the country, extends to five-past-the-decimal-point, and even then pages have trouble properly shelving materials. The long Dewey number is error prone for the classifier, processor, shelver, and reader. Further, the justification for these long numbers can only be sustained—at best—when one considers their use in large research libraries. One omitted the reference librarian, who, even more importantly than the cataloger, must have a working memory of the more common Dewey numbers. Requiring this person to do floor work, "schlepping" around ten-digit numbers, seems unreasonable . . . . Ten digits are just too many for practical application in a browsing library . . . . Even in a closed-stack situation, the page or shelver is still prone to error . . . .
>
> The larger issue, and one can only guess this was an unstated motivation of Prof. Comaromi in his advocacy of these long numbers, is the elegance and manipulability of extended numbers for machine retrieval purposes. In Great Britain there is an interest in classification research and the use of computers for retrieval purposes which has no parallel here. In a closed-stack collection for which classification is primarily or solely a means of subject analysis and retrieval rather than shelf location, lengthy classification numbers can be quite useful and of significant value. But in the American public library context, one finds them most impractical and confounding for all of the people who must deal with them.

And Katharine Gaines has similarly argued for *more* mnemonics and *shorter* notations. See "Dewey: For—or against—the Public Library?" *HCL Cataloging Bulletin*, nos. 23-24 (September 1, 1976): 7-8, 10.

4. Benjamin A. Custer, "*DDC 19*: Characteristics," *HCL Cataloging Bulletin*, no. 35 (July/August 1978): 9.

5. Custer, pp. 9-10.

6. Freedman ("Better Latent than Never," p. 7.) has commented that:

> the *DDC*, or for that matter any classification system which functions primarily as a shelf arrangement device for a browsing . . . library, should minimize dislocation and change so as to avoid the attendant hardship on the library's users—both the public and the staff who use the collections in order to help the public. Changes must be based on more than just aesthetic or theoretical considerations . . . . The basic point is that classification is . . . both a physical and conceptual arrangement of library materials, and, as such, each shift, be it unique or part of a body rising from its own ashes, should be viewed from a principle of necessity and utility: *is this change absolutely necessary, and will the benefits far outweigh the ensuing problems?*

And Marvin Scilken, editor of the *Unabashed Librarian* and director of the Orange (NJ) Public Library, adds that "*DDC 19, AACR2*, etc. will only make us look more foolish in the eyes of our users, that small percentage of the public that's willing to put up with us now." Letter in *HCL Cataloging Bulletin*, no. 37 (November/December 1978): 12.

7. Comaromi recommends reclassification and shelf dummies in "*DDC 19*: The Reclass Project," pp. 12-5. Berman replied in *HCL Cataloging Bulletin*, no. 36 (September/October 1978): 37:

> Ordinary libraries, already faced with reduced income and inflationary costs, plainly cannot implement the sort of 'reclass project' recommended by Prof. Comaromi. They don't have the staff nor time. And even the dummy approach may be unfeasible when dealing with literally hundreds of relocations per library in systems composed of 10, 20, or more agencies.

And Scilken (p. 12) characterized the Comaromi approach as "unworldly," explaining:

> It's my impression that most public libraries are lucky if they have *one* cataloger. And most school libraries have *none*.
>
> Comaromi assumes that libraries have a reclass platoon on the beach waiting for its eight-year cycle to come up so it can "get in there" and reclass for the old Dui. This would be great, but we all know what a mess most of our catalogs are in and *DDC 19* will only add to the morass of trash.
>
> If we lived in a perfect world, with books and cards reclassifying themselves, change would be wonderful. In the world of Jarvis/Gann, it seems foolish to foist extensive changes that increase both librarians' guilt and libraries' disorganization.

For another reclass critique, from the perspective of clerical and page staff, see Steve Thompson's letter in *HCL Cataloging Bulletin*, no. 37 (November/December 1978): 13-4.

8. HCL did so in early 1979 by inserting the unused number, 301.432, between 301.4315, "Adolescents" and 301.434, "Mature and middle-aged persons." See *HCL Cataloging Bulletin*, no. 39 (March/April 1979): 33.

9. For HCL's 1975 expansion of the 301.41s, including specifications for topics like "Androgyny," "Men's and women's studies," "Men's liberation," "the Women's movement," "Sexism," "Homemakers," and "Consciousness-raising groups," see "New and Revised *DDC* notations," *HCL Cataloging Bulletin*, nos. 11-13 (March 15, 1975): 13-6.

10. For HCL's handling, see "New and Revised *DDC* Notations," *HCL Cataloging Bulletin*, nos. 11-13 (March 15, 1975): 16. Also: S. Berman's "Gay Access: New Approaches in Cataloging," *Gay Insurgent*, nos. 4–5 (Spring 1979): 14–5 [*Joy of Cataloging*, pp. 110–2].

Unsurprisingly, the *DDC 19* index includes absolutely no "Gay" entries or cross-references. It does, however, predictably site "Homosexuality" in no less than four separate medical/clinical numbers (e.g., 157.7, "Disorders of character and personality"), in Social issues" (363.49), and in "Social theology," as well as referring to

"Moral issues" and " Sexual deviations" for "other aspects" of the topic.

11. HCL in late 1973 reactivated 301.413 (formerly denoting "Celibacy") to "cover sociologically oriented material on Transvestism and Transvestites" and innovated 301.416 to represent "Transsexuality." See "Classification," *HCL Cataloging Bulletin*, no. 4 (November 21, 1973): 12. A notation for "Bisexuality" (301.4156) was created about two years later. See "New and Revised *DDC* Notations," *HCL Cataloging Bulletin*, no. 17 (October 1, 1975): 13.

12. S. Berman, *HCL Cataloging Bulletin*, no. 36 (September/October 1978): 37. For another critique, see Freedman, "Better Latent than Never," p. 7.

13. Only one "Alternative" entry appears in the *DDC 19* index: "Alternative education."

14. Prepublication input from *DDC* users seems to have been minimal. And even unwanted. There appears to be no mechanism for Dewey consumers to directly elect representatives to advisory or policymaking bodies. And there is little or no visible effort to secure advance opinion on proposed changes. Indeed, the whole revision process comes across as marvelously secretive and hush-hush, almost as if national security would be threatened by leaks or—much worse—public discussion. For further comment on *DDC* governance, see Freedman ("Better Latent than Never"), p. 9, and Gaines ("Dewey: For—or against—the Public Library"), p. 7, who sagely noted that "since catalogers have so little clout (and too many have their feet stuck in detail), the designer doesn't hear enough about what's wrong and goes on merrily constructing abstract cobwebs. These designers of revised schedules probably never use them . . . in actual public library practice."

REVIEWS

Special Cataloguing

Horner, John Leonard. *Special Cataloguing, with Particular Reference to Music, Films, Maps, Serials, and the Multi-Media Computerized Catalogue*. Hamden, CT: Linnet Books, 1973. 327 p.

If this had been a 50-page, 75¢ pamphlet written and published last month, it could be warmly recommended. Horner, an Australian lecturer and experienced cataloger, knows what he's talking about. He's refreshingly "biased" toward the user, rightly favoring a minimum of apartheid-type searching "sequences," convincingly arguing for an "integrated, multi-media" catalog, wisely accenting the virtues of "uniform titles" (though he might have mentioned Schwann as a handy authority), and nicely obliterating Jay Daily's Neolithic opinion of media as something essentially weird and unassimilable with Holy Print. Much of what Horner writes is solid common sense. But he writes *too much*. And his particularly detailed analyses of many decedent and some extant "codes" are of largely academic, if not strictly archeological, interest, for his manuscript dates from 1972, prior to the appearance of the LA's *Non-book Cataloging Rules* (1973), AECT *Standards* (3d ed., 1973), and the Weihs/Lewis/Macdonald *Non-book Materials: The Organisation of Integrated Collections* (1st ed., 1973), all reviewed, incidentally, in the Autumn 1973 *Catalogue & Index*. It may be intellectually stimulating to discuss at length Cutter's 1904 *Rules* and MLA's 1958 music code, but that's not where the action is *now*. It's the lately issued codes that demand immediate analysis and harmonization. Moreover, even two years ago Horner might have managed enough of the new "sensitivity" to avoid the invariable, annoying equation: Catalogers = Men. (Not a "she" nor "her" graces the whole shtick.) Also, coupled with an inordinate verbosity that inflates the tome by perhaps two-thirds what it ought to be, there's a constant, cloying self-consciousness manifest in myriad "we dub" and "we suggest" phrases, together with irritatingly repeated locutions like "as already stated," "mentioned above," and "already mentioned," sometimes three or four of these per page.

Wit is ordinarily welcome in such studies. Here, though, it tends to be strained; e.g., Horner suggests that if *Beethoven for Ten Little Fingers* does not itself adequately "clarify the intention of the work,"

Reprinted from *HCL Cataloging Bulletin*, nos. 11–13 (March 15, 1975): 91–2.

one of the following notes may be added: "For children" or "For dwarfs." (Another, incredibly morbid, example appears on p. 94.) Well, librarianship has yet to produce an Art Buchwald.

Though not intended as a manual, the opus would nonetheless have benefitted from more graphic examples of actual or possible catalog treatment for media. Notably omitted is a sample page from the very kind of mixed-media product the author propounds. (For anyone interested, HCL will gladly supply such photocopies from its latest, multimedia book catalog supplement or upcoming, totally integrated second edition.)

While a lot of Horner's advice is surely sound, he's occasionally shortsighted or simply hung-up on traditional nonproblems. For instance, he typically recommends that film- or record-size only be shown in the collation when the item in hand differs from most of the library's stock (e.g., a 10-inch disc when the library mainly has 12-inch, or a Super-8 millimeter film when holdings are largely 16 millimeter), and also doubts that the number of phonodisc sides need be indicated, except for very "extensive" works. The first proposition, implying long-term stasis, could prove catastrophic if the library later expanded its stock of 10-inch discs or Super-8s, while the second could produce terrific confusion at the circulation desk, the clerks not necessarily knowing just how many physical discs belong in a given album that's to be charged out or in. And he frequently agonizes—as with maps—over proper main-entry forms: whether author, title, or perhaps subject area. But generous assignment of added entries, whatever the chosen main-entry principle, should furnish ample access or retrieval points.

A few good things: The idea of adding a date to subject heads for maps; e.g., MEXICO—MAPS—1941. The inclusion, resources permitting, of evaluations, review citations, summaries, distribution data, "grading," and certifications on film entries. The succinct glossary and nine-page bibliography. Opting for contents' notes to better reveal a composite work's scope. Specifying "duration of performance" on scores, etc., for the benefit of program planners. An informative section on serial main entries, naturally emphasizing the terrible hassle of title changes (which may, however, subside if the aggressive editors of that sprightly new mag, *Title Varies*, achieve their hoped-for impact). A happily cogent critique of LC music headings, as well as discussion of various forms and suitable cross-referencing for MUSIC DRAMAS, LIGHT OPERAS, GRAND OPERAS etc. (pp. 69-70). The realistic acknowledgement that while *LCSH* ought to be scuttled, it probably won't be, and thus must be reformed. And the admirable statement (on p. 109), which deserves to become a cat-and-class maxim: "Catalogues are not produced by cataloguers for their satisfaction in a completed work of art, like a wood carving . . . . They are merely tools in themselves serving as a medium to facilitate use of stock, and any information in them which is not used—however pleasing it may be to the manufacturer—is in fact worthless." (Too bad the *ISBD* manufacturers didn't operate on that basis.)

If Horner can transmute this basically valuable labor into a condensed, updated, and desexified edition, it's a natural for all library schools and practicing catalogers. But as it is now, uh-uh.

Questionable Milestones

Lehnus, Donald J. *Milestones in Cataloging: Famous Catalogers and Their Writings, 1835-1969.* Introduction by Phyllis A. Richmond. Littleton, CO: Libraries Unlimited, 1974. 137 p.

"Utilizing the method of citation analysis, Dr. Lehnus has identified the more important writings in the area of cataloging for the period from 1835 to 1969. On the basis of this core literature, the author subsequently identified the most influential catalogers of the period, studies the interrelationships between them (invisible colleges) and, by noting the duration of citations, nominates super-classics, classics, and potential classics in the field. An additional concern is to demonstrate the importance of a few libraries and related institutions, either because they published many of the important monographs or because they employed a significant number of these influential catalogers. Appendix I lists the 184 most frequently cited works, while Appendix II presents the most often cited authors (141). Appendix III is a selective bibliography of citation analysis studies, arranged chronologically. . . ."—*Publisher's News Release*, March 8, 1974.

"Topics which could be considered as a part of cataloging but which have been definitely excluded from this study are: subject cataloging; filing rules; card reproduction; union catalogs; classified catalogs; shelf lists; centralized and cooperative cataloging; and all aspects of classification."—*Milestones* . . . , p. 4.

Solid waste.

Black Literature Resources

Clack, Doris H. *Black Literature Resources: Analysis and Organization.* New York: Marcel Dekker, 1975. 207 p. $17.50.

Things are seldom what they seem. Despite the promising title, the many Du Bois quotations, the laudatory *LJ* review (5-1-76, p. 1097), the firm commitment to Black Studies, the 45 footnotes, the nine-page bibliography, the impressive, photoreproduced classification schedules and *LCSH* excerpts, and the declared intent to "initiate change and increase the effectiveness of library usage," this is *not* an incisive, thoroughgoing study of tools and praxis, *not* a tough, militant expose of racism and neglect in subject cataloging, and *not* an innovative, dynamic approach to the genuinely serious problem of constricted and distorted catalog access to Black (and other ethnic) resources. Rather, it's disappointingly sterile, essentially passive, and already dated, a *Potemkin* tome that's almost totally useless as either a theoretical critique or practical handbook.

Section I allegedly "offers a critical review of the state-of-the-art of subject analysis in libraries . . . a compelling account of the development of black literature . . . and a discussion of those influences—especially black studies—that have heightened problems of subject analysis. . . ." In fact, those three narrative chapters constitute an extremely superficial, even sophomoric, treatment of subject analysis, Black literature, and Black Studies. And at least one assertion—that the "few citations [on pages 8-9] virtually exhaust the critical references to the state of subject analysis for black resources"—is simply false.

Yes, the author rightly claims at the outset that Black resources have suffered "gross neglect," even declaring that "too rigid adherence to the framework of the Library of Congress [subject heading] list can seriously hamper the efficacy of subject analysis for this body of literature, especially with regard to specificity and relevance." But although "specificity and relevance" thereafter becomes a veritable leitmotiv, that "gross neglect" is never convincingly proven, few concrete examples being furnished of overly general or otherwise inadequate descriptors assigned to actual works and absolutely no illustration provided of specific, relevant

Reprinted from *HCL Cataloging Bulletin*, no. 22 (July 1, 1976): 32–3.

headings that might be employed as *LCSH* alternatives, of typical LC *under*cataloging (e.g., insufficient nonfiction subject tracings and seldom *any* for ethnic novels, drama, and poetry), or of counter-cataloging systems developed elsewhere (e.g., at the Makerere Institute of Social Research Library). Indeed, what forms the bulk of the work is little more than a pure tabularization of *status quo* LC subject heads and classification numbers related to "black resources." Admittedly, the codified and indexed class notations could prove of some nitty-gritty worth to classifiers using the LC scheme. However, the subject rosters are altogether valueless, for several reasons:

- "Black" is throughout construed to mean strictly "Black *American*." Hence, no "Africa" nor natural Diaspora (e.g., Afro-Brazilian, Afro-Canadian) links appear, a colossal and remarkable omission that completely isolates Afro-America from both its roots and relatives.

- The multitudinous "Negro" and "Negroes" rubrics have since been jettisoned by LC in favor of "Afro-American" and "Black" constructions, thus rendering much of the tabular data obsolete.

- Primary forms and *see* references alike are dutifully transcribed with utterly *no* comment—*none*—on the variously racist, inept, and inaccurate nature of the terms themselves and the often "peculiar" syndetic structure. Unbelievably, the author says nothing about "Negro" as an inherently objectionable word, nothing about the degrading implication of "Negroes as . . .," nothing about the indefensible MAMMIES, nothing about the victimizing subhead, RACE QUESTION, and nothing about the host of Black-related topics that LC has either introduced with disgraceful tardiness (e.g., GOSPEL SONGS) or so far failed to sanctify at all (e.g., KWANZA, BLACK THEOLOGY, RHYTHM AND BLUES MUSIC, AFFIRMATIVE ACTION, RACISM, BUSING, AFRO-AMERICANS AND AFRICA, SLAVE RESISTANCE AND REVOLTS).

In short, the book does *not* do what it was supposed to. The author complains that "traditional library tools" don't promote maximum access to Black resources. That charge, however, is *not* resoundingly demonstrated. Instead, those very "traditional tools"—virtually uncontested—occupy most of the volume's space. And how to avoid "too rigid adherence" to them or induce reforms goes undiscussed.

It's frankly impossible to imagine *what* library—anywhere—could justify spending the outrageous $17.50.

South African Cataloging

Scott, Patricia E. *Cataloguing Monographs: A Manual Illustrating the Anglo-American Cataloguing Rules British Text 1967.* 2d ed. Grahamstown, South Africa: Rhodes University, 1976. 103 p.
———. *Facsimile Title Pages to Accompany Cataloguing Monographs.* Grahamstown, South Africa: Rhodes University, 1976. 88 p.

The basic volume, "confined to monographic works" and "intended for the beginning student," seeks both to illustrate and explain *AACR*'s major principles and rules. Only *one* woman and absolutely *no* Africans appear among the abundant main-entry examples. Arabic numerals misleadingly (for Americans, at least) precede nonsubject added-entries. Neither traditional nor newly introduced format elements—like *ISBD* punctuation, brackets, cumbersome collations, and "bibliography" notes—are challenged in terms of actual relevance and utility to most libraries. (Indeed, the author coolly remarks that "introduction of [the ISBN] rule reflects the growth in importance of ISBN's for computer programming," making no comment on the equally obvious growth of user mystification reflected by such unintelligible addenda to the public cataloging record.)

Because of the heavy emphasis on South African corporate and governmental forms, catalogers handling many RSA documents may find the manual of some use. Otherwise, due to the essentially stagnant, uncritical approach, skewed personal-name examples, and imminent publication of a totally revised *AACR*, both items seem practically worthless outside South Africa. And even of dubious value inside.

Cat/Class Curricula

Thomas, Alan R. *The Library Cataloguing Curriculum,* USA: A *Survey of the Contemporary Compulsory Instruction.* London: The Panizzi Press. 1976. 77 p.

If both the quality and usefulness of cataloging, as well as the very status of catalogers, are seriously declining, our library schools not only aren't doing much to correct the situation, but may actually share the blame for it. Thomas, who teaches indexing at Ealing Technical's School of Librarianship, doesn't quite put it in those terms, yet his 1973/74 survey of cat/class curricula in 47 ALA-accredited schools easily supports such a view.

In surely the most recent—if not first-ever—analysis of course content, orientation, and purpose, Thomas provides a most welcome overview of what *is* being taught and why, plus a candid, independent examination of what's either *not* being taught at all or is woefully underemphasized (e.g., sensitivity to real library and user needs, and criticism of "standard services and systems"). Careful, thorough, and in its conclusions and suggestions equally constructive and exciting, this study deserves close and immediate attention by library school faculty, practicing catalogers, and everyone else concerned about information access.

Reprinted from *Library Journal* (January 15, 1977): 182. Published by R.R. Bowker Co. (a Xerox company). Copyright © 1977 by Xerox Corporation.

Subject Analysis

Chan, Lois Mai. *Library of Congress Subject Headings: Principles and Application*. Littleton, CO: Libraries Unlimited, 1978. 347 p.

This is a meticulous, well-illustrated guide to how LC subject headings are constructed, applied, cross-referenced, and maintained. Also, even though not "prescriptive" in intent, it critically relates mainstream theory to LC operations, particularly noting anomalies in heading structure, comparing other systems (like PRECIS), and advocating a code to complement *AACR*. On both practical and theoretical planes, the tome should prove useful to libraries that subject catalog within the *LCSH* framework. However, it could have been better.

First, the tone is pedantic and the prose dull, belying the real joy and excitement of subject analysis. And second, the criticism—based largely on orthodox sources—is much too cautious and limited, accenting morphology and mentioning "obsolescent" terms, but wholly ignoring four glaring problems: biased and awkward nomenclature; skimpy heading assignment; the failure to represent literally hundreds of old and new topics for which there is undoubted "literary warrant"; and the irrelevance of many patterns and forms (e.g., —AMATEURS' MANUALS and —ADDRESSES, ESSAYS, LECTURES) to popular collections. Further, there is no hint of possible "new frontiers"; e.g., the creation and assignment of genre headings like "REGENCY" NOVELS, "BEAT" POETRY, or TRIVIA to meet legitimate public and school library needs. Nor does the author intimate that LC descriptors and policies have been widely modified outside of Washington to make subject access at once faster, fairer, and more intelligible.

RESEARCH

A welter of highly statistical, heavily footnoted, uniformly dull, and usually irrelevant catalog-use studies inspired the following spoof, but two particular examples of the genre deserve special mention:

- Bates, Marcia J. "Factors Affecting Subject Catalog Search Success." *Journal of the American Society for Information Science* (May 1977): 161-9.

Abstract

The study examined the effects of two variables on success in searching an academic library subject catalog that uses Library of Congress subject headings. The variables were "subject familiarity," and "catalog familiarity," representing patron knowledge of a subject field and of the principles of the subject heading system, respectively. Testing was done in a laboratory setting which reproduced a real search situation. The n varied with the particular test, but about 20 university students in each of the following majors participated: psychology, economics, librarianship. Success was measured as degree of match between search term and term used by the library for desired books on the subject.

Catalog familiarity was found to have a very significant beneficial effect on search matching success, and subject familiarity a slight, but not significant, detrimental effect. An interview substudy of subject experts suggested causes for the failure of subject expertise to help in catalog search-term formulation.

Surprising results were that overall matching success was strikingly low. Since the methodology used enabled a more precise determination of match success than has been typical of catalog use studies, it appears that people may be less successful than we have thought in using subject catalogs.

Excerpts

The research design called for students to be presented with the titles and abstracts of books, to which they would respond by stating the subject term they would use in finding books just like the test ones . . . There were two major constraints on selection: (1) The book had to have a publication date between 1954 and 1962, in order to control for vocabulary change and to accommodate peculiarities of the abstracting services. (2) The most important criterion was that the book had to have been indexed with only one subject heading. In this way the student term could be matched unambiguously with the library's term.

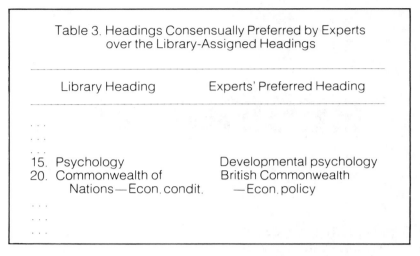

Table 3. Headings Consensually Preferred by Experts over the Library-Assigned Headings

Library Heading	Experts' Preferred Heading
. . .	
. . .	
. . .	
15. Psychology	Developmental psychology
20. Commonwealth of Nations — Econ. condit.	British Commonwealth — Econ. policy
. . .	
. . .	
. . .	

The LC system uses the rule of specific entry, which holds that a book is to be entered under the most specific term that describes its entire contents . . . It is thus expressly forbidden, for example, to apply the terms "Mental tests" or "Psychology" to a book on the Rorschach test, either alone or in conjunction with the term "Rorschach test." By the rule of specific entry, the only term that may be applied to a book is "Rorschach test." So the searcher looking under either of the broader terms will not find listed there any monographs on the Rorschach test. In addition, if the library has eliminated *see also* references to save money—as the University of Calfornia at Berkeley Library had done at the time of the study—then the user will find no references to the more specific term, "Rorschach test," in the catalog. Incidentally, *see also* references that go upward hierarchically, i.e., superordinate references, are forbidden altogether in LC. So searches going in at too specific a level get no help, whether the library uses *see also* references available in the list or not.

With automation . . . we can now use a subject approach . . . that allows the naive user, unconscious of and uninterested in the complexities of synonyms and vocabularly control, to blunder on to desired subjects, to be guided, without realizing it, by a redundant but carefully controlled subject access system. And now is the time to change—indeed, with MARC already so highly developed, past time.

Comment

1. This is not the highly refined study it claims to be since:

   a. The book titles employed (and hence their cataloging treatment) were seriously dated: i.e., "had to have a publication date between 1954 and 1962."

   b. The surveyed library had *eliminated see also* references, and there is no indication of whether it had also eliminated direct *see* references.

   c. *If see* references appeared in the catalog (as they should in a reasonably well-maintained operation), the testers apparently didn't investigate whether users successfully reached actual, primary headings *via* such x-refs.

    d. The researchers seem to be less than familiar/conversant with *LCSH*; e.g., the expert-preferred heading, DEVELOPMENTAL PSYCHOLOGY, *is* a valid LC form—and if it wasn't assigned to a given work that warranted it, the trouble or fault lay not with the scheme, but (in this case) with the cataloger.

    e. There was clearly no control introduced to genuinely test subject-search efficacy in an LC-type catalog that embodied reformed, contemporized terminology; included bountiful cross-references; was arranged/filed in essentially dictionary or alphabetical, nonhierarchical fashion; and wherein most titles (not merely 50 percent) had been assigned two or more subject tracings.

2. The reason for few (if any) superordinate *see also* references in subject catalogs is never stated and so made to seem unreasonable, if not even perverse. But it makes good sense: namely, that such references are potentially "blind."

3. "Profs" and "experts" may have been overvalued vis-à-vis their judgment; e.g., an "expert" *should* have realized that the "British Commonwealth" became the "Commonwealth of Nations" years ago. (The catalog, of course, ought to reflect that change by means of an x-ref or "history"-note.)

- Gorman, Michael, and Hotsinpiller, Jami. "ISBD: Aid or Barrier to Understanding?" *College & Research Libraries*, v. 40, no. 6 (November 1979): 519-26.

Abstract

This article investigates the validity of claims that *ISBD (International Standard Bibliographic Description)* punctuation and conventions are a barrier to the understanding of catalog information. A group of undergraduate students were asked specific questions about the elements on catalog cards. Two sets of catalog entries were used for the test. The sets were identical in content, but one followed unrevised 1967 *AACR Chapter 6* rules and the other followed *ISBD*. The degree of correctness of the response and the response time were recorded. The test results showed a slightly greater degree and number in correctness of response to the *ISBD* format cards. The study indicates that the *ISBD* format aids, rather than hinders, reader understanding.

Excerpts

All persons approached agreed to take part in the study. Whether this was due to their eagerness to help the library, general affability, or the Snickers candy bar each subject was given is not known.

Each question was designed to test the subject's understanding of the description. Typical questions were: Who is the publisher? In what city was this book published? Is this book illustrated? If you were recommending this book to a friend, what would you write down as the title?

The study demonstrates to our satisfaction that the primary problem in reader use of the descriptive data in catalog entries lies in the nature of that data, not in the manner in which it is presented. Further, that a systematic set of conventions, such as those embodied in the *ISBD*, will aid rather than hinder reader understanding. The pre-*ISBD* conventions were an uneasy combination of normal prose usage and arbitrary convention. The *ISBD* conventions have the merits of system and consistency.

It seems to us that our study could be criticized on two grounds: first, that the sample was too small, and second, that undergraduate students at a large university are not a fair example of "typical" catalog users.

If . . . the study proves that the *ISBD* aids, rather than halts, the understanding and speed of use of descriptive data as compared with pre-*ISBD* descriptions, then the long-drawn-out "controversy" over the *ISBD* is at an end.

Comment

1. Despite the elaborate "method," the well-reproduced card examples, and the nice statistical tables, the "study" does *not* prove that "*ISBD* aids, rather than halts, the understanding and speed of use of descriptive data as compared with pre-*ISBD* descriptions." Not because of too small a sample nor the exclusive testing of undergraduates, but rather because the *questions* employed—e.g., "Is this book illustrated?" or "What is the subtitle?"—inevitably prejudice the results. That is, the questions themselves tend to induce "correct" answers. For instance, it's a very different matter to ask an "ordinary user" *what* "ill." means (in context) than to ask "Is this book illustrated?" The former question genuinely tests understanding and recognition, while the latter "gives away" the answer, merely testing (if anything) the respondent's ability to apply *external* cues, to guess rightly with the benefit of Very Heavy Hints.

2. For examples of truly objective research into ordinary users' comprehension of standard bibliographic elements, particularly abbreviations, see Larry Legus' "Sure, They Save Space, but Who Knows What They Mean?," *HCL Cataloging Bulletin*, no. 40 (May/June 1979): 24–9; and "The Mystery of Ips and Mono; or, Do Students Understand AV Card Catalog Terms?" by Jane Schlueter and Robert D. Little, in Deirdre Boyle's *Expanding Media* (Phoenix: Oryx Press, 1977), pp. 273-5. These studies, incidentally, demonstrated a significant nonrecognition or nonunderstanding of such taken-for-granted cataloging conventions as *c* (copyright), *d* (died), *v* (volume), *l* (leaves), and *n.d.* (no date).

3. The "long-drawn-out 'controversy' over the *ISBD*" is hardly ended by such amateur and transparently flawed "research."

Megasucrose Levels and Manual Bibliographic Searching

by Ike Bohrmann
and Jay Pfortzmacher

Abstract

A literature search revealed that few catalog-use studies have investigated physiological factors in "hit" rates. Research was therefore undertaken to remedy these apparent lacunae in the field of information-seeking behavior.

Object

Since a thorough review of all material published in *Die allgemeine Obersturmbahnsbibliothekszeitschrift* and *Sipapu* for the years 1931–1938 failed to show any major research into the biochemical determinants of effective card catalog use, it was decided to probe this neglected aspect of patron performance using sophisticated sampling and analytical techniques.

Hypothesis

Based upon six months of continuous participant observation by the two principal researchers at the 15,000-drawer card catalog of the University of Southwestern Missouri at Ripple-Suburbana Library, it was tentatively concluded that increasingly higher levels of sugar intake by undergraduate snackers affected bibliographic searching at a progressive null-null ratio. That conclusion would be subjected to a rigorous empirical test.

Sample

To secure a test population of ordinary catalog-using undergraduates, only two requirements were posited: that the students (1) be duly enrolled and paid up; and (2) have visible acne. Of the total student universe of 35,637, fully 34,755 met these dual criteria. The test group was thus necessarily and objectively reduced to a more manageable scale by eliminating all Leos, Libras, Cancers, and Geminis, as well as redheads, Jews, Blacks, Orientals, and women. Of the remaining 27,342 students, everyone with mononucleosis was disqualified, and of the 46 persons then left, only those whose surnames began with X were accepted. The final test population consisted of 2 students, with a similarly sized control group selected at random from the locker room following an Intercollegiate Men's Towel-Snapping Competition.

Methodology

Promptly at 9 AM on a typical weekday morning, the test population was situated at the library card catalog. The students were instructed to search for either the main-entry or title-entry card for the 1965 Urdu-language translation of Jack Kerouac's *On the Road,* published at the Sri Aurobindo Ashram in Pondicherry. A "hit" would be recorded if one or the other entry were found. To make the search even more realistic, the bibliographic data were first transliterated into Cyrillic characters and then the cards deliberately misfiled. Key to the entire protocol was the periodic ingestion of *Snicker* bars, one every 15 minutes for the first hour, every 10 minutes for the second, and every 5 minutes for the third. During the same period, the control group, positioned in the student lounge, was fed *Butterfinger* bars at the identical rate while watching "All My Children," "Days of Our Lives," and "Ryan's Hope." Research staff, assembled from the Library School faculty, monitored the entire operation with stopwatches, metric rulers, and microfiche readers. The experiment terminated exactly at 12 noon.

Findings

Both the catalog searchers and TV viewers became extremely sick after two to two-and-one-half hours, a comparable and statistically significant number from each group—as calculated according to the Morgenstern Tau Coefficient— vomiting copiously into their backpacks. Additionally, both groups developed quite sticky fingers and produced a numerically critical amount of candy wrapper litter.

Future Research

While the investigators believe this study represents a notable breakthrough in the discipline of Bio-Library Toxicology, it is necessary to caution that the conclusions cannot be completely validated until the research is satisfactorily replicated under similar conditions elsewhere. Further, it is recommended that as a cross-check the next groups be tested on *Baby Ruth* and *Almond Joy.*

Policy Implications

These results, if sustained by later research, mandate two policy changes:
1. The immediate introduction of online bibliographic systems.
2. The concurrent removal of all automatic vending machines from library premises.

Tables, Charts, Graphs

Although much too detailed and complex to reproduce here, the tabular and mathematical data generated by this study will shortly be issued by Knowledge Industry Publications as a separate, three-panel color brochure @ $24.50.

Acknowledgement

The researchers wish to gratefully acknowledge the support and encouragement of the Council on Library Resources and Onan Family Foundation. Without their generous grants, totalling $575,000, this project would not have been possible. Nor profitable.

APPENDICES

APPENDICES

Cataloging Criticism and Alternatives: A Source List

Alternative Press Centre:
 Indexing Guide for Publications. 1980. 36 p. @2.50. Order from: APC, P.O. Box 7229, Baltimore, MD 21218.
Atherton, Pauline:
 "Catalog Users' Access from the Researcher's Viewpoint: Past and Present Research Which Could Affect Library Catalog Design." In *Closing the Catalog,* pp. 105–22. Phoenix, AZ: Oryx Press, 1980.
Berman, Sanford:
 "Africana Subject Headings." *Africana Libraries Newsletter,* no. 4 (February 1976): 25–8.
 "Cataloging Alternative Media: Part 1." *Collectors' Network News,* v. 1, no. 1 (January/February 1977): 7–8.
 "Cataloging Alternative Media: Part 2." *Collectors' Network News,* v. 1, no. 2 (March/April 1977): 4–6.
 "Cataloging for Public Libraries." In *The Nature and Future of the Catalog,* pp. 225–39. Phoenix, AZ: Oryx Press, 1979.
 "The Cataloging Mystique—And Automation." *HCL Cataloging Bulletin,* no. 32 (January/February 1978): 15–25.
 "CIP, Subjects, and Little Presses." *COSMEP Newsletter,* v. 7, no. 10 (July 1976): 8.
 "The Gays and the Straights." *Wilson Library Bulletin,* v. 50, no. 9 (May 1, 1976): 699
 "God and LC." *Library Journal,* v. 107, no. 4 (February 15, 1980): 454.
 "ISBD: Aid or Barrier?" *College & Research Libraries,* v. 41, no. 3 (May 1980): 245.
 "Living amid Closed Catalogs: A Talk Given at LITA's 'Closing the Catalog' Institute." *HCL Cataloging Bulletin,* no. 39 (March/April 1979): 6–10.
 "More on CIP." *Library Resources & Technical Services.* v. 16, no. 3 (Summer 1972): 103–4.
 "On Familiar Terms." *Wilson Library Bulletin,* v. 54, no. 1 (September 1979): 5.
 "1. Libraries—Forecasts. 2. Elitism in Librarianship." *Library Journal,* v. 105, no. 1 (January 1, 1980): 23–7.

Prejudices and Antipathies: A Tract on the LC Subject Heads concerning People. Metuchen, NJ: Scarecrow Press, 1971. 249 p.

Supplements: *Ugandan Libraries,* v.1, no. 1 (September 1972): 21–6; v. 1, no. 2 (March 1973): 18–23.

Subject Headings Employed at the Makerere Institute of Social Research Library: A Select List. Kampala, Uganda: Makerere University Library, 1972. 102 p.

"Top Priorities for LC." *Library Journal,* v. 99, no. 13 (July 1974): 1764.

"Warped Cataloging." *Library Journal,* v. 98, no. 12 (June 15, 1973): 1856.

Berry, John N.:

"The Cataloging Revolution." *Library Journal,* v. 99, no. 15 (September 1, 1974): 2017. Editorial.

Chan, Lois Mai:

"*ISBD:* Implications for Cataloging Children's Materials." *School Media Quarterly,* v. 3, no. 1 (Fall 1974): 21–6.

Committee for the Development of Subject Access to Chicano Literatures:

Chicano Thesaurus for Indexing Chicano Materials. 1979. 77 p. $7.50. Order from: Office of the Librarian, University Library, University of California, Santa Barbara, CA 93106.

Davis, Emmett:

"Disability-related Subject Cataloging: Defective, Deformed, Degenerate, Delinquent." *HCL Cataloging Bulletin,* no. 38 (January/February 1979): 27–31.

Davis, Emmett and Davis, Catherine M.:

"Subject Cataloging" and "Perscriptive Cataloging." In their *Mainstreaming Library Service for Disabled people,* pp. 80–169. Metuchen, NJ: Scarecrow Press, 1980.

Dickinson, Elizabeth:

"Of Catalogs, Computers, and Communication." *Wilson Library Bulletin,* v. 50, no. 6 (February 1976): 463–70.

"An Inexpensive 'User-oriented' Authority File." *Unabashed Librarian,* no. 21 (1976): 5–6.

Statement to the RTSD/CCS Subject Analysis Committee on Sex-biased Library of Congress Subject Headings (1974). 9 p. Typescript copies available from the author at Stockton & San Joaquin Public Library, 605 N. El Dorado, Stockton, CA 95002.

"Word Game." *Canadian Library Journal,* v. 31, no. 4 (August 1974): 338–43.

Ferrington, Gerda:

"A List of Canadian Subject Headings." *Canadian Library Journal,* v. 33, no. 5 (October 1976): 457–60.

Freedman, Maurice J.:

"Opening a Catalog." In *Closing the Catalog,* pp. 152–69. Phoenix, AZ: Oryx Press, 1980.

"Processing for the People." *Library Journal,* v. 101, no. 1 (January 1, 1976): 189–97.

"Some Thoughts on Public Libraries and the National Bibliographic Network." In *Library Lit. 9—The Best of 1978,* edited by Bill Katz, pp. 138–53. Metuchen, NJ: Scarecrow Press, 1979.

"What Do Libraries Really Need?" *Library Journal,* v. 99, no. 18 (October 15, 1974): 2579–80.

Harris, Jessica L. Milstead and Clack, Doris H.:

"Treatment of People and Peoples in Subject Analysis." *Library Resources & Technical Services,* v. 23, no. 4 (Fall 1979): 374-90.

Hennepin County Library:

Authority File. 1977- quarterly. $30 per annum,—$7.50/single cumulations. 42x microfiche service.

Cataloging Bulletin. 1973- bimonthly. Back issues @ $1.50.

Indexes: #1-10 ($3), 11-20 ($5), 21-30 ($5). Orders for both *Authority File* and *Bulletin* to: The Secretary, Technical Services Division, Hennepin County Library, 7009 York Ave. S., Edina, MN 55435.

Hey, Consumer! A Selection of Consumer-related Headings in the Hennepin County Library Materials Catalog. December 1977. Six-panel folded bookmark.

We're UNREAL! A Selection of Subject Headings in the Hennepin County Library Catalog for Fictional People, Places and Things. July 1978. Six-panel folded bookmark.

Johansen, Deborah and Gottstein, Ruth:

"Gander Gets Gosling." *Booklist,* v. 72, no. 15 (April 1, 1976): 1074. Letter on CIP subject tracings, from Glide Publications, an alternative press.

Kanwischer, Dorothy:

"Subject Headings Trauma." *Wilson Library Bulletin,* v. 49, no. 9 (May 1975): 651-4.

Legus, Larry:

"Sure, They Save Space, but Who Knows What They Mean?" *HCL Cataloging Bulletin,* no. 40 (May/June 1979): 24-9.

Library of Congress. Congressional Research Service:

Legislative Indexing Vocabulary. 12th ed. Washington, DC: 1978. 572 p.

Makerere Institute of Social Research Library, Kampala, Uganda:

Accessions List/Bulletin. February-September 1972. monthly.

Marshall, Joan K.:

"The Catalog in the World around It." In *The Nature and Future of the Catalog,* pp. 20-33. Phoenix: Oryx Press, 1979.

"LC Labeling: An Indictment." In *Revolting Librarians,* edited by Celeste West and Elizabeth Katz, pp. 45-9. San Francisco, CA: Booklegger Press, 1972.

"A New Look at Organizing Materials in Academic Libraries." In *New Dimensions for Academic Library Service,* edited by E.J. Josey, pp. 132-41. Metuchen, NJ: Scarecrow Press, 1975.

On Equal Terms: A Thesaurus for Nonsexist Indexing and Cataloging. New York: Neal-Schuman, 1977. 152 p.

New Periodicals Index. 1977- semiannual. $25 per annum. Orders to: Mediaworks Ltd., P.O. Box 4494, Boulder, CO 80306.

Roberts, Don:

"If You Want Non-print Media, Don't Look in the Catalog!" *HCL Cataloging Bulletin,* no. 26 (February 1, 1977): 10-3.

Running, Linda:

Review of *Public Library Subject Headings for 16mm Motion Pictures.* In *American Reference Book Annual,* v. 6 (1975): 111-2.

San Diego County Library Community Information Project:

List of Subject Headings. 1976. 54 p.

Schlueter, Jane and Little, Robert D.:

"The Mystery of Ips and Mono: or, Do Students Understand AV Card Catalog Terms?" *Wisconsin Library Bulletin,* November/December 1973: 381-3; reprinted in *Expanding Media,* edited by Deirdre Boyle, pp. 273-5. Phoenix: Oryx Press, 1977.

Scilken, Marvin H.:

"The Catalog as a Public Service Tool." In *The Nature and Future of the Catalog,* pp. 89–101. Phoenix: Oryx Press, 1979.

"Cataloging for 'Real People.' " *Library Journal,* v. 98, no. 12 (June 15, 1973): 1856–7.

"Catchwords, Subtitles, and Synthetic Subtitles." *Unabashed Librarian,* no. 1 (November 1971): 32.

"Demystifying the Catalogue." *Emergency Librarian,* v. 4, no. 4 (March/April 1977): 3-5.

"Let's Try COP." *Library Journal,* v. 99, no. 18 (October 15, 1974): 2582-3.

"Relevant Subject Headings." *Unabashed Librarian,* no. 1 (November 1971): 11-3.

Scott, Randall W.:

"Comic Book Cataloging." In his *Subject Index to Comic Books and Related Materials based on the Holdings of the Michigan State University Library's Comic Art Collection,* pp. 31-7. East Lansing, MI: MSU, 1975.

Thomas, Alan R.:

Library Cataloguing Curriculum, USA: A Survey of the Contemporary Compulsory Instruction. London: Panizzi Press, 1976. 77 p.

Unabashed Librarian. 1971- quarterly. $15 per annum; back issues @ $4.00. Orders to: Marvin Scilken, Editor, G.P.O. Box 2631, New York, NY 10001.

Weihs, Jean Riddle:

Nonbook Materials: The Organization of Integrated Collections. 2d ed. Ottawa, Ontario: Canadian Library Associaion, 1979. 134 p.

"Problems and Prospects in Non-book Cataloging." In *The Nature and Future of the Catalog,* pp. 272-90. Phoenix: Oryx Press, 1979.

"Problems of Subject Analysis for Audio/Visual Materials in Canadian Libraries." *Canadian Library Journal,* v. 33, no. 5 (October 1976): 453, 455.

Wiggin, Tom:

From BAT-BANDING to ZOONOSES: the Winners in the PLAFSEP Silly Subject Heading Contest. Illustrated for posterity by Tom Wiggin, Paul Wiggin, and Anne Reynolds. Edited by John R. Likins. Wellesley, MA: PLAFSEP Press, 1979. 17 p.

Wolf, Steve:

"Catalogers in Revolt against LC's Racist, Sexist Headings." *Interracial Books for Children Bulletin,* v. 6, nos. 3-4 (1975): 3, 16.

"Sex and the Single Cataloger; New Thoughts on Some Unthinkable Subjects." In *Revolting Librarians,* edited by Celeste West and Elizabeth Katz, pp. 39-44. San Francisco, CA: Booklegger Press, 1972.

A Model Authority File for Names, Subjects, and Dewey Numbers*

Single asterisks (*) indicate totally new HCL forms.

Double asterisks (**) indicate replacements for LC forms.

No asterisks indicate existing HCL forms with added notes or cross-references.

cn = cataloger's note (for internal use only)

pn = public note (appearing in the catalog)

sa = *see also*

sf = *see from* (x-reference)

xx = *see also from*

Abortion.
cn Not subdivided by —UNITED STATES. Class general, comprehensive, and sociological works in 301.4265, ethical aspects in 179.76, criminal abortion in 364.185, medical aspects in 618.33 (spontaneous) or 618.88 (surgical).

Absaroke Indians.
cn LC form: CROW INDIANS. Class in 970.3 A.

Acid rain.*
cn HCL form. Authority: Gene E. Likens' "Acid rain," *Scientific American*, v. 241, no. 4 (Oct. 1979), p. 43-51.
pn Additional material on this subject may be found in the Pamphlet Collection.
sf Acid precipitation
   Rain, Acid
xx Air—Pollution
   Rain and rainfall
   Water—Pollution

Adopted children.**
cn LC form: CHILDREN, ADOPTED. Assignment: J.G. Ansfield's *Adopted child* (1971); C. Bunin's *Is that your sister* (1976); *We're adopted!* (1973 kit); A.M. McWhinnie's *Adopted children: how they grow up* (1967).
sa Adoptees
   Names, Personal—Law
sf Children, Adopted
xx Adoption
   Children

Adult literacy programs.*
cn HCL form. Authority/precedent: *Thesaurus of ERIC descriptors* (7th ed., 1977), p. 5: ADULT READING PROGRAMS. Assignment: Don A. Brown's *Handbook for organizing and managing literacy programs for adults* (1979).
sa Adult basic education materials
sf Literacy programs, Adult
   Reading programs, Adult

xx Adult education
   Reading programs

Aerial photography.**
cn LC form: PHOTOGRAPHY, AERIAL. Class in 778.35.
sf Photography, Aerial
xx Photography

Agent Orange.*
cn HCL form. Usage examples: "Agent Orange survey goes out," *Hennepin family*, v. 7, no. 9 (Dec. 1979), p. 1; William Steif, "Agent Orange disaster," *Progressive*, Feb. 1980, p. 8. Assignment: Ruth Winter's *Cancer-causing agents: a preventive guide* (1979), which includes "Agent Orange" entry
xx Dioxin
   Vietnamese Conflict, 1961-1975 —Chemistry
   Vietnamese Conflict, 1961-1975 —Destruction and pillage
   Vietnamese Conflict, 1961-1975 —Medical aspects

*Compiled from 1979–80 additions and changes at Hennepin County Library.

Agricultural policy.**
  cn LC form: AGRICULTURE AND
     STATE. Not subdivided by
     —UNITED STATES. Authority:
     Political science thesaurus
     (1975), p. 25; Alternative Press
     Centre subject heading list
     (1973), p. 9; *Legislative index-*
     ing vocabulary (12th ed., 1978),
     p. 13. Class in 338.18.
  sa Agricultural administration
     Agricultural experiment stations
     Agricultural extension work
     Agricultural laws and legislation
     Agricultural price supports
     Food as a weapon
     Land reform
     Rural development
  sf Agriculture and state
     Farm policy
     Federal agricultural policy
     Government agricultural policy
     State and agriculture
  xx Economic policy
     Land reform

Air freight.**
  cn LC form: AERONAUTICS, COM-
     MERCIAL—FREIGHT. Class in
     387.744.
  sa Air freight lines
     Air mail service
  sf Air cargo
     Cargo, Air
     Freight, Air
  xx Commercial aviation
     Freight and freightage

Air traffic.*
  cn HCL form. Authority: *Legislative*
     indexing vocabulary (12th ed.,
     1978), p. 18. Assignment (with
     —FORECASTS): annual *FAA*
     aviation forecasts
  xx Aeronautics

Alcohol fuels.**
  cn LC form: ALCOHOL AS FUEL.
     Authority: Donal L. McClamrock's
     Glossary of energy terminology
     (2d ed., 1978), p. 7
  sa Gasohol
  sf Alcohol as fuel
     Ethanol
     Ethyl alcohol fuel
  xx Alternative energy sources
     Biomass energy
     Fuel
     Motor fuels

Alternative education.*
  cn HCL form. Authority: *New*
     periodicals index (e.g., v. 1, no.
     1, p. 20); Alternative Press
     Centre subject heading list for
     publications (1973), p. 9. Assign-
     ment (with —INFORMATION
     SERVICES): *Communities'*
     Guide to cooperative alterna-
     tives (1979). Class in 371.04
  sa Education, Non-formal
     Free schools
     Free Universities
  sf Education, Alternative
  xx Education

Anilingus.*
  cn HCL form. Authority: Erwin J.
     Haeberle, *Sex atlas* (1978), p.
     220; "Asking for anilingus,"
     Forum magazine, v. 9, no. 1
     (Oct. 1979), p. 124-5; Kate
     Miller, "Anilingus: something
     special for your lover," *Human*
     digest, v. 3, no. 1 (Jan. 1979), p.
     32+. Assignment: Charles
     Silverstein's *Joy of Gay sex*
     (1977), which includes material
     on "Rimming."
  sf Oral sex
     "Rimming"
  xx Sexuality

Anti-Nuclear Movement.*
  cn Previous HCL form: ANTI-
     NUCLEAR POWER MOVE-
     MENT. Assignment: Robert
     Jungk's *New tyranny: how nu-*
     clear power enslaves us (1979)
  sf Anti-Nuke Movement
     "No Nukes" Movement
  xx Environmental protection
     groups and agencies
     Nuclear power
     Nuclear power industries
     Nuclear power plants
     Nuclear weapons
     Pressure groups
     Social movements

Astral projection.
  cn Class in 133.89.

Barrier free design.**
  cn LC form: ARCHITECTURE AND
     THE PHYSICALLY HANDI-
     CAPPED. Previous HCL form:
     ARCHITECTURE AND DIS-
     ABLED PERSONS. Class in
     721.0484. Assignment: Betty
     Garee's *Ideas for making your*
     home accessible (1979).
  sa Disabled persons and travel
     Houses—Remodeling (for dis-
     abled persons)
  sf Accessibility for disabled
     persons
     Architectural barriers for dis-
     abled persons
     Architecture and disabled
     persons
     Architecture and physically
     disabled persons
     Architecture and the disabled
     Architecture and the "handi-
     capped"
     Architecture, Barrier free
     Design, Barrier free
     Disabled persons and archi-
     tecture
     Physically disabled persons
     and architecture
  xx Disabled persons
     Disabled persons and travel
     Home economics for disabled
     persons
     Houses—Remodeling (for
     disabled persons)
     Physically disabled persons
     Wheelchairs

Bates Method.*
  cn HCL form. Assignment: *Well-*
     being (1979); A. Huxley's *Art of*
     seeing (1975).
  sf Bates Eye-Healing Method
  xx Alternative medicine
     Eye—Accommodation and
     refraction
     Eye—Care
     Eye—Diseases and defects
     Eyeglasses
     Vision disorders

Bay of Pigs Invasion, 1961.**
  cn LC form: CUBA—HISTORY—
     INVASION, 1961. Authority:
     Alternative Press Centre subject
     heading list (1973), p. 11.
     Assignment: Peter Wyden's *Bay*
     of Pigs: the untold story (1979).
  sf Cuba—History—Invasion, 1961
  xx CIA
     Cuba—Foreign relations—
     United States
     Cuba—History— 1961-
     The Sixties
     United States—Foreign rela-
     tions—Cuba

Bermuda Triangle.
  cn Class in 001.946.

Big game fishing.
  sf Game fishing
     Gamefishing
     Ocean game fishing

Bill collecting.**
  cn LC forms: COLLECTING OF
     ACCOUNTS; COLLECTION
     AGENCIES. Assignment: John
     M. Striker and Andrew O.
     Shapiro's *Power plays: how to*
     deal like a lawyer in person-to-
     person confrontations and get
     your rights (1979), which
     includes chapter titled "Up
     against the bill collector."
  sf Account collecting
     Collecting bills

Collection agencies
Collection of accounts
xx Consumer credit
Debt

Biomass energy.
cn Class in 621.49.
sa Alcohol fuels

Birds
cn Class in 598.2.

Bisexuality.
cn Class in 301.4156.

Bligh, William, 1754-1817.
sf Captain Bligh, 1754-1817

Bradshaw, Terry.
cn Class biographies in 921 B726.

Broomball.*
cn HCL form. Class in 796.963.
Assignment (with —RULES):
biennial *MRPA broomball rules.*
pn Here are entered materials on a
game "played with an inflated
ball by two teams of six players
each on a sheet of ice 200 feet
long and 85 feet wide. Points are
scored when a ball entering
from the front passes between
the cage posts and goes completely across the goal line."
sf Broom ball
xx Winter sports

Bungling and bunglers.*
cn HCL form. Assignment (with
—FICTION): B. Girion's *Joshua,
the Czar, and the chicken bone
wish* (1978).
sa Clumsiness
Misfits (Persons)
sf Awkwardness
Ineptitude
Klutziness

Business English.**
cn LC form: ENGLISH LANGUAGE
—BUSINESS ENGLISH. Assignment: A. DeCaprio's *Modern
approach to business English*
(1973) and *Modern approach to
business spelling* (1979). Not
subdivided by —HANDBOOKS,
MANUALS, ETC.
sf Commercial English
English, Business
English language—Business
English
xx Business letters
English language
Secretaries—Handbooks,
manuals, etc.

CIA.**
cn LC and previous HCL form:
UNITED STATES. CENTRAL IN-
TELLIGENCE AGENCY. Class
in 327.12. Assignment (with

—FICTION): G. Gordon Liddy's
Out of control (1979).
pn Additional material on this subject may be found in the Pamphlet Collection.
sa Bay of Pigs Invasion, 1961
sf Central Intelligence Agency
"The Company"
United States. Central Intelligence Agency.
xx Intelligency service—United
States
International intrigue

Children of working parents.*
cn HCL form. Assignment: Gloria
Norris and Jo Ann Miller's *Working mother's complete handbook* (1979), which includes
chapters on childcare and
"Succeeding with your
children."
sa Child care centers
Working mothers
Working parents
sf Working mothers' children
Working parents' children
xx Working mothers
Working parents

Christian television.*
cn HCL form. Assignment (with
—PERSONAL NARRATIVES): T.
Bakker's *I gotta be me* (1978).
sf Broadcasting, Christian
Christian broadcasting
Television, Christian
xx Evangelistic work
Television broadcasting

Class struggle.*
cn HCL form. Authority: *British
alternative press index* (e.g., v.
3, no. 3, July/Sept. 78, p. 13):
Alternative Press Centre subject
heading list (1973), p. 14: *Politi-
cal Science thesaurus* (1975),
p. 57. Assignment (with
—EUROPE): Jean Ziegler's
Switzerland: the awful truth
(1979).
sa Black Liberation
Chicano Movement
Communism
Red Power
Socialism
xx Communism
Social classes
Social conflict
Socialism
Working classes

Color therapy.*
cn HCL form. Authority: Martin A.
Jackson's "How color affects
your life and love." *Pillow talk*, v.
3, no. 6 (Sept. 1979). p. 76+.

Assignment: Linda A. Clark's
*How to improve your health: the
wholistic approach* (1979),
which includes chapter on
"Color healing."
sf Chromotherapy
Therapy, Color
xx Alternative medicine
Therapeutic systems

Communication satellites.**
cn LC form: ARTIFICIAL SATEL-
LITES IN TELECOMMUNICA-
TION. Authority: *McGraw-Hill
encyclopedia of science &
technology* (1977). v. 3. p. 346-
9: *Legislative indexing vocabulary* (12th ed., 1978). p. 95.
sa INTELSAT
Project Telstar
sf Artificial satellites in telecommunication
Communications-relay systems
Global satellite communication
systems
Satellite communication
systems
Satellites in telecommunication
xx Artificial satellites
Telecommunication

Corruption (in labor unions).*
cn HCL form. Not subdivided by
—UNITED STATES. Assign-
ment: J. Kwitny's *Vicious circles:
the Mafia in the marketplace*
(1979: "Meat—the union":
p. 71+: "The Teamsters":
p. 141+).
sf Labor corruption
Labor union corruption
Labor unions—Corrupt
practices
Union corruption
xx Labor unions

Court musicians.*
cn HCL form. Authority: 1978 *Music
index subject heading list.* p. 28.
Assignment (with —FICTION):
David Lasker's *Boy who loved
music* (1979).
sf Musicians. Court
Royal musicians
xx Courts and courtiers
Musicians

Disabled children.**
cn LC form: HANDICAPPED CHIL-
DREN. Authority: "Subject
index." *Sources* (e.g., v. 2. no. 3
1979. p. 191): "Subject index."
Serials for libraries (1979).
p. 474.
pn Additional material on this subject may be found in the
Pamphlet Collection

sa Camps for disabled children
Developmentally disabled
children
Disabled teenagers
Hyperactive children
Physically disabled children
Physically disabled teenagers
sf Children, Disabled
Children, "Handicapped"
"Handicapped" children
xx Children
Disabled persons

Disabled children's writings **
cn LC form: PHYSICALLY HANDI-
CAPPED CHILDREN'S WRIT-
INGS.
sf Children's writings, Disabled
Children's writings, "Handicapped"
Developmentally disabled
children's writings
"Handicapped" children's
writings
Physically disabled children's
writings
Physically "handicapped"
children's writings
xx Children's writings

Disabled workers.*
cn Previous HCL form: HANDI-
CAPPED WORKERS. Authority:
"Subject index," Sources (e.g.,
v. 2, no. 3, 1979, p. 191): George
Monaghan, "Disabled workers
uniting," Minneapolis star, May
16, 1979, p. 1C+.
sa Blind artists
Blind authors
Blind musicians
Blind physicians
Blind photographers
Blind psychiatrists
Blind sculptors
Blind teachers
Deaf actors
Deaf detectives
Deaf lawyers
Deaf workers
Disabled persons—Employ-
ment
Physically disabled artists
Vocational rehabilitation
sf "Handicapped" workers
Workers, Disabled
Workers, "Handicapped"
xx Disabled persons—Employ-
ment
Physically disabled persons—
Employment

Disco skating.*
cn HCL form Class in 793.36
Assignment: Dale A. Marzano's
Roller disco (1979).

sf Disco roller skating
Roller skate disco
Skating, Disco
xx Disco dancing
Roller skate dancing

Electric vehicles.**
cn LC form: AUTOMOBILES,
ELECTRIC. Authority: Sources
(e.g., v. 2. no. 3, 1979, p. 192):
Legislative indexing vocabulary
(12th ed., 1978), p. 163; V.
Daniel Hunt's Energy dictionary
(1979), p. 139.
sf Automobiles, Electric
E.V.'s
Electric automobiles
Electric autos
Electric cars
Vehicles, Electric
xx Automobiles
Automobiles—Fuel consump-
tion
Energy conservation
Motor vehicles

Ellis Island Immigration Station,
New York.**
cn LC form: UNITED STATES. IM-
MIGRATION STATION, ELLIS
ISLAND, N.Y. Assignment (with
—PERSONAL NARRATIVES):
David M. Brownstone's Island of
hope, island of tears (1979).
sf United States. Ellis Island Immi-
gration Station, New York.
United States. Immigration
Station, Ellis Island, New York.
xx United States—Immigration and
emigration

Energy planning.*
cn HCL form. Assignment (with
—TWIN CITIES METROPOLI-
TAN AREA): Metropolitan Council's Planning for solar access
protection (1979).
sa Energy policy
sf Planning, Energy
xx Energy policy

Energy technology.**
cn LC form: POWER (MECHANICS).
Authority: V. Daniel Hunt's
Energy dictionary (1979), p.
147. Class in 621.
pn Here are entered works on the
physics and engineering as-
pects of energy.
sa Electric power
Energy resources
Geothermal engineering
Nuclear engineering
Water power
Wind power
sf Energy engineering
Engineering, Energy

Engineering, Power
Power (Mechanics)
Power technology
Technology, Energy
Technology, Power
xx Mechanical engineering

English, John W.
cn Joint author of Bicycling laws in
the United States.

English, John Wesley, 1912-
cn Joint author of The coming real
estate crash.

Environmental education.*
cn HCL form. Authority: Sources
(e.g., v. 2, no. 3, 1979, p. 193):
Thesaurus of ERIC descriptors
(7th ed., 1977), p. 71. Assignment (with —MINNESOTA):
Environmental education . . . a
state plan for Minnesota (1972)
sa Ecology—Study and teaching
Energy education
sf Education, Environmental
xx Ecology—Study and teaching
Education

Environmental planning.*
cn HCL form. Authority: Sources
(e.g., v. 1, no. 3, Fall 1977, p.
183). Not subdivided by
—UNITED STATES. Assign-
ment: John O. Simonds' Earth-
scape: a manual of environ-
mental planning (1978)
sa City planning
Conservation of natural
resources
Environmental impact state-
ments
Environmental policy
Environmental protection
Landscape architecture
Planned unit development
Regional planning
Transportation planning
Urban renewal
sf Eco-planning
Ecological planning
Planning, Environmental
xx City planning
Conservation of natural
resources
Development planning
Ecology—Action projects
Environmental policy
Environmental protection
Pollution
Regional planning

Ex-convicts—Rights.*
cn HCL form. Class in 342.0874
Assignment: David Rudenstine's
Rights of ex-offenders (1979)
sa Ex-convicts—Legal status,
laws, etc.

sf   Rights of ex-convicts
xx   Civil rights
     Ex-convicts—Legal status.
         laws, etc.
FBI.**
cn   LC and previous HCL form:
     UNITED STATES. FEDERAL
     BUREAU OF INVESTIGATION
sf   Federal Bureau of Investigation
     United States. Dept. of Justice
         Federal Bureau of Investiga-
         tion.
     United States. Federal Bureau
         of Investigation.

Farm buying.*
cn   HCL form. Assignment: George
     Laycock's How to buy and enjoy
     a small farm (1978)
xx   Consumer education
     Homesteading

Farm organizing.*
cn   HCL form. Assignment (with
     —MIDDLE WEST—PERSONAL
     NARRATIVES): Pandora Pro-
     ductions' 3-tape People. pride &
     politics: building the North Star
     country (1978), which includes
     "Early farm organizing" and
     "Farm organizing in the Depres-
     sion."
sa   Agricultural co-ops
     Grange
sf   Organizing farmers
xx   Radicalism
     Social movements

Farm workers.**
cn   LC form: AGRICULTURAL
     LABORERS. Not subdivided by
     —UNITED STATES. Class in
     331.763. Authority: New
     periodicals index (e.g., v. 1, no.
     1, Jan./June 1977, p. 57); Alter-
     native Press Centre subject
     heading list (1973), p. 18;
     "Subject index," Sources (e.g.,
     v. 2, no. 3, 1979, p. 193).
sa   Afro-American farm workers
     Housing, Rural
     Labor unions—Farm workers
     Mexican-American farm
         workers
     Mexican farm workers
     Migrant workers
     Peasantry
     Plantation workers
sf   Agricultural laborers
     Agricultural workers
     Farm laborers
     Farmhands
     Farmworkers
     Workers, Farm
xx   Working classes

Fashion models.**
cn   LC form: MODELS, FASHION.
     Class in 659.152.
sa   Afro-American fashion models
     Model agencies
sf   Manikins (Fashion models)
     Mannequins (Fashion models)
     Modeling, Fashion
     Models, Fashion

Flash photography.**
cn   LC form: PHOTOGRAPHY,
     FLASH-LIGHT. Assignment: E.
     Voogel's 200 flashtips (1978):.
     Edgerton's Electronic flash,
     strobe (1970).
sf   Flash-bulb photography
     Photography, Flash
xx   Photography
     Photography—Lighting

Food as a weapon.*
cn   HCL form. Assignment: Jean
     Mayer's Human nutrition (1972),
     which includes chapters on
     "Crop destruction in Vietnam,"
     "Starvation as a weapon: herbi-
     cides in Vietnam," and "Famine
     in Biafra."
sa   Defoliation
sf   Hunger as a weapon
     Starvation as a weapon
xx   Hunger
     War
     Weapons

Food co-ops.
cn   HCL form. Class in 658.8707.

Gay couples.*
cn   HCL form. Assignment: Betty
     Fairchild and Nancy Hayward's
     Now that you know: what every
     parent should know about
     homosexuality (1979), which
     includes "Gay couples."
sa   Gay marriage
sf   Couples, Gay
xx   Gay marriage

Gay prisoners.*
cn   HCL form. Assignment (with
     —FICTION): M. Puig's Kiss of
     the spider woman (1979).
sf   Prisoners, Gay

Government libraries.
cn   LC form: LIBRARIES, GOVERN-
     MENTAL, ADMINISTRATIVE,
     ETC. Not subdivided by
     —UNITED STATES. Class in
     027.5.
sf   Libraries, Government
xx   Libraries
     Special Libraries

Gray Reef Shark.**
cn   LC form: CARCHARHINUS
     MENISORRAH. Assignment:

W.A. Starck's Blue reef: a report'
from beneath the sea (1979).
xx   Sharks
Gullibility.**
cn   LC form: CREDULITY. Assign-
     ment (with —FICTION): Abraham
     Soyer's Adventures of Yemima,
     and other stories (1979).
sa   Belief and doubt
     Deception
     Faith
     Fraud
     Hoaxes
     Misconceptions
     Propaganda
     Quacks and quackery
     Skepticism
     Superstition
     Swindlers and swindling
sf   Credulity
xx   Belief and doubt
     Deception
     Fraud
     Hoaxes
     Skepticism
     Swindlers and swindling

Handicraft for disabled persons.**
cn   LC form: HANDICRAFT FOR
     THE PHYSICALLY HANDI-
     CAPPED. Class in 745.5041.
     Assignment: Elizabeth Gault
     and Susan Sykes' Crafts for the
     disabled (1979).
sa   Handicraft for developmentally
     disabled persons
sf   Crafts for disabled persons
     Disabled persons' crafts
     Disabled persons—Handicraft
xx   Disabled persons—Recreation

Holmes. Sherlock, born 1854
(Fictional character).
cn   LC form: HOLMES, SHERLOCK
     (FICTITIOUS CHARACTER).
     Class in 823.812 D772. Un-
     glossed form assigned, with
     genre subheads, to material in
     which Holmes appears as a
     protagonist: glossed descriptor
     applied only to works that dis-
     cuss. interpret, or analyze
     Holmes as a person.

Holocaust. Jewish (1933-1945).**
cn   LC and previous HCL form:
     HOLOCAUST, JEWISH (1939-
     1945). Authority/discussion:
     1979 Simon Wiesenthal Center
     for Holocaust Studies brochure
     ("The term 'Holocaust' refers to
     the period from January 30,
     1933 when Hitler became
     Chancellor of Germany to May
     8, 1945 . . . when the war in
     Europe ended"): Anti-Semitism

(Keter Books, 1974), p. 46-7; *The record: the holocaust in history, 1933-1945* (Anti-Defamation League of B'nai B'rith in cooperation with the National Council for the Social Studies, 1978), p. 1-16; Jessica L. Milstead Harris and Doris H. Clack's "Treatment of people and peoples in subject analysis," *Library resources & technical services*, v. 23, no. 4 (Fall 1979), p. 381. Not subdivided by —HISTORY. Class in 940.5315.

pn Here are entered materials on the Nazi destruction of European Jewry, dating "from January 30, 1933, when Hitler became Chancellor of Germany to May 8, 1945 (V-E Day), when the war in Europe ended."

sa Auschwitz (Concentration camp)
Auschwitz Trial, Frankfurt am Main, 1963–65
Babiy Yar Massacre, 1941
Buchenwald (Concentration Camp)
Christian Church and the Jewish Holocaust (1933-1945)
Concentration camp survivors
Crystal Night, 1938
Leon Jolson Award Books
Maydanek (Concentration camp)
Nazism
Theresienstadt (Concentration camp)
United States and the Jewish Holocaust (1933-1945)
Warsaw Ghetto Uprising, 1943

sf Destruction of the Jews (1933-1945)
Extermination, Jewish (1933-1945)
"Final solution" (1933-1945)
Jewish Holocaust (1933-1945)
Shoah (1933-1945)

xx Antisemitism
Genocide
Jews in Europe—History
Jews in Europe—Persecutions
Jews in Germany—History—1933-1945
Jews—Persecutions
World War, 1939-1945—Jews

Holocaust, Jewish (1933-1945)—Personal narratives.
sa Holocaust, Jewish (1933-1945)—Hungary—Personal narratives
Holocaust, Jewish (1933-1945)

—Kazimierz, Poland—Personal narratives
Holocaust, Jewish (1933-1945)—Lvov—Personal narratives
Holocaust, Jewish (1933-1945)—Warsaw—Personal narratives
sf Holocaust narratives

Hot tubs.*
cn HCL form. Assignment (with —DESIGN AND CONSTRUCTION): *Sunset ideas for hot tubs, spas & home saunas* (1979).
sa Home spas
Hot baths
sf Tubs, Hot
xx Home spas
Hot baths

Inuit—Alaska.
sf Alaska—Inuit
Alaskan "Eskimos"
Alaskan Inuit

Inuit—Canada.
sf Canada—Inuit
Canadian "Eskimos"
Canadian Inuit

Inuit craft.
sf Handicraft, Inuit
Inuit handicraft

Inuit language.
sf Inuktitut

Inuit—Legends.
sf Legends, "Eskimo"

Inuit poetry.
sf "Eskimo" poetry
Poetry, "Eskimo"
Poetry, Inuit
xx Inuit literature

Juan, Don, 1891?-.
cn Previous HCL form: JUAN, DON, 1891- . Alleged Yaqui sorcerer.
sf Don Juan, 1891?-
Juan Matus, 1891?-
Matus, Juan, 1891?-

Junior Olympics.*
cn HCL form. Authority: Ralph Hickok's *New encyclopedia of sports* (1977), p. 299. Class in 796.484. Assignment (with —RULES): AAU *Junior Olympics supplement: gymnastics* (1977). Further assignment (with —FICTION): Charles M. Schulz's *You're the greatest, Charlie Brown* (1979), which begins: "Okay, gang. We have somebody from our school entered in every event for the Junior Olympics . . ."
sf AAU Junior Olympics

Amateur Athletic Union of the United States Junior Olympics
Olympics, Junior
xx Olympic Games
Sports, Children's
Track and field athletics

KGB.**
cn Previous HCL form: RUSSIA. COMMITTEE FOR STATE SECURITY.
sf Commission of State Security (Russia)
Committee for State Security (Russia)
Russia. Commission of State Security
Russia. Committee for State Security
Russia. K.G.B.
Russia. Komissija Gosudarstvennoj Bezopasnosti
State Security Committee (Russia)
xx Intelligence service—Russia
International intrigue
Secret service—Russia
Spies, Russian

Kauffman, Max.*
cn Fictional character. Creator: Thomas Chastain.
sf Inspector Kauffman
Inspector Max Kauffman
Kaufman, Max
Kauffman, Max
Max Kauffman

Kirigami.*
cn HCL form. Assignment: F. Temko's *Magic of kirigami; happenings with paper and scissors* (1978). Class in 736.98.
pn Here are entered materials on the Japanese art of making ornamental designs by cutting and folding paper.
sa Origami
sf Paper-cutting, Japanese
Japanese paper-cutting
xx Origami
Paper work

Korean Lobbying Scandal.*
cn HCL form. Assignment (with —PERSONAL NARRATIVES): Leon Jaworski's *Confession and avoidance; a memoir* (1979).
sf Korea Lobbying Scandal
"Koreagate" Scandal
Park Lobbying Scandal
Tongsun Park Lobbying Scandal
xx Corruption (in politics)—United States

Korea—Foreign relations—
United States
Lobbying
United States—Foreign rela-
tions—Korea
United States—Politics and
government— 1977-

Lesbian mothers.*
cn HCL form. Authority: Joan K.
Marshall, *On equal terms*
(1977), p. 74. Assignment: Emily
L. Sisley and Bertha Harris' *Joy
of Lesbian sex* (1977).
sf Mothers, Lesbian
xx Mothers

Life after death.**
cn LC form: FUTURE LIFE. Assign-
ment: Christopher Milbourne's
Search for the soul (1979), "an
insider's report on the . . . quest
by psychics and scientists for
evidence of life after death."
sa Eschatology
Future punishment
Heaven
Hell
Immortality
Reincarnation
Resurrection (Christian
theology)
Soul
Spiritualism
sf Afterlife
Eternal life
Future life
Survivalism
xx Death
Eschatology
Immortality
Soul

Loch Ness Monster.
cn Class in 001.944.
sf Monster of Loch Ness
"Nessie"

McCarthyism.*
cn HCL form. Authority: Alternative
Press Centre subject heading
list (1973), p. 26; Stanley
Hochman's *Yesterday and
today: a dictionary of recent
American history* (1979),
p. 197-9; *World book dictionary*
(1974), p. 1275. Assignment:
Robert C. Goldston's *American
nightmare* (1973); Athan G.
Theoharis' *Seeds of repression*
(1971); Charles E. Potter's *Days
of shame* (1965).
pn Here are entered materials on
both the public investigation of
Communist activities con-
ducted in the early 1950s by
Sen. Joseph R. McCarthy and

the "art or practice of publicly
accusing individuals or groups
of political disloyalty and subversion, usually without sufficient evidence."
sa McCarthy, Joseph Raymond,
1908-1957
xx Anti-Communist movements—
United States
The Fifties
McCarthy, Joseph Raymond,
1908-1957
Repression, Political—United
States
United States—Politics and
government— 1945-1953
United States—Politics and
government— 1953-1961

Madison Square Garden, New York
(City).**
cn LC form: NEW YORK (CITY).
MADISON SQUARE GARDEN.
Class in 791.067.
sf "The Garden," New York (City)
New York (City). Madison
Square Garden.

Mass media reform.
cn HCL form. Assignment: Congressional quarterly's *Rights
revolution* (1978) and *Consumer protection, gains and
setbacks* (1978), both of which
include section on "Media re-
formers."
sa Fairness doctrine (Broadcasting)
Fraud in television advertising
Sexism in mass media
Television advertising and
children
Violence in mass media
sf Media reform
Reform of the mass media

Math anxiety.**
cn LC form: MATHEMATICS—
STUDY AND TEACHING—
PSYCHOLOGICAL ASPECTS.
Assignment: S. Tobias' *Over-
coming math anxiety* (1978); S.
Kogelman's *Mind over math*
(1978).
sf Anxiety, Math
Mathematics anxiety
Mathematics—Study and
teaching—Psychological
aspects
xx Mathematics—Study and
teaching

Military expenditures.*
cn HCL form. Assignment (with
—UNITED STATES): Boston
Study Group's *Price of defense:*

*a new strategy for military
spending* (1979).
sa Defense contracts
sf Defense appropriations
Defense budget
Defense expenditures
Defense spending
Military appropriations
Military budget
Military costs
Military spending
xx Defense contracts
Expenditures, Public

Minority women.*
cn HCL form. Authority: "Subject
index," *Sources* (e.g., v. 2, no. 3,
1979, p. 200). Assignment (with
—HEALTH): Ellen Frankfort and
Frances Kisslig's *Rosie: an
investigation of a wrongful death*
(1979).
sa Women, Afro-American
Women, Amerindian
Women, Chinese-American
Women, Japanese-American
Women, Jewish
Women, Jewish-American
Women, Latino
Women, Mexican-American
sf Women, Minority
xx Minorities
Women

"New Age" (Concepts, Lifestyles,
etc.).
cn Class in 132.

New Left.*
cn HCL form. Class in 322.4. Not
subdivided by —UNITED
STATES. Authority: Walter
Laqueur's *Dictionary of politics*
(Rev. ed., 1973), p. 355;
*Barnhart dictionary of new
English since 1963* (1973), p.
315; *6,000 words* (1976), p. 134;
Political science thesaurus
(1975), p. 205; Alternative Press
Centre subject heading list
(1973), p. 28; Leon W. Blevins'
*Young voter's manual: a topical
dictionary of American government and politics* (1975), p.
123-4; Wiliam L. Safire's *Political
dictionary* (1978), p. 457.
Assignment: Assar Lindbeck's
*Political economy of the New
Left* (1971); Priscilla Long's *New
Left: a collection of essays*
(1969); Carl Oglesby's *New Left
reader* (1969); Massimo
Teodori's *New Left: a documentary history* (1969).
pn Here are entered materials on
"a broad grouping of political

tendencies and organizations embracing many varieties of neo-Marxism, socialism, syndicalism, anarchism, pacifism and more personal forms of opposition to established society" that flourished during the 1960s.
- sa Black Panther Party
  GI resistance and revolts
  Peace movement—United States
  The Sixties
  Student Nonviolent Coordinating Committee
  Students for a Democratic Society
  Youth International Party
- sf American New Left
  Left, New
  Radical Left
- xx Pressure groups
  Radicalism—United States
  Right and left (Political Science)
  The Sixties
  United States—Politics and government—1961-1963
  United States—Politics and government—1963-1969

New Right.*
- cn HCL form. Class in 322.4. Not subdivided by —UNITED STATES. Authority: *Barnhart dictionary of new English since 1963* (1973), p. 315; Walter Laqueur's *Dictionary of politics* (Rev. ed., 1973), p. 355-6; Paul Sand's "Right-Fundamentalism poses dangers for U.S.," *Minneapolis star*, Oct. 19, 1979, p. 8-9A; J. Charles Park's "Clouds on the Right: a review of pending pressures against education," in James E. Davis: *Dealing with censorship* (1979), p. 96-107; Minnesota Women's Political Caucus conference-flyer: *Exploring The New Right* (Nov. 1979). Assignment: Thomas J. McIntyre's *Fear brokers* (1979) and E.T. Jorstad's *Politics of doomsday: fundamentalists of the Far Right* (1970); further assignment (with —PERIODICALS): Liberty Lobby's weekly *Spotlight*.
- pn Here are entered materials on "a political movement," dating from the late 1960s, that stands for "conservatism and nationalism in response to both the New Left and the traditional or established conservatives."

- sa Liberty Lobby
- sf American New Right
  Far Right
  Radical Right
  Right-Fundamentalists
  Right, New
  Ultraconservatism
- xx Anti-Communist movements
  Conservatism—United States
  Evangelicalism
  Fundamentalism
  Pressure groups
  Right and left (Political Science)
  The Seventies
  United States—Politics and government—1969-
  United States—Politics and government—1977-

New words.**
- cn LC form: WORDS, NEW. Not subdivided by —ENGLISH.
- sa Afro-Americans—Language (New words, slang, etc.)
  Gays—Language (New words, slang, etc.)
  Lumber workers—Language (New words, slang, etc.)
  Soldiers—Language (New words, slang, etc.)
  Truck drivers—Language (New words, slang, etc.)
- sf Coinage of words
  English language—New words
  Neologisms
  Word coinage
  Words, New
- xx English language—Words
  Slang
  Vocabulary

The Nineties (19th Century).*
- cn HCL form. Not subdivided geographically. Assignment: American Heritage's *Nineties: glimpses of a lost but lively world* (1967); C. Hoffmann's *Depression of the nineties* (1970); C. Beals' *Great revolt and its leaders: the history of popular American uprisings in the 1890's* (1968).
- sf 1890s
  "Gay Nineties"
- xx Nineteenth Century
  Nostalgia
  United States—Social life and customs—1865-1918.

Nuclear power and birth defects.*
- cn HCL form. Assignment: *Shut down! Nuclear power on trial* (1979).
- sf Birth defects and nuclear power
- xx Birth defects
  Industrial toxicology

Nuclear power plants—Physiological effect
Radiation—Physiological effect

Nuclear power and cancer.*
- cn HCL form. Assignment: *Shut down! Nuclear power on trial* (1979).
- sf Cancer and nuclear power
- xx Carcinogens
  Industrial toxicology
  Nuclear power plants—Physiological effect
  Radiation—Physiological effect

Nuclear power and civil rights.*
- cn HCL form. Assignment: Robert Jungk's *New tyranny: how nuclear power enslaves us* (1979).
- sf Civil rights and nuclear power
  Nuclear power and authoritarianism
  Nuclear power and freedom
- xx Civil rights

Nursing home reform.
- cn HCL form. Class in 362.61.
- sf Reform, Nursing home

Occupational health and safety.*
- cn LC forms: INDUSTRIAL HYGIENE; INDUSTRIAL SAFETY; OCCUPATIONAL DISEASES. Previous HCL form: INDUSTRIAL HEALTH AND SAFETY CONDITIONS. Not subdivided by —UNITED STATES. Authority *New periodicals index* (e.g., Jan./June 1977, p. 97); *Sources* (e.g., v. 2, no. 3, 1979, p. 202); Alternative Press Centre subject heading list (1973), p. 29; *Legislative indexing vocabulary* (12 ed., 1978), p. 365.
- sa Anthrax
  Asbestos industry—Hygienic aspects
  Black Lung Disease
  Employer negligence
  Factories—Safety measures
  Industrial accidents
  Industrial toxicology
  Mine accidents
  United States. Occupational Safety and Health Administration.
  Work—Physiological aspects
  Working classes—Health and safety conditions
  Workmen's compensation
- sf Diseases, Occupational
  Employee health
  Employee safety
  Health of workers
  Hygiene, Industrial
  Industrial health and safety

Industrial hygiene
Occupational diseases
Occupational hazards
Occupational safety
Safety of workers
Work hazards
Worker health
Worker safety
Workers' health
Workers' safety
xx Environmental health
Industrial accidents
Industrial management
Public health
Working classes—Health and
safety conditions

Offshore oil.**
cn LC form: PETROLEUM IN
SUBMERGED LANDS.
sf Oil fields, Offshore
Oil, Offshore
Petroleum in submerged lands
Tidelands oil
Underwater oil fields
xx Marine resources
Oil

Oil.**
cn LC form: PETROLEUM.
Authority: *New periodicals
index* (e.g., Jan./June 1977, p.
97.) Assignment: Roma Gans'
Oil: the buried treasure (1974);
B.H. Kraft's *Oil and natural gas*
(1978); B. Lowery's *Oil* (1977);
P. Windsor's *Oil* (1976).
pn Additional material on this
subject may be found in the
Pamphlet Collection.
sa Offshore oil
Shale oil
sf Coal-oil
Fossil fuels
Non-renewable energy sources
Petroleum

Olympic Games, Moscow, 1980.*
cn Assignment (with —FICTION):
John Redgate's *Last decathlon*
(1979).
sf Moscow Olympics, 1980
Moscow Summer Olympics,
1980
1980 Olympics, Moscow
xx The Eighties

PBB's**
cn LC form: POLYBROMINATED
BIPHENYLS. Assignment: F.
and S. Halbert's *Bitter harvest*
(1978), "the investigation of the
PBB contamination: a personal
story."
sf Polybrominated biphenyls
xx Food contamination.

Paranormal phenomena.**
cn LC form: PSYCHICAL RE-
SEARCH.
sa Apparitions
Astral projection
Astrology
Automatic writing (Psychic
phenomena)
Biorhythm theory
Clairvoyance
Cosmobiology
Dowsing
Extrasensory perception
Ghosts
Haunted houses
Kirlian photography
Occult sciences
Paraphysics
Plants—Communication
(Alleged)
Poltergeists
Precognition (Extrasensory
perception)
Psychic archaeology
Psychic children
Psychic detectives
Psychic espionage
Psychic healing
Psychic surgery
Psychics
Psychokinesis
Psychometry (Occult sciences)
Pyramid energy
Reincarnation
Science—Methodology
Spirit photography
Spontaneous human combus-
tion
Telepathy
U.F.O.'s
Witchcraft
sf Metapsychology
Parapsychology
Psi phenomena
Psychical research
Supernormal phenomena
xx Curiosities and wonders
"New Age" (Concepts, life-
styles, etc.)
Supernatural

Parent education.
cn LC form: CHILDREN—MAN-
AGEMENT—STUDY AND
TEACHING. Authority: "Subject
index," *Sources* (e.g., v. 2, no. 3.
1979, p. 202). Class in 649.107.
sf Education of parents
Education, Parent
Parenting education

Photojournalism.**
cn LC form: PHOTOGRAPHY,
JOURNALISTIC. Assignment:
A.E. Loosley's *Business of*

photojournalism (1971); L.
Payne's *Getting started in
photojournalism* (1967); Time-
Life Books' *Photojournalism*
(1971).
sa Documentary films
Film journalism
Newsreel
Newsreels
sf Journalistic photography
News photography
Photography, Journalistic
Press photography
xx Journalism
Photography

Pick-up trucks.*
cn HCL form. Assignment (with
—CUSTOMIZING): Mike
Anson's *Customizing your
pickup* (1977).
sf Trucks, Pick-up
xx Trucks

Pilots.**
cn LC form: AIR PILOTS. Authority:
New periodicals index (e.g., v.
1, no. 1, Jan./June 1977, p.
102): Alternative Press Centre
subject heading list (1973), p.
30.
sa Aeronautics—Vocational
guidance
Afro-American pilots
Astronauts
Kamikaze pilots
Labor unions—Pilots
Military pilots
Women pilots
sf Air pilots
Aircraft pilots
Airplane pilots
Aviators
Fliers
xx Aeronautics
Aeronautics—Biography
Air lines—Employees
Airplanes—Piloting

Plastic surgery.**
cn LC form: SURGERY, PLASTIC
Class in 617.95.
sf Cosmetic surgery
Restorative surgery
Surgery, Cosmetic
Surgery, Plastic
xx Surgery

Police shootings.*
cn HCL form. Assignment: *Police
use of deadly force: what police
and the community can do
about it* (1979).
sf "Deadly force" (Law
enforcement)
Shootings, Police

xx Police accountability
    Police misconduct

Political action committees.*
    cn HCL form. Assignment (with
        —DIRECTORIES): *Washington
        lobbyists/lawyers directory*,
        which includes PAC list
    sf PACs
    xx Elections—United States—
        Campaign funds
        Lobbying

Psychic archaeology.
    cn Class in 133.87.

Pyramid energy.
    cn HCL form. Class in 118.2

Recession (Economics).*
    cn HCL form. Not subdivided by
        —UNITED STATES. Authority:
        Alternative Press Centre subject
        heading list (1973), p. 22; Scott
        Long, "By definition . . . reces-
        sion/depression" [cartoon],
        Minneapolis tribune, Aug. 26,
        1979, p. 22A. Assignment:
        George Katona and Burkhard
        Strumpel's *New economic era*
        (1978), which includes "The
        experience of the Recession."
        Class in 338.542.
    pn Here are entered materials on
        periods of at least two consecu-
        tive quarters during which there
        is negative GNP growth.
    sf Business recession
        Economic recession
    xx Business cycles
        Economics
        Gross national product

Reptiles.
    cn Class in 598.1.

Retirement.
    cn Class in 301.4356.

Satirical art.*
    cn HCL form. Assignment: Cynthia
        Jaffee McCabe's *Fernando
        Botero* (1979).
    sf Art, Satirical
        Satire in art
    xx Art
        Satire

Science fiction television programs.*
    cn HCL form. Assignment (with
        —HISTORY AND CRITICISM):
        James A. Lely's *Battlestar
        Galactica* (1979).
    xx Television programs.

Self-care.*
    cn HCL form. Assignment: Toni M.
        Roberts, Kathleen McIntosh
        Tinker, and Donald W. Kemper's
        Healthwise handbook (1979),
        which deals with "how to pre-

vent, recognize, and treat
common illnesses."
    sa Childbirth education
        Drug education
        First aid in illness and injuries
        Health—Handbooks, manuals,
            etc.
        Holistic health
        Medical records
        Nutrition
        Physical fitness
        Self-care movement
    sf Medical self-care
        Self-diagnosis
        Self-help medicine
        Self-treatment
    xx Health
        Medical care
        Medicine
        Self-reliance
        Simple life
        Survival (Economics)

Self-help psychology.
    cn HCL form. Class in 158.1.

The Seventies.
    sa Aeronautics—Accidents—
            1970
        Aeronautics—Accidents—
            1972
        Aeronautics—Accidents—
            1974
        Mount Everest Expedition, 1978
        Olympic Games, Montreal,
            1976
        Olympic Games, Munich, 1972

Shandy, Peter.*
    cn Fictional character. Creator:
        Charlotte MacLeod.
    sf Peter Shandy
        Professor Shandy

Shaw, George Bernard, 1856-1950.
    pn Portraits of this person may be
        found in the HCL Picture File.*
    sf G.B.S.
        Shaw, Bernard, 1856-1950

Singing—Auditions.
    cn Class in 784.07.
    sf Auditions—Singing
        Singers' auditions
        Vocal auditions

Skokie Case.**
    cn LC form: SKOKIE, ILLINOIS—
        DEMONSTRATION, 1977. As-
        signment: Aryeh Neier's *De-
        fending my enemy: American
        Nazis, the Skokie case, and the
        risks of freedom* (1979).
    xx Antisemitism—United States
        Concentration camp survivors
        Freedom of assembly
        Freedom of speech
        Jewish-Americans—Political
            and social conditions

Skydiving.
    cn Class in 797.56.
    sf Sky diving
        Sport parachuting
    xx Air sports
        Parachuting

Smoking and health.
    cn HCL form.
    af Health and smoking
        Smoking—Physiological effects

Southern Africa.**
    cn LC form: AFRICA, SOUTHERN.
    pn Here are entered materials on
        the area south of Zaire and
        Tanzania.
    sa Angola
        Botswana
        Lesotho
        Malawi
        Mozambique
        Namibia
        South Africa
        Swaziland
        Zambia
        Zimbabwe

Space colonies.
    cn Class orbiting colonies in
        629.447, colonies established
        on natural extraterrestrial
        bodies in 325.99.

Space shuttles.
    cn LC form: REUSABLE SPACE
        VEHICLES. Class in 629.442.
    sa Model space shuttles
    sf Reusable space vehicles.

Space warfare.*
    cn HCL form. Assignment (with
        —FORECASTS): David Lang-
        ford's *War in 2080: the future of
        military technology* (1979).
    sf Interplanetary warfare
        War in space
        Warfare, Space
    xx Military art and science
        Outer space
        War

Spanish-language periodicals
    sf Periódicos en español
        Revistas en español

Special libraries.
    cn LC form: LIBRARIES, SPECIAL.
        Class in 027.6
    sa Government libraries

Special Olympics.
    cn Class in 796.486.
    sf Olympics, Special
    xx Developmentally disabled
            persons—Projects and
            services
        Developmentally disabled
            persons—Recreation
        Disabled persons' sports
        Olympic Games

Stained glass.**
　cn　LC form: GLASS PAINTING
　　　AND STAINING. Class in 748.5.
　　　Authority: Julia M. Ehresmann's
　　　Pocket dictionary of art terms
　　　(1971); Dorothy B. Kersten's
　　　*Subject headings for church or
　　　synagogue libraries* (1978), p.
　　　18; Jewish Library Association
　　　of Greater Philadelphia's *Sub-
　　　ject headings for a Judaica
　　　library* (3d ed., rev., 1972), p. 18;
　　　New periodicals index (e.g., v.
　　　1, no. 1, Jan./June 1977, p. 126.
　　　Assignment: Claude Lips' *Art
　　　and stained glass* (1973);
　　　Robert Sowers' *Stained glass:
　　　an architectural art* (1965).
　sa　Glass painting
　sf　Glass, Stained
　　　Windows, Stained glass
　xx　Church decoration and
　　　ornament
　　　Decoration and ornament
　　　Glass craft
　　　Glass, Ornamental
　　　Glass painting
　　　Painting
Suggestology.*
　cn　HCL form. Assignment: S.
　　　Ostrander's *Superlearning*.
　pn　Here are entered materials on a
　　　holistic therapeutic and educa-
　　　tional system that attempts "to
　　　get the body and left-brain and
　　　right-brain abilities working
　　　together as an orchestrated
　　　whole to make people more
　　　capable of doing whatever
　　　they're trying to do." As devel-
　　　oped in Bulgaria, Suggestology
　　　"is basically 'applied' altered
　　　states of consciousness for
　　　learning, healing, and intuitive
　　　development."
　sf　Holistic learning
　　　Suggestopedia
　xx　Consciousness
　　　Educational acceleration
　　　Human Potentials Movement
　　　Learning ability
　　　Memory
　　　Mind and body
　　　"New Age" (Concepts, life-
　　　styles, etc.)
　　　Paranormal phenomena
Supplemental Security Income
Program.*
　cn　HCL form. Not subdivided by
　　　—UNITED STATES. Authority:
　　　Legislative indexing vocabulary
　　　(12th ed., 1978), p. 509. Assign-
　　　ment: *Social Security hand-
　　　book: retirement insurance,*

*survivors insurance, disability
insurance, health insurance,
supplemental security income,
black lung benefits* (6th ed.,
1978).
　pn　Here are entered materials on a
　　　federal program of assistance to
　　　the aged, blind, and disabled,
　　　operating since January 1974
　　　under the Social Security
　　　Administration, which replaces
　　　three earlier programs: Old Age
　　　Assistance, Aid to the Blind, and
　　　Aid to the Permanently and
　　　Totally Disabled.
　sa　Aid to the Permanently and
　　　Totally Disabled
　　　Old age assistance
　　　Social Security
　sf　Aid to the Blind
　　　Aid to the Disabled
　　　S.S.I. Program
　xx　Aid to the Permanently and
　　　Totally Disabled
　　　Disabled persons—Projects and
　　　services
　　　Old age assistance
　　　Public welfare—United States
　　　Social Security
Television collectibles.*
　cn　HCL form. Assignment: M.
　　　Resnick's *Official price guide to
　　　comic & science fiction books*
　　　(3d ed., 1979), including "Radio
　　　and television premiums," "Star
　　　Trek."
　sa　Star trek (Television program)
　　　—Collectibles
　sf　Collectibles, Television
　　　Television premiums
　xx　Collectors and collecting
－　"Test tube" babies.**
　cn　LC form: FERTILIZATION IN
　　　VITRO, HUMAN. Class in
　　　618.178. Assignment: Jeremy
　　　Rifkin's *Engineering test tube
　　　babies* (1978 tape cassette).
　　　Further assignment (with
　　　—CASES, CLINICAL REPORTS,
　　　ETC.): Lesley and John Brown's
　　　*Our miracle called Louise: a
　　　parents' story* (1979), a "first-
　　　hand account of the . . . events
　　　that brought two people . . . in
　　　the West of England into the
　　　world's limelight" when, "on July
　　　25, 1978, Louise Brown, the
　　　world's first 'test-tube' baby,
　　　was born."
　sf　Fertilization in vitro
　　　In vitro fertilization
　xx　Gynecology
　　　Infertility
　　　Pregnancy

Tinieblas (Imaginary country).*
　cn　HCL form. Creator: R.M. Koster.
　xx　Imaginary places
Track and field athletics.**
　cn　LC form: TRACK-ATHLETICS.
　　　Authority: *Thesaurus of ERIC
　　　descriptors* (7th ed., 1977), p.
　　　219; Ralph Hickok's *New
　　　encyclopedia of sports* (1977),
　　　p. 469-95; *Sources* (e.g., v. 2,
　　　no. 3, p. 208). Class in 796.42.
　sa　Decathlon
　　　Discus throwing
　　　High jumping
　　　Hurdle-racing
　　　Javelin throwing
　　　Junior Olympics
　　　Marathon running
　　　Olympic Games
　　　Pole-vaulting
　　　Running
　　　Shot putting
　　　Special Olympics
　　　Track and field athletes
　　　Walking (Sports)
　sf　Field athletics
　　　Track athletics
　xx　Running
　　　Sports
Travel—Guide-books (for disabled
persons).*
　cn　Previous HCL form: TRAVEL—
　　　GUIDE-BOOKS (FOR HANDI-
　　　CAPPED PERSONS). Make dual
　　　entry under DISABLED PER-
　　　SONS AND TRAVEL.
　sf　Disabled persons' travel guides
　　　"Handicapped" persons' travel
　　　guides
　xx　Travel
Trucking industry.*
　cn　HCL form. Not subdivided by
　　　—UNITED STATES. Assign-
　　　ment: J. Kwitny's *Vicious circles*
　　　(1979; "Trucking": p. 139+).
　xx　Transportation.
Two-career couples.*
　cn　HCL form. Assignment: C. Bird's
　　　Two-paycheck marriage
　　　(1979); Rhona and Robert
　　　Rapoport's *Dual-career families
　　　re-examined* (1976).
　sf　Couples, Two-career
　　　Dual-career couples
　　　Marriage, Two-career
　　　Two-career marriage
　xx　Marriage
Underwater photography.**
　cn　LC form: PHOTOGRAPHY,
　　　SUBMARINE. Assignment: D.
　　　Rebikoff's *Underwater photog-
　　　raphy* (2d ed., 1975); W.A.
　　　Starck's *Art of underwater*

photography (1966); H.R. Roberts' *Beginner's guide to underwater photography* (1978).
  sf Photography, Submarine
      Photography, Underwater
      Submarine photography
  xx Photography

Unification Church.**
  cn LC form: SEGYE KIDOKKYO T'ONGIL SILLYONG HYOPHOE. Class in 289.91. Assignment (with —PERSONAL NARRATIVES): Allen Tate Wood's *Moonstruck; a memoir of my life in a cult* (1979).
  sf "Moonies"
  xx Christian sects

United States—Description and travel—Views.
  pn Here are entered works consisting wholly or largely of graphic material.
  sf United States—Description and travel—Pictorial works
      United States—Pictorial works

Unnecessary surgery.**
  cn LC form: SURGERY, UNNECESSARY. Class in 617.0013. Assignment: Duane F. Stroman's *Quick knife; unnecessary surgery U.S.A.* (1979).
  sf Surgery, Unnecessary
  xx Medical malpractice
      Surgery

Vietnam veterans.*
  cn HCL form. Authority: Alternative Press Centre subject heading list (1973), p. 38. Assignment (with —FICTION): Allston James' *Attic light* (1979).
  sa Veterans

  sf Veterans, Vietnam
      Vietnamese conflict, 1961-1975—Veterans
  xx Veterans
      Vietnamese conflict, 1961-1975—United States

Vital force.
  cn Class in 118.2.

Volunteer workers.
  cn Class in 331.53. Not subdivided by —UNITED STATES.

Western Hemisphere.**
  cn LC form: AMERICA.
  sa Caribbean area
      Central America
      Latin America
      North America
      South America
      West Indies
  sf Americas
      "New World"

Wild food.**
  cn LC form: FOOD, WILD. Not subdivided by —UNITED STATES.
  sa Cooking (Wild foods)
      Gathering (of wild foods, seeds, medicinal plants, etc.)
      Plants, Edible
  sf Food, Wild
  xx Food
      Wilderness survival

Winter Olympics, Lake Placid, 1980.*
  cn HCL form. Class in 796.98. Assignment: Eugene H. Baker's *XIII Olympic Winter Games, Lake Placid, 1980* (1979).
  sf Lake Placid Winter Olympics, 1980
      1980 Winter Olympics
      Winter Olympics, 1980
  xx The Eighties

Women—Lifestyles.
  cn LC form: WOMEN—CONDUCT OF LIFE. Class in 301.4126.

Wood fuels.**
  cn LC form: WOOD AS FUEL.
  sa Fireplaces
      Wood stoves
  sf Fire wood
      Firewood
      Wood as fuel
      Wood burning
      Woodburning
      Wood energy
      Wood power
  xx Alternative energy sources
      Biomass energy
      Fireplaces
      Fuel
      Wood stoves

World War, 1914-1918—Prisoners and prisons.
  cn Adjectival forms denote prisoners held and prisons operated by the specified power. E.g., use —PRISONERS AND PRISONS, GERMAN for works dealing with military personnel imprisoned by the Germans and/or German-operated prisons.

Yiddish theater.**
  cn LC form: THEATER—JEWS. Assignment: L. Rosenfeld's *Bright star of exile: Jacob Adler and the Yiddish theatre* (1977); E.T. Beck's *Kafka and the Yiddish theater: its impact on his work* (1971).
  sf Jewish theater
      Theater, Jewish
  xx Jews—Civilization
      Theater

Index

Compiled by Sanford Berman